The
Baby Boon

How Family-Friendly America
Cheats the Childless

Elinor Burkett

The Free Press

New York   London   Sydney   Singapore

*f*P

THE FREE PRESS
A Division of Simon & Schuster Inc.
1230 Avenue of the Americas
New York, NY 10020

THE FREE PRESS and colophon are trademarks
of Simon & Schuster Inc.

Designed by Kyoko Watanabe

Manufactured in the United States of America

20 19 18 17 16 15

Library of Congress Cataloging-in Publication Data

Burkett, Elinor.
The baby boon: how family-friendly America cheats the childless/Elinor Burkett.
p. cm.
Includes bibliographical references and index.
1. Childlessness—United States.
2. Family—United States I. Title.
HQ755.8.B857   2000
306.87—dc21   99-050273
CIP

ISBN 978-0-7432-4264-6

For Bernard Cohen (1911–1993),
the role model of the perfect contrarian

Woe to him who seeks to appease rather than appal.

—HERMAN MELVILLE

Contents

All Animals Are Equal   1

PART ONE

America's New Family-Friendly Face
In the Workplace and in Public Policy

1. Unequal Work for Unequal Pay   25
2. Pregnant Payoffs   62

PART TWO

For the Children?
Hardly—Pure Politics Are Driving This Train

3. For the Sake of Which Children?   91
4. Family Frenzy   118
5. The Maternal Mystique   147

PART THREE

Balancing Act

6. No Kidding   179
7. When the Bough Breaks   199

   Notes   219
   Bibliography   243
   Acknowledgments   247
   Index   249

The
Baby Boon

All Animals Are Equal

All animals are equal
but some animals are more equal than others.

—George Orwell

It was just after four o'clock on a warm afternoon in April, and all Cheryl Brant wanted was to find something watchable in the video store and go home to her apartment on the outskirts of Baltimore. She had spent a long, hard week on her job as a concrete inspector hassling with companies about the percentage of water in the mix, and it was made longer and harder by the fact that the inspector who was her partner had pleaded childcare problems for the umpteenth time, forcing her to start work early and to stay late.

Cheryl didn't mind putting in extra hours when her coworkers had problems—sick kids, appointments with doctors, even dogs needing to be defleaed. But the dads she worked with had been having a lot of problems lately, problems and soccer games and school plays. She knew what they'd think if she, a single, childless woman who spent her free time building sculptures or cutting stained glass, refused to fill in for them: "What's with Cheryl? Doesn't she understand how hard it is to be a parent? Does she hate kids?" No sane person would risk being branded a kid-hater in modern America, even if it meant doing somebody else's work while that somebody got the pay. And she knew better than to insist that she too had pressing matters to attend to. What was she going to say, "Sorry, I've got an image in my head that has to be put on paper before it dissolves"? Right, she thought. As if anyone would think that her artwork was as important as junior's football practice.

Her nerves were frayed even further because she'd just filed her income tax return, which had left her no room to even fantasize about buying antique glass at thirty dollars a square foot for the stained-glass windows she creates. She'd been tempted to give herself a couple of kids to ease the pain. Dependent deductions, childcare credits, and kiddie credits would've added up to a pile of glass and enough latex to create molds for her concrete plaques. But the prospect of an audit erased that temptation. Cheryl's not moved much by unwritten laws. But she has a healthy dose of respect for the written ones.

So Cheryl, a slim blonde who would look delicate if not for the hard hat and steel-toed work boots, wasn't in the most tolerant of moods when she pulled into the parking lot at the mall housing her video store only to be forced to ride up and down rows of parked cars waiting for a space. Out of the corner of her eye, she finally spotted ten feet of empty blacktop and steered her truck in that direction. Then she confronted The Sign: "Parking Reserved for Expectant Mothers and Parents with Infants."

Was the special parking just an exquisitely sensitive gesture to aching backs? Had the mall authorities begun to post valets with electric wheelchairs inside the entrance to speed the disabled women through the endless corridors? If not, what was the point? Walking, after all, is the sine qua non of mall shopping.

Or were the parking spaces the mall's way of blessing pregnancy and motherhood as exalted status?

By the time she found a parking space for which she was eligible and entered the video store, Cheryl was still only peeved at the latest reminder of her inferior station in American life. And then it happened, the incident that pushed Cheryl over that invisible barrier between pique and full-bodied disgust. As she waited in line to check out a movie, a woman with an empty infant carrier strapped across her chest approached the counter. The clerk didn't hesitate. Looking past Cheryl and the other women in line, he virtually ushered the Mom, who advertised her astral state prominently even in the absence of her progeny, to the head of the pack.

Cheryl vowed on the spot to purchase an infant carrier that she could flaunt as what she calls "an antishunning device." "Does not having kids make me a second-class citizen, unworthy of the most basic consideration?" she asks. "When does it get to be my turn to have my choices and interests respected and honored in America?"

Cheryl's grandmother, Anna Diehl, might have uttered those last words seventy-five years earlier. In fact, women who don't conform to America's rigid female stereotypes have been uttering them, or at least thinking them, for decades. For all of the lip service paid to women's liberation, Cheryl is still as trapped by social expectations of what women should be and do and feel as were her foremothers. The specific expectations have changed; the disrespect for deviation from them remains.

Cheryl's grandmother Anna veered off the socially blessed path of her day in the summer of 1914, when she took over a one-room school in the farm country twenty miles from her home in Lonaconing, Maryland, and entered the ranks of America's working women. Born in 1895 in the heart of America's coal country, Anna came of age with the new millennium, at a time when the hunger of a nation convinced of its own destiny, manifest or not, was creating a widening middle class. America was rife with movement—from east to west, rags to riches, farm to factory—and that possibility was Anna's birthright. Her father's general store kept him safe from the hazards of work underground and his family firmly planted in the town's solid, respectable middle class.

Like many daughters of her class, when Anna finished seventh grade, she fixed her eyes on a higher education. For a generation of Americans like Anna's parents, formed in the 1870s, the nadir of women's employment, spending money on a girl's schooling must have seemed virtually wanton. But traditions were crumbling as quickly as distance and homogeneity, and promise, long America's most illusive bit of false advertising, was beckoning the new generation.

That promise, however, went only so far, at least for women. Twenty percent of Anna's peers continued their studies, and 25 percent of American women were working for wages—laboring in cigar factories and textile mills, scrubbing the floors of the wealthy, or in such middle-class occupations as teaching, nursing, or clerical work. But wherever they worked, women rarely earned even half the wages of the men beside them. Teachers, for example, women like Anna, were penalized for their gender with pay that was 30 percent below the going male wage, which meant that their salaries barely covered room and board.

And over 90 percent of female workers were single, almost all living at home, adding their meager wages to the family pot. In the early twentieth century, women's lives were still either/or propositions. A single woman might work to help feed her family. She might continue working her whole life, if she was willing to suffer the social isolation of a spinster. But if she married, her place was in the home. If her own common sense didn't guide her in that direction, her employers' almost inevitably did. Teachers, clerks, and shop girls knew, in no uncertain terms, that being single was the price of employment.

For a few years, Anna was an exception. Living on her own, she worked from interest rather than need and paid her own way thanks to the pennies her students' parents paid as tuition. But shortly after she turned twenty, she met George Diehl, who lived in Cumberland, Maryland's second-largest city, nestled in the valley east of Lonaconing. Properly chaperoned, the young couple courted for almost a year until they decided to marry. With that decision, Anna's fate was sealed. Law and custom left her no room to battle the prohibition against married teachers. So on the eve of her wedding, she bid farewell, both to her moment of rebellion and to her pupils, packed up her meager possessions, and joined the exodus of young women from the world of work into domesticity.

She was a member of the last generation to do so without question—and her daughter Susan was definitely a questioner. When Susan graduated from high school in 1950, she examined her career options with dismay. During World War II, young girls had been able to dream of flying airplanes, pounding rivets, or balancing the finances of major companies. But when the nation's soldiers returned home, those dreams quickly faded into distant, almost wanton, fantasies. "I could be a nurse, a teacher, a telephone operator or a clerk," Susan says, the sarcasm dripping. "I chose the one I disliked least," which was nursing. That was the last time she hesitated to push the envelope.

While still in nursing school, "Miss Know-It-All," as Susan calls her youthful self, fell in love with a dashing young Glenn Brant and decided to get married, assuming that that personal decision would have no impact on her professional plans. She assumed wrong. In that age of sleek car fins and an obsession with all things modern, Americans believed they had moved into a progressive new world. But for women, the new world wasn't much shinier than the old one. Female tea chers like Susan's mother were no longer summarily dismissed when they married, but they were out the door the minute they got pregnant. And in Cumberland, at least, nursing hadn't inched even that far. The day Susan got married, she was kicked out of her training program.

She had already made one compromise with her future, and unlike her mother, Susan had some social space in which to maneuver around another. When the training program in Cumberland rejected her demand for reinstatement, she found a hospital in Baltimore that allowed married trainees and transferred across the state to the Hospital for the Women of Maryland. For four years, Susan was the modern young woman, living in an apartment far from home, donning her uniform each morning and going off to work, while her husband commuted to his job on the U.S. Army base in Aberdeen.

Only when Glenn was released from the service and the young couple moved back to Cumberland did Susan give the fifties domestic life a try. It was a disaster. "I was bored out of my mind," she says, sitting back on a couch in her pin-neat living room, Oriental embroideries framing her head. At the age of sixty-nine, she is a striking woman, radiating some of the inner steel of a Katharine Hepburn. "I hate housework. I prefer to work and pay money for someone else to do it."

When Cheryl was four years old, Susan divorced Glenn and began struggling to raise her kids while working full-time as a surgical nurse. By then, one in three marriages ended in divorce, but America was still unready to admit how far reality diverged from mythology. Single mothers threatened the already shaky social order, so Susan was pretty much on her own. Her salary, thirty-two hundred dollars a year, covered the taxes on her house, utilities, food, and the salary of her baby-sitter, with no margin for emergency. There were no employer-sponsored daycare centers at hospitals. No tax credits for her children beyond the standard exemptions. Susan had nowhere to turn but to family and to Mrs. Chaney, an older woman, who faithfully appeared each morning in time for her to hit the operating room by 6:30. Beyond that, Susan carried the full weight. "I made my own choices," she says, a mixture of confidence and pride tingeing her voice. "I accepted responsibility for them. "People looked at me funny. People get uncomfortable when you don't do what everyone else is doing. But my attitude was, 'If people don't approve, that's just too bad.'"

Susan passed that attitude along to Cheryl, who is the walking embodiment of strong and invincible. The men on the job sites she works as a construction supervisor cower in her wake. She does not suffer fools, gladly or otherwise.

Born in 1960, Cheryl came of age constrained by few of the conventions that had governed the lives of her Susan and Anna. But she was hardly free of social expectations and constraints. Women of her generation and social class were supposed to go to college and become professionals, but they were also supposed to get married, and probably divorced, and to have children, who would spend as much time with the nanny as with her.

Cheryl, however, never responded well to supposed-tos. She has tried her hand at romance more times than she cares to count, and a week doesn't go by that someone doesn't ask her, "Don't you want to get married? Don't you want children?" She's not opposed to marriage, and she's crazy about kids, an affection she indulges by working in a children's theater group. But, a member of the first generation of American women confident in their ability to support themselves, and able to have sex without the attendant diapers, she is alternately puzzled and annoyed by the incessant harping on her lack of husband and progeny. "I don't get it," she says, flatly. "What's the point of getting married just to get married or having kids for the sake of having kids?"

For Cheryl, the stories of her grandmother and mother are not just parables about independence and self-reliance, or even the human price of discrimination. They are cautionary tales about more insidious dangers, the dangers of a society that promotes any one lifestyle, of exalting and rewarding one set of personal inclinations and decisions above all others. Ask any gay person what it means to live in a world that overtly favors heterosexuality, or a Jewish person what it feels like to live amidst the presupposition that everyone is Christian. The assumption that all women will reproduce—and the granting of special privileges to those who do so—galls Cheryl in precisely the same fashion. She feels belittled and demeaned, and appalled that even feminists seem to have forgotten that where there is privilege for some, there will inevitably be unprivilege for others, and that such privilege is the type of subtle social pressure that has long circumscribed women's lives. "What kind of liberation is that?" she asks, plaintively.

"People act as if my life isn't valid because I'm not doing this thing, raising kids, as if nothing I could possibly do is as important as what parents are doing," she says, the frustration rising in her voice. "And then they accuse me of being selfish if I dare to ask why they should be put up on some pedestal. Well, I think that's a pretty selfish attitude—refusing to respect other people's lives and demanding that everyone organize *their* lives around *your* interests and *your* needs."

The penchant of others to accept—blithely, thoughtlessly or self-interestedly—the existence of such implicit discrimination nags at her daily. Her coworkers regularly come in late, leave early, or beg out of Saturday work because of their kids. Their paychecks include medical benefits that cost her boss twice what hers do because they have kids. Their taxes are dramatically lower because of their kids, while hers help pay for their kids' education, recreation, and medical care. And everywhere she turns, from the supermarket to the IRS, she's expected to make accommodations for the decisions of others to have it all: professions and children, time at the gym, evenings to party, and money for vacations.

"What does it mean to say we respect people's choices, women's choices, if we only respect the choice to procreate? If asking for respect is today's definition of selfish, I'll just have to live with that, just like my grandmother and mother lived with the prejudices of their days."

Over the past decade, Cheryl Brant has become a second-class American citizen. No legislation enacted explicitly proclaims Cheryl less than equal. But as the nation undergoes political cosmetic surgery to give itself a "family-friendly" face, measure by measure, bill by bill, executive order by executive order, personnel policy by personnel policy, she and the nation's other thirteen million childless adults over the age of forty have been consigned to the nether reaches of public life.

They have watched President William Jefferson Clinton and his Republican Congress forge the most massive redistribution of wealth since the War on Poverty—this time not from rich to poor, but from nonparents, no matter how modest their means, to parents, no matter how affluent. In 1997, with enormous public hoopla, they unveiled a massive middle-class tax break totaling more than $5 billion a year. There was just one catch: Delivered as a tax credit for children, it left the taxes of the childless unchanged, thus shifting the national tax burden even more heavily onto their shoulders.

Then parents of college-age children received a second windfall, in the form of a tax credit for college tuition. The result: A professional couple in suburban Boston with a six-digit income receives a $1,000 tax credit for their two younger children, a $960 tax credit for childcare because the wife works two evenings a week, and an additional $1,500 tax credit because their daughter is in college, on top of five standard dependent exemptions. But a nonparent in poverty can receive only three months of food stamps every three years because he has no kids, and a nonparent earning as little as $10,000 a year receives a maximum Earned Income Tax Credit of $341—while an adult with a single child in that same income bracket can claim up to $2,210.

In June 1999, childless Americans saw their status further eroded when Clinton launched the nation's first system of federally paid parenting by authorizing states to extend unemployment insurance benefits to parents who want to stay home with their newborn. Nonparents, of course, can get those government checks only if disaster strikes them in the form of layoffs, which has long been the rationale for the unemployment insurance system—a kind of umbrella if the worst kind of rain begins falling. So, now, in this wonderful world in which welfare has allegedly been reformed, the Clinton unemployment insurance revamping also means that the poor lose federal benefits if they don't work, but doctors and lawyers who don't work after they have kids can receive checks from Uncle Sam.

Things are even bleaker in the workplace. Violating the principle of equal work for equal pay, American employers increasingly compensate workers according to family status, offering parents health insurance, childcare centers, and leave packages worth thousands of dollars more than the benefits packages offered to the childless—and employers might soon be given tax breaks by the federal government if that discrimination includes subsidized daycare. They are also required, by law, to grant parents long postpartum leaves with full benefits, but they are not required to transfer their salaries to the childless workers who pick up the added work while those parents stay home with the kids.

And the situation at work is about to get worse. In May 1999, the White House announced that it was drafting a new piece of civil rights legislation to protect parents from workplace discrimination, even while admitting that no evidence of rampant discrimination exists. But the president and Senator Chris Dodd of Connecticut, who will sponsor the bill in the Senate, are using the specter of such discrimination to try to bar employers from requiring parents to work overtime or attend weekend business meetings that might interfere with their parenting obligations— although they would be free to extract all those extra hours, and then some, from the childless. They would then be prohibited by law from rewarding nonparents for all that extra time and work with compensatory raises or promotions because paying parents less money for less work, or promoting employees who worked hardest, would be "discriminatory."

As the presidential election of 2000 heats up, the words parent and citizen have become virtually interchangeable, leaving nonparent citizens dangling in political limbo. Vice-President Al Gore hit the presidential campaign trail in spring 1999 flying his "family banner." On May 16, in his commencement address at Graceland College in Lamoni, Iowa, he promised high-quality preschool care for all children. On June 22, at his annual Family Re-Union symposium in Nashville, Tennessee, he exhorted, "Let's create a family lobby as powerful as the gun lobby." On his website, he devoted a full policy section to his proposals for building "stronger families." What was his definition of the families those proposals would help? Not brothers and sisters, cousins, or even husbands and wives. The proposals were geared exclusively to parents.

As political parties and candidates read the electoral tea leaves and vie for the votes of women, they cast their appeals on the basis of motherhood, equating being female with being a mother. In the months after the shooting at Columbine High School in Littleton, Colorado, the Democrats reframed their warnings about the dangers of a nation without gun control in terms of child safety rather than crime in order to reach out to women who, as Representative Carolyn McCarthy said, "find they have a maternal instinct about this." As they battled for a patients' bill of rights with their health insurance companies, Democrats made the same pitch once again. "Health care is a women's issue," said Senator Barbara Mikulski. "Women will do anything to make sure their children have the kind of health care they need." In fact, the Democrats seemed intent on reframing every issue on their agenda—from air quality and toxic waste to suburban sprawl—as "women's issues" that became instantly transmogrified into "mothers' issues." Even *The New York Times* took note of the reality the Democrats seemingly had missed— "The irony that the same political party that claimed ownership of the position that women could be more than mothers is . . . casting them primarily in that role," and reminded readers that a record number of women are eschewing motherhood entirely.

The hoppers of the House of Representatives and the Senate are rife with Democratic legislative initiatives that will inevitably diminish the childless, and their checking accounts, even more. For two decades, the Republicans have portrayed themselves as the party of family values, which might have annoyed the childless, but at least didn't cost them much money. In recent years, however, the Democrats have jumped on that bandwagon, reshaping themselves as the party that puts a dollar value on families. During the 106th Congress alone, dozens of Democratic bills designed to lighten the tax burden of parents were introduced into the House of the Representatives and the Senate: bills to increase the child tax credit from five hundred dollars to nine hundred dollars, to increase the childcare tax credit, to place a higher income cap on the maximum childcare tax credit, to award stay-at-home parents special grants to go back to school, to give stay-at-home parents their own tax credits, to expand the 1993 Family and Medical Leave Act (which is used predominantly by parents), and to move the nation closer to a national system of publicly funded daycare.

In this breathless rush to make America a kinder and gentler place for parents, the existence of the childless, who foot a heavy percentage of the bill for that remodeling, is never mentioned. No matter that in Cheryl's demographic group alone—women in their late thirties with graduate degrees—one-third are still childless, that one in five baby boomer women is a nonmother by choice, or that the U.S. Census Bureau projects that up to one-quarter of their daughters will follow their lead. Just as the needs and interests of women like Cheryl's mother and grandmother have suffered from laws, traditions, and social assumptions that punished them for "aberrant" inclinations, so, too, are the needs and interests of today's nonparents brushed aside, with proposals and policies that violate every democratic principle fought for over the past two centuries, from "one person, one vote" to equal pay for equal work. Parents, after all, produce the next generation. Parents, after all, have weightier responsibilities. Parents, after all, *deserve* special privilege for the unique contribution they make to us all.

Or so the theory goes.

I never thought of myself as "intentionally childless." I just didn't have children. Like most women of my generation and ilk—upper-middle-class, overeducated baby boomer feminists—while I was in my twenties and early thirties, I was too busy building a career and proving that women could be more than baby machines to think about reproduction. As we inched up on forty, most of my friends and colleagues confronted their biological clocks with alarm. I, on the other hand, faced that watershed with indifference. I wasn't interested in parenting. And my interest in kids was satisfied by my work as a college professor. That didn't feel like a big deal at the time. My parents were only mildly disappointed. My colleagues were only marginally curious. And while I was peripherally aware that I was underwriting parenting—by paying to educate other people's children, for example—that was just fine with me.

Then came the presidential election of 1996, when Bob Dole and Bill Clinton littered the campaign trail with initiatives allegedly designed to ease the burden on "working families." I quickly realized that that political catchphrase did not include me. It was irrelevant that I worked and that I was a member of several families. Dole was prattling on about special tax credits for children, and Clinton wowed the masses with the promise of parental leave. "Working families," I realized, was a code phrase for parents. Somehow, I'd been written out of the political equation.

I admit this shyly not because I am embarrassed by my decision to forgo parenthood—although, God knows, I am often enough treated as if I should be—but because I abhor the notion that I have become afflicted with the "what about me?" virus that seems to have infected wide swaths of the nation. But when the six-figure-income crowd is receiving multi-thousand-dollar tax breaks while the childless poor are losing their public benefits and my share of the national tax burden rises, it isn't easy to hold my tongue. And it is that much harder because this family-friendly fervor has erupted at an ironic moment in history, a moment when a record number of American men and women, members of the first generation with effective tools to prevent conception, are using them intentionally and consciously to avoid procreation entirely.

For decades, we've paid more taxes each year to educate children we don't have without complaint. We've done our share to give poor children some shot at the possibilities the kids of our friends accept as their birthright. We've volunteered to work weekends and holidays so parents could spend the time with their kids. But it still isn't enough. Suddenly we are asked to finance school choice, which means that parents will use *our* money to make *their* choices. Suddenly, we are expected to bear an even greater share of the national tax burden although we continue to receive the fewest government services. Suddenly we are accused, implicitly by Bill Clinton and explicitly by men like Allan Carlson, president of the Rockford Institute, of being "free riders" on the system because we have exercised our right to reproductive choice.

For months I struggled with questions about this encroaching reality: Are the benefits and tax breaks being offered to parents really "for the children"? Or is this brave new "family-friendly world" a new welfare program for baby boomers who want to eat their cake and have it too—to have their progeny without losing steam at work or being too strapped to pay for the new cars and vacations that defined their lives before childbirth? After all, if the goal is the well-being of children, why is the government slashing welfare, cutting food stamps, and withdrawing financial aid from inner-city school programs? What is this, some sort of childhood apartheid?

I know that supporting the health, education, and emotional well-being of the next generation, who are our future, is essential to the social good, and far be it from me to argue with the social good. But at what level and to what extent is reproduction a social good? Is expecting non-parents to pick up the slack at the office so that parents working to fulfill themselves can attend school plays, for example, intrinsic to the social good? Does supporting the future necessitate subsidizing the private college educations of the children of wealthy families? Is our growing support for parents, which skews taxation toward a significant childless minority and services away from them, really reflective of our collective concern for the future, or is it a sop to those who have kids? What does it mean that we're devising policies that force the poor to take responsibility for themselves and their decisions while establishing programs to relieve the relatively affluent of the consequences of theirs? And shouldn't we at least have a social discussion about these matters?

Finally, I began posing these questions—important, substantive questions worthy of at least a modicum of social discourse—directly to friends and colleagues. Among parents, they made me as popular as a flagburner at a convention of the Daughters of the American Revolution. "That's so selfish," mothers berated me with barely disguised rage. "After all, we're raising the next generation. Don't you care about the future?" I seethed quietly: Oh, is that why you want flex-time and tax breaks, to ensure the future of the human race? Is this blackmail: Give me my tax breaks, or I won't bear the future's children?

"How can you say that parents shouldn't earn more money than the childless, their expenses are greater, they need to earn more," one woman responded. The words slipped out of my mouth before I could shut it: "Do you advocate a Marxist wage system—you know, from each according to his ability, to each according to his need?"

That was the last time I dared broach the topic in a social setting. The posing of the questions was translated into answers, and, no matter the truth, the answers were child- and parenting-hating. The scenario was shockingly familiar, yet one more case of the majority entrenching itself in self-righteous justification to stifle complaint from the minority.

The spring of 1963 was an odd moment of stasis for a nation about to fall over a dozen political and social brinks. In my tiny corner of suburban America, on the outskirts of Philadelphia, students had traded in their

Loden coats and cardigan sweaters for cotton Madras skirts and white blouses with Peter Pan collars, the proper dress for an eminently proper group of white teenagers. Caught in the grip of graduation fever, seniors were pulling all the predictable pranks, from the obligatory water balloon attacks to the festooning of the campus with toilet paper.

Martin Luther King, Jr., had just taken the struggle for justice into the heart of the beast, and civil war had broken out in Birmingham, Alabama. But, as privileged kids, we were still hopelessly stuck in the 1950s. The election of the prom queen was the only burning political issue of the day in our lush environs. Anyway, with Camelot firmly entrenched in the White House and "Blowin' in the Wind" at the top of the charts, we were convinced we had already entered the ranks of the truly enlightened.

Few of my classmates paid much attention to the news that spring, or, in all probability, during any other season. But my father, Bernard Cohen, conducted our dinner table as a seminar in current events, a free-floating roundtable that veered seamlessly from the power struggles in the Middle East to the history behind the black and white images of firehoses washing human beings along hate-filled streets in exotic places like Alabama. That May, however, the conversations over roast chicken and brisket that were seared into my memory dealt not with the plight of African-Americans, whose lives I could barely imagine, but with the struggle of women to achieve full equality. After almost two decades languishing in the congressional hopper, the Equal Pay Act was finally poised to become law, an advance in which my father, the father of two daughters, was thoroughly invested.

As the daughter of one of the first female graduates of the University of Pennsylvania, I was not unaware of the implications that bill had for the shape of my future. The old Philco television set in my father's library broadcast no weekly news magazines to unravel the myriad facets of the discrimination against women. And my local daily paper, the *Philadelphia Inquirer*, contributed little to public understanding of such inequity within the Cradle of Liberty. I picked up an awareness of discrimination and harassment, both niggling and concrete, from the conversations of my parents and their friends, from the almost casual comments of guidance counselors, from the newspaper want ads, which still divided employment opportunity by gender.

My enthusiasm over the prospect of legislation that would guarantee me equal pay for equal work, however, was tempered by the cautions of my father, who was too well-read to be an optimist, yet too naturally optimistic to be a full-blown cynic. Just after the Civil War, he warned me, Congress had mandated equal pay for equal work in the federal civil service, but few women saw any benefit from that reform. And the private sector had remained stubbornly committed to a pay scale that rewarded white men for their gender and skin color, no matter their position or skills.

The Equal Pay Act itself had first been introduced into Congress by Claude Pepper of Florida and Wayne Morse of Oregon the year before I was born, after women had proven their mettle in the most male-dominated segments of the workforce during World War II. The Women's Bureau of the Department of Labor had pulled out all the stops to ensure the bill's passage, organizing a National Equal Pay Commission that, in turn, launched a major media campaign in the popular press, women's magazines, and labor union papers. They got as far as hearings in 1945—but not a step further.

Year after year, session after session, the bill was reintroduced. Year after year, session after session, it languished despite the support of both political parties, leading labor leaders, and President Dwight David Eisenhower. Congressional committees held hearings again in 1948 and 1950, but, for the following decade, the bill couldn't be budged an inch closer to the floor.

Every study, every report demonstrated with no equivocation that separate, unequal pay scales were maintained for male and female workers in manufacturing, education, office work, and the professions. In a survey conducted by the National Office Management Association in 1961, for example, one-third of more than nineteen hundred employers queried admitted openly to the practice. Despite the war experience, Americans still clung stubbornly to their beliefs about women and work, and those included the belief that men should be paid more than women because they had families to support. The latter, a signal socialistic concept, was strangely out of synch with the anticommunist hysteria of the Cold War era in which it was raised. And it was strangely irrational to apply that logic to single men without families, and not to single mothers who had them. But it was proffered nonetheless by such companies as Westinghouse in justifying its practice of reducing wage rates for women's jobs by 20 percent.

Corporate America was following, in a helter-skelter fashion, the model of the "Australian wage" popular in most of Europe as well. In Australia, state and federal tribunals set minimum rates of pay for almost all occupations. Until 1975, those tribunals categorized occupations by gender and set the wages accordingly, on the assumption that all men, and no women, supported families. The minimum wage for a "male occupation" was based, then, on the cost of living for a man, his wife, and their children. The minimum wage for a "female occupation" was set to allow a single woman to scrape by on her own. In New York City at the turn of the last century, for example, male public school teachers were paid $900 a year while their female counterparts earned just $600 and male telephone operators received $75 to $100 per month while female operators were paid $30 to $50. And things didn't change much for the next half-century.

Today the Equal Pay Act—indeed, the very concept of equal pay for equal work—hardly feels revolutionary. It is a simple statement of the simplest equation of justice. But even as late as 1963, it drove yet another wedge into a nation already splintering under the force of its own hypocrisy. And it provided me with my first direct lesson in the fine points of the ongoing war between equality and self-interest.

My homeroom teacher, whom I shall call Mr. H., seemed perpetually offended by the incursion of Jewish Democratic families like mine into the sea of Episcopalian Republicans that was the Main Line of Philadelphia, and never missed an opportunity to strike a blow for the honor of white men slaving to build homes and futures for their families. For two years I'd endured his diatribes about malleable southern blacks being whipped up by communist agitators determined to topple the social order. And now the president, he said, a Catholic (a word he pronounced with undisguised disdain), was being led around by the nose by a bunch of pinko females who oughta be home taking care of the kids.

Earlier that same year, Mr. H. and I had come to verbal blows over the case of Alger Hiss, whose innocence then seemed apparent to me, naively, perhaps, in the face of evidence collected from random pumpkin patches. So it was inevitable that we'd come to verbal blows over the Equal Pay Act. I, a naive teenager certain that politics was governed by Big Principles, saw the controversy as a clear-cut contest between right and wrong. Mr. H., of course, tried to set me straight. Justice, he insisted, was not the issue. What was at stake was the very backbone of our nation, the American family, which counted on men to bring home the bacon. Should single women be paid as much as these workers, who, by any measure, *needed* more income than they did? he asked. Isn't it selfish, he asked, for a woman working for pocket change to demand the same pay as a man who had four or five mouths to feed?

I learned a lesson, although not exactly the one Mr. H. intended. It was, in a sense, a new appreciation of Gilbert and Sullivan's admonition about skim milk masquerading as cream. I saw clearly, for the first time, how naturally the self-interested find ways to cloak their privilege in moral superiority—without even realizing what they are doing. Mr. H. hadn't calculated a strategy in order to defend the special benefits he received because of his gender. He believed his own rhetoric. That much was obvious. And that mantle of self-righteousness—his sincere belief that he was defending some version of truth, justice, and the American way—provided him full ethical cover to trample on the rights of women without reluctance or moral compunction.

Ours was the high-school version of the argument being played out both in the halls of Washington and in the nation's newspapers. "The apparently general approval of 'equal pay for equal work' seems to me to overlook a reality of our socio-economic order: the inequality, by and large, of the economic responsibilities of men as compared with women," one Copal Mintz wrote in a letter printed in *The New York Times* on June 12, 1963. "Pay to the sole supporter of a family equal to the pay to one who supports only herself means inequality of access to the necessities (and material niceties) of life."

The supporters of the Equal Pay Act countered as did I, with appeals to fundamental moral principles, rather than reminders of the growing number of women who were supporting their families. Secretary of Labor Lewis Baxter Schwellenbach declared, "Pay is for work done, rather than for the number of dependents of the workers." And, writing in response to Mintz, H. Gordon of Brooklyn exposed the absurdity of the whole "family wage" argument; "What Mr. Mintz is saying is that if a man wants to earn more, all he has to do is have more children, not do a better job."

That rhetoric, of course, made nary a dent in the opposition to equal pay. The battle had been joined over the preservation of the American family, which its defenders equated with the preservation of the American Way of Life, whatever that meant. The issue was so charged that employers who disapproved of the new scheme declared themselves ready to find new, presumably legal, ways to keep the old system alive—by awarding extra perks to men supporting families or awarding special "head of household" bonuses to theoretically "equalize" wages.

As the Equal Pay Act moved inexorably toward passage, surmounting Senate subcommittees, House committees, and the full votes on both sides of the Capitol, I raced to school each morning, anxious to gloat over the mounting discomfort of my homeroom nemesis. Alas, I was denied my final triumph. By the time that President John F. Kennedy, surrounded by the avant garde of a women's movement that did not exist in the public consciousness—Dr. Minnie Miles, president of Business and Professional Women; Dr. Dorothy Height, president of the National Council of Negro Women; Congresswomen Edith Green and Edna Kelly; Assistant Secretary of Labor Esther Peterson—signed into law that simple piece of legislation that permanently changed the legal landscape for working women, school had adjourned for the summer.

But I savored that moment as my first personal triumph of honor over expediency, of principle stripping away the facade of moral haughtiness to reveal its brazen self-interest. With that stroke of the presidential pen, America committed itself to guaranteeing the nation's women the simplest and most basic foundation of economic justice, equal pay for equal work. At least on paper. At least for some women. I was still too young to understand precisely how right my skeptical father would turn out to be.

Every time I hear Bill Clinton or some other political hack pontificate about "shoring up the beleaguered American family" (which, by my calculations, has been beleaguered for at least a century), every time I watch Katie Couric gush over *Working Mother* magazine's efforts to foster "family-friendly" companies, every time I argue with high-paid lawyers or journalists about the tax cuts they need "for the children," I think back to that spring of the Equal Pay Act, to the exquisite pirouettes executed by opponents of equal treatment, and to our national inability to learn the lessons of our own history.

All these "family-friendly" policies strike a blow for the needs of parents—mothers, actually, although we are too politically correct to codify that truth into law—precisely as the wage structure before the Equal Pay Act protected the needs of men who were raising families. The gender of the advantaged might have become more inclusive, but the principle those special protections violates has not changed one whit.

In an age in which the stresses and traumas of parenting have become a near-obsession, however, hammered home by weekly magazine features about moms exhausted by double duty and by politicians staking their electoral fortunes on tough talk not about crime but about the plight of our children, I realize that arguing with those entitlements sounds churlish. The attempts of the childless to provoke some discussion, any discussion, of the competing principle of *fairness,* then, are dismissed out of hand, or simply not registered on the national radar screen. Against the incessant recitations of parental woes, they go against the grain of communitarian thinking in this age of Hillaryesque villages.

But the first stirring of demands by any minority always sound selfish, or at least out of touch with the *zeitgeist.* That is the nature of majoritarian tyranny, which is not just the monopolization of resources and power, but, more perniciously, of thought and morality.

If history is any guide, that monopoly isn't broken easily. Reasoned appeals to justice are rarely sufficient to break through the predominant thinking, or the interests and self-interests it serves. African-Americans, women, and gays had to take to the streets. They had to grab Americans by the scruff of their collective necks and shake them out of old patterns of thinking so that competing principles of need and fairness, equity and equality, could be rebalanced in that tense dance that is American democracy.

We are approaching a new round in that tango. As parents continue to raise the bar, pressing for more time off for PTA meetings and more postpartum leave to bond with their newborns, a growing number of childless adults are declaring, "Enough." They are crying "foul" over the extra hours heaped onto their schedules and filing complaints about employee benefits plans that reward fertility, rather than merit or longevity. They are organizing against Republican proposals to give tax breaks to parents who send their children to private schools and against school choice. And as they listen to political rhetoric about relief for working families and then examine the resulting legislation, they are asking in increasingly strident voices how and when they got written off by their elected representatives.

The first skirmishes have run the gamut from the sublime to the vaguely ridiculous. In Colorado, a childless couple in their fifties who had enrolled at the university took on the student housing service over its policy of reserving married student housing for married students with children. Although housing discrimination against families with children is against the law, they discovered that housing discrimination against families without children is not—which has provoked a furor among nonparents already feeling like second-class citizens.

The stirrings have even made it into the popular media. Two seasons ago, the newfound fury of nonparents cropped up on *The Drew Carey Show*, with an episode about the boss sending workers with kids home because a storm was coming in, turning the freeways into skating rinks. "What about us?" their childless counterparts asked. "Is it okay for us to get killed on the ride home since we won't leave behind any orphans?" And Bill Maher managed to ruffle more than a few female feathers on *Politically Incorrect* first by insisting that the Child Tax Credit was designed not to help factory workers and cashiers teetering on the brink so much as to relieve yuppie parents so that they could buy Jet Skis.

A voting gap—a parent gap, actually—has emerged in electoral politics. In the 1996 congressional elections, for instance, voters with no children at home cast their ballots 48 percent for the Democrats and 40 percent for Republicans, while parents with children at home preferred the Republicans 54 percent to 35 percent for Democrats. And in that year's presidential election, married parents favored Bob Dole over Bill Clinton 49 percent to 40 percent, while married voters without children favored Clinton over Dole 48 percent to 44 percent.

The message is clear and simple: Raising kids used to be the responsibility of those who bore them, and so it should remain. Sure, Americans paid for public education. That's a cost of a vibrant democracy. And we underwrote Head Start and Upward Bound and scores of other programs essential to help the needy, the unable. That's a matter of justice. Handing out goodies to parents just because they are parents, however, is not about justice, about helping the disadvantaged, creating a less steeply sloped playing field, or helping kids. It's affirmative action—the preferential treatment of one group designed to correct real or perceived discrimination or inequity—based on reproductive choice.

Obviously, such a conclusion will not endear me to the minions of the growing parental rights movement. But the job of the contrarian journalist isn't to win popularity contests. It is to stick a foot in the path of facile assumptions and glib rhetoric to send complacency sprawling. So the coming pages may well be disconcerting because they ask, in a skeptic's voice, whether such catchphrases as "for the children" and "in the name of the family" underpin a serious attempt to address pressing social problems or a political dance staged, like Mr. H.'s jig against equal pay, in the name of some illusory and unnamed "greater good."

At the risk of being less than prosaic, let me end with a bit of housekeeping, by laying out the logic behind what you are about to read. The first section details the shape, texture, and shading of the new face of family-friendliness, in the workplace and in social policy. The second asks what has impelled America on this course. Is this a sincere effort to bolster the future and fortunes of today's children, or are less noble motivations driving this train? Finally, the third and last section explores what the nation's new obsession with parenting means both for the childless and for such basic principles as fairness, equity, and personal responsibility, and posits the steps we might take to redress the imbalance between parents and nonparents.

America's New Family-Friendly Face

In the Workplace and in Public Policy

1

Unequal Work for Unequal Pay

By midmorning, even the brightly colored plastic blocks seem too heavy for the preschoolers enrolled at the daycare center run by Neuville Industries in Hildebran, North Carolina, and Barney's antics, which normally draw wild giggles of delight, have become a soporific. It's already been a long day for most of the seventy kids there, who have been busy since before 6:00 A.M. at what Americans in the nineties like to think of as "structured play" while their mothers have been toiling at knitting or seaming machines, or hassling with personnel problems or accounting glitches on the other side of the building.

Just after 11:00 A.M., a white panel truck pulls up alongside the low metal sheds on a hill above the small town that is little more than a blip on a rural highway. As the driver begins unloading stainless-steel trays piled high with the day's lunch, the odors of chicken-fried steak, biscuits, and gravy signal dozens of women on the factory floor to shut down their machines and wander down to the infant room to breastfeed their newborns before nourishing themselves, to pick up toddlers with sniffles for checkups with the company nurse, or grab their sons and daughters for quick family lunches in the company cafeteria. As the women race through corridors that jig-jag around the warrenlike offices and manufacturing rooms, Steve Neuville stops to chat, comparing notes on their children and his grandchildren, who throw food at one another and take naps together at the on-site daycare center sponsored by the textile company Steve owns.

The modest waiting room at Neuville is adorned with none of the brightly colored socks that the textile company manufactures for such companies as Keds. Rather, the walls there are decorated with the awards and newspaper plaudits Steve has received for building one of the nation's most "family-friendly" companies. The small mill is the kind of workplace we're told most working mothers would kill for, offering a first-rate on-site daycare center and the freedom to carve your eight-hour shift out of a twelve-hour time slot so you can grab that precious midday hour to take a child to the dentist or meet with a teacher at school. Neuville employees can sign their kids up for swimming lessons, have their photographs taken for Christmas cards, arrange for their school immunizations with the company nurse, have their oil changed by a mobile lube service that comes to the plant—and eat lunch with their kids at the company cafeteria.

Compared to most American companies, where working mothers have to fend for themselves, that largesse is startling. But it is modest in comparison to what other mothers and children around North Carolina—where six of *Working Woman* magazine's favorite companies are located—have come to enjoy in a state caught up in a frenzy of mother-friendly initiatives. Over in Cary, on the edge of the famed Research Triangle, the five hundred children at the daycare centers run by SAS, the world's largest privately held software company, play and study in an environment blessed by Montessori. They picnic with their parents by the six-acre lake in the center of a two-hundred-acre "campus" dotted by those oversized, brightly colored geometric nightmares that are called "public art." They toss plastic discs with their fathers on the Ultimate Frisbee green, or sip hot and sour soup with their mothers in the company café, soothed by live piano music. Until the Internal Revenue Service put the kibosh on such generosity, parents paid absolutely nothing for the kind of daycare few elsewhere can possibly imagine.

Such pampering isn't all that extreme in the high-tech world where competitors routinely steal programmers and designers from one another. SAS employees, whose average age is thirty-three, take breaks in rooms stocked with soft drinks and bottomless jars of M&Ms, a natatorium, and free laundry service in the company gym for granted. They think those are standard working conditions in Corporate America. Only the rest of us know better.

But it isn't just SAS that knows how to treat working parents. Less than an hour from Neuville's plant, in the bustling city of Charlotte, employees of NationsBank enjoy six weeks of paid maternity and paternity leave, adoption leave, unpaid fostercare leave. When they return to work, they can gear back up on reduced schedules and place their children nearby in the company daycare center. Those working out of Atlanta can choose to use a childcare center in which the bank is a partner. Workers assigned to sites without company daycare receive tax-free corporate subsidies that allow them to purchase better childcare than they might normally be able to afford. By 1996, the bank had spent more than $25 million to provide childcare to the parents among its sixty-five thousand employees. Parents at all of the bank's worksites receive two paid hours off each week to meet with their children's teachers or attend school events, and the company matches any gifts and contributions they make to their kids' schools.

In Winston-Salem, the men and women still left working at R.J. Reynolds, the unsung corporate hero of "family-friendly" programs, can take advantage of a daycare resource and referral service that Joe Camel built in cooperation with several other local businesses. Office workers wanting more flexible schedules to accommodate the busy lives of their kids are encouraged to "just ask" about working from home, coming in early, or working late. And those toiling in manufacturing—where salaries average forty-five thousand dollars a year—can trade the standard thirty-seven-and-one-half-hour, Monday-through-Friday workweek in favor of two twelve-hour shifts on the weekend, for the exact same pay.

Unlike SAS, of course, Neuville isn't a high-tech industry with a professional workforce likely to be filched by a competitor. It is a mill where undereducated workers spend their days tending knitting machines, manipulating sewing machines and airhoses, or standing on their feet to slip socks onto the obligatory slice of cardboard. And Hildebran isn't the Research Triangle, or even urban Winston-Salem. Theirs is the North Carolina that has a Baptist church at each intersection—Redeemed, Free Will, Calvary, or First. For more than a century, women in this region in the foothills of the mountains have labored in textile mills while their husbands worked in furniture manufacturing.

So Steve Neuville didn't get into the "family-friendly benefits" business to keep highly skilled employees from being stolen by Microsoft, or because a "women's committee" demanded it, as has happened in heavily white-collar companies. When he opened his manufacturing plant in 1979, moving a family business as a hosiery middleman into production, his budget didn't leave room for him to match the going wage, even in the low-wage hosiery industry. With keen business acumen tinged by altruism, Steve and his wife seized on the idea of opening a daycare center to pull women who might not otherwise be willing or able to work out of their homes and into his plant.

They had no idea that they were breaking new ground. Robert Owen, who ran a major cotton-mill complex in New Lanark, Scotland, pioneered the concept of employer-run childcare in 1816, when he created a preschool for children over the age of one. "This baby school is of great consequence to the establishment," a visitor commented after a tour of the unique facility, "for it enables the mothers to shut up their houses in security, and to attend to their duties in the factory, without concern for their families."

But few employers followed Owen's lead in the 163 years between the founding of the New Lanark school and the opening of Steve Neuville's first plant. The Kellogg Company of Battle Creek, Michigan, gave childcare a try in 1924 with a free center open from 7:00 A.M. to 11:00 P.M., but it closed in 1932. During World War II, defense plants and aircraft companies, many tapping public funds available for that purpose, provided care for the children of the women who were turning out the planes, ships, and guns that gave the Allies their victory.

In the years after the war, however, as the ideology of domestic bliss swallowed the nation, few companies offered working mothers anything but overt hostility. A handful of hospitals created daycare centers for nurses working night shifts and weekends. KLH, the stereo-equipment manufacturer, opened a daycare center for its workers in 1968. And in 1971, Polaroid began a subsidy program for workers to help offset the cost of daycare.

Although Steve didn't know it at the time, in 1979, there were only nine noninstitutional daycare centers connected to businesses in the United States. His, then, rounded the number off to ten. Back in those days—before daycare centers became the targets of reams of federal and state regulations, and before the concept of daycare as preschool had seized the national imagination—Steve's offering was a pretty modest affair. He set aside a spare office in his new building, hired a few women to watch the kids, and opened for business. Nonetheless, other mill owners in the area guffawed, betting that such generosity would run the kid from New York out of business in six months.

Twenty years later, that daycare center is the linchpin in a broad range of "family-friendly" programs available at Neuville. Workers pay sixty dollars a week to send their children or grandchildren to a center that teaches them Spanish and begins them on computers at the age of two. That's half the going rate for a high-quality center in that area, thanks to corporate subsidies that run about hundred thousand dollars a year—almost fifteen hundred dollars per child. Each child receives twenty-one days a year free, to help out parents running short of money around Christmas time, or dealing with a sudden bill for a family illness or a major car repair. And a consulting pediatrician helps keep children well enough that their parents don't have to leave work. "If we send a sick child home, we are losing a parent from the plant floor," says Chris Gates, who runs the center, a reminder that Neuville's concern is not entirely altruistic.

Parents who don't use the center regularly know that Chris will always find room for a child whose baby-sitter is sick or whose grandmother is off visiting an aunt. And parents of older children understand that if public schools are closed because of ice, snow, or a holiday, they can bring children to work, where they will be supervised and entertained by a substitute teacher Chris will call in.

Steve Neuville's scheme for luring workers into low-wage jobs—which, ironically, have become defined as the hallmark of a progressive company—has brought his small hosiery business nationwide recognition. *Working Mother* magazine has named Neuville one of the most mother-friendly companies in the nation for eight straight years. Reporters fly in to tour the facility. Other businessmen come by to quiz him about the intricacies of family-friendly programs. And Steve himself has become something of a poster boy for the type of corporate programs for which Bill Clinton's White House kept pressing.

Clinton has been stumping for these programs for more than three years, since he proclaimed the creation of "Family-Friendly Workplaces" as the first of his "Five Corporate Citizenship Challenges." Companies must create "workplaces that allow workers to be both productive workers and caring and responsible family members," the president declared in a speech at Xavier University in Ohio on March 23, 1996. "Companies that recognize our broader obligations as parents, family members and citizens off-the-job get more committed employees on-the-job." Steve Neuville has echoed the president, in both deed and word. "It would be easy to say that childcare isn't our business, that we shouldn't get involved with people's families," he says. "The idea of a wall between work and family still exists in old-line textile industries in the South. But it is silly to say that one shouldn't intrude on the other. It does."

But it is the bottom-line impact to which the president alluded in his speech in Ohio that nags at the endless stream of corporate honchos who come calling on Steve Neuville. "What's the payoff?" they ask him bluntly. His response is both canned and candid. "We decided years ago that we can't quantify that," he says. "In the end, it is a matter of faith."

That faith rests on shaky foundations. Even with daycare, flextime, and an on-call pediatrician, and with an amply publicized stamp of approval from *Working Mother* magazine, the putative arbiter of what every working mother desires, the women of western North Carolina aren't beating down the door to join Steve Neuville's workforce. Indeed, when Steve decided to build a second sock factory, he was forced to do so in Tennessee because he couldn't find enough workers to staff a new plant in North Carolina. That made no sense to me. Working women are supposed to flock to companies like Neuville and to cling to their jobs there with almost desperate loyalty. At least that's what an almost endless stream of news reports has taught us. So, after a morning visiting Neuville, I spent an afternoon and evening at the grocery store looking for explanations.

"Why would I care about the daycare center?" answered a female worker at a neighboring hosiery plant when I inquired if she wouldn't prefer to work at Neuville. "I don't have children." A neighbor shopping with her chimed in. "I do have kids, but my mother takes care of them, so fat good a daycare center would do me."

The Neuville workers, including some with children, were equally unimpressed. "It's a good place to work and the daycare is convenient, but I could think of other things I'd rather have," a young female employee responded. "What things?" I asked. "Oh," she said, laughing, almost embarrassed. "An extra dollar an hour to start." Overhearing the laughter, a coworker shopping nearby piped in, "A dollar an hour? I'd trade the daycare center for twenty-five cents an hour. But nobody seems to be asking me."

I turned back to the first woman, who had two children. "But wouldn't you have to spend a hefty part of that hour to make up for the daycare?" The response, in a classically bubbly mountain drawl, was out of her mouth before I could finish the word daycare. "No, I'd get a neighbor to watch them," she said. "Anyway, even if I wound up spending more money, it would be mine to do with as I please." The women, the granddaughters of rebellious female mill workers of the twenties and thirties who'd instigated walkouts and strikes throughout North Carolina, have lost most of the fire of their forebears in confronting management. They have accepted the eight- to ten-dollar-an-hour wage they earn without struggle or argument. They would not allow their names to be printed.

Steve Neuville is convinced that his daycare center was critical to his success, but it is unclear how effective his center ever was in pulling female workers out of the home. After all, when the plant was first built, in the late 1970s, the nation was in the midst of a deep recession. Money was tight and women in that region had relatively few employment opportunities. And, no matter the initial appeal of such family-friendliness, its allure has changed dramatically over the past twenty years. In the early 1980s, for example, 85 percent of the children in the center had mothers who worked on the plant floor. Today, although 85 percent of Neuville's employees labor in manufacturing, only 50 percent of the children enrolled in the daycare center have parents who work there. Of those, few are African-American or Hispanic, and none are Hmong refugees from Cambodia, despite the large number of women of color employed at Neuville. The other half of the children belong to women who work in accounting, human resources, and information systems, who make up less than 15 percent of the workforce. They, Steve Neuville readily acknowledges, are the women he would lose if not for the center. "I guarantee you," he says, "that they'd be grabbed up by the cable industry or other employers in a second."

Neuville is far from unique. Companies small and large have jumped onto the "family-friendly" train and ridden it right past their lowest-paid employees into the offices of the most affluent women on their staffs. Ask Donna Klein of Marriott Corporation, who has been trying to redirect the locomotive for almost a decade. Ten years ago, the management at Marriott assigned Donna, who was then involved in management training for the company, to design a work/family program that would help the company meet the needs of its increasingly female labor force. That was no mean feat for a corporation with six thousand worksites scattered across the world and 135,000 employees, 85 percent of them hourly workers whose schedules varied in any given month from full-time to part-time, from day shift to night shift.

Those were the days when the idea of on-site daycare centers had captured the imaginations of female human resources executives, many of them feminists building the newest incarnation of their movement on their concern for working mothers. They managed to win over corporate bigwigs when company lawyers suggested the legal wisdom of proving their commitment to women in a material fashion. Caught up in that excitement, Donna began exploring how Marriott could jump on that bandwagon. Intuitively, at least according to upper-middle-class professional intuitive logic, it made sense that twenty-four-hour, seven-day-a-week daycare centers would be salvation for women working for peanuts on terrible schedules. They could drop their children off at well-equipped, high-quality daycare centers on their way to work and labor through the night without the stress of worrying if their kids were in danger or getting proper care. They could look in on them during breaks, then pick them up at the end of the shift and take them home. The logic seemed impeccable.

Donna spent years struggling to turn that logic into reality, trying to make a business case for spending the kind of money such a center would entail. Finally, in 1992, "I put a stake in the sand," she says. "I decided we had to resolve whether it was really possible for us, as a company, to deliver high-quality childcare to low-income workers." By then, she says, the challenge had become personal. Klein convinced executives from Omni,

Hyatt Regency, and Hilton to join Marriott in a consortium to build and run a pilot center for the children of hotel employees in the middle of downtown Atlanta. The need was certainly there: Everyone had heard rumors about night housekeepers tucking their children in on the backseats of cars they'd parked in downtown garages. The city and state governments were willing to cough up public funds. And the workers, surveyed by their employers, expressed keen excitement.

The $2.5 million center, the Atlanta Inn for Children, opened in 1997 to enormous hoopla. Mayor Bill Campbell showed up to cut the ribbon. Hotel executives ate peanut butter and jelly sandwiches with the kids— apparently unaware of the dangers of peanut allergies. The newspapers declared that, thanks to corporate good citizenry, a new day had dawned for minimum-wage workers in Atlanta. Donna Klein waited for housekeepers and waitresses, front desk clerks, office managers, and maintenance men to show up in herds at the door.

She is still waiting. The center's tuition, charged on a sliding scale, is highly subsidized, with Marriott contributing five thousand dollars toward the cost of caring for each enrolled child. Yet when the inn threw open its doors, only 109 children had been enrolled in a facility built for 250. The companies involved barraged their workers with information about the new facility, the regular well-baby checkups their kids would receive, the immunizations, the educational programs. They even threw up billboards to advertise the scholarship slots open to nonhotel employees. Three months later, enrollment had increased to only 170. It still is not full.

Meanwhile, the childcare center at Marriott's headquarters in Bethesda, Maryland, had a waiting list. The only problem Donna faced there were the constant demands of white-collar and professional parents for more services, including covered parking.

What's going on? Experts advance varying—all equally speculative— explanations. "I don't know whether it is cultural or what," says Donna Klein, pointing out, as all experts do, that white workers are more likely to enroll their children in institutional daycare centers than black workers of similar incomes, and that immigrant women shy away from such sites. Women workers interviewed at Neuville offered their own clue: Many don't have children, and many of those who do prefer the cash to the ben-

efit, unlike high-income women obsessed either with daycare as education or with minimizing their taxes.

An extensive survey commissioned by the AFL-CIO in 1997, *Ask a
Working Woman,* suggests that the women on the factory floor of Neuville
are not alone. When fifty thousand working women were asked what was
important to them on the job, they ranked equal pay, health insurance, a
safe workplace, job security, and paid sick leave at the top of their wish
list. Childcare was second from the bottom of their concerns, just below
continuing education and just above eldercare. That should have come as
no surprise, since, if the fifty thousand working women surveyed mir-
rored the female workforce, most did not have young children.

Karen Nussbaum, head of the Working Women's Department of the
AFL-CIO, seems unmoved by that demographic reality. Refusing to accept
the survey responses at face value, she explains them away, alternately, by
insisting that the very notion of the good, inexpensive corporate daycare
center is such a pipedream that most working women dismiss it as unat-
tainable, and, then, by bemoaning the lack of awareness among her own
members. "It is clear that we have a lot more education to do. It is obvious
that these women don't know about the brain research," she says, referring
to studies suggesting that experiences and interactions with caregivers
from the day of a child's birth profoundly affect how his or her brain ma-
tures.

Corporate daycare is just the tip of the iceberg. Few of the new "family-
friendly benefits" have much to do with the lives of most American workers. In fact, most of the highly touted innovations are entirely irrelevant to
them since most workers aren't the kind of middle-class working mothers
who dream up these benefits in the first place. Look at what the "best"
companies—the companies honored by *Working Mother* magazine, by
Business Week, or the Women's Bureau of the Department of Labor, which
actually printed an Honor Roll of well-behaved corporations—are offering their employees.

Fel-Pro Incorporated is precisely the type of company Americans expect not to have superb "family" benefits. This is no white-collar corporation heavy with kid-gloves executives nor a high-tech business packed with

professionals and technicians who could move to, say, North Carolina, Boston, or Silicon Valley with a single phone call. Fel-Pro's twenty-one hundred employees—40 percent of them female—manufacture engine gaskets, sealants, and lubricants in the industrial section of Skokie, Illinois.

But it is a parental heaven, with on-site daycare, a summer camp for kids at the company's two-hundred-acre park, subsidized in-home childcare for those days when the baby-sitter doesn't show up or a child is ill. New parents receive a one-thousand-dollar check as a gift for their baby and two months of unpaid leave. Adoptive parents receive fifteen hundred dollars to help out with the legal bills. Parents of older children can take advantage of a special program that helps them explore college options. And if their children are outstanding students, they even receive corporate scholarships.

IBM boasts the nation's most generous family-leave policy, granting parents three years with full benefits. It has spent millions of dollars to help its employees with childcare, spending five hundred thousand dollars on one North Carolina daycare center in conjunction with Duke Power, Allstate, and American Express. Parents can carve out their work schedules any time from 6:30 A.M. to 10:30 P.M., or opt for a "midday flex."

The largesse of major companies is dramatic. Eli Lilly provides up to ten thousand dollars in financial aid for adoption. BE&K, one of the nation's largest building contractors, owns a modular daycare center that it moves from site to site to provide for the children of construction workers. Stride-Rite, the shoe manufacturer, allows new parents eight weeks of paid leave and eighteen weeks more unpaid but with full benefits and job protection. And Hallmark lends tuition money, interest-free, to parents with five or more years of service.

When *Working Mother* began its best companies list in 1985, editors say they could find only thirty companies marginally qualified for the title of mother-friendly. Now hundreds vie for those slots. According to Hewitt Associates' annual survey of the benefits packages of America's employers, 72 percent allow parents some sort of flexible schedules, 86 percent sponsor a childcare benefit program, 31 percent provide family-leave benefits that are more generous than the federal government requires, 25 percent subsidize adoptions, and a wide array of programs, everything from after-school hotlines to family care days, vacation camps, and tuition reimbursement, for the children of their workers, are spreading like wildfire.

Survey after survey confirms that same picture of a family-friendly workplace movement reshaping the nature of work for American parents. A 1998 survey of more than one thousand companies conducted by the Families and Work Institute found that 88 percent of all companies with more than one hundred employees allow parents time off for school functions; 15 percent offer more than twelve weeks of maternity leave, and more than half with some pay; 24 percent award scholarships or other educational assistance to the children of their employees; and 87 percent paid for at least part of the health insurance of their employees' families.

The magazine editors, human resources officers, consultants, and politicians who promote these programs, and themselves in the process, argue their value not just on humanistic or moral grounds, but as wise bottom-line decisions. Family-friendliness, they say, pays by promoting loyalty and productivity, reducing absenteeism, tardiness, and turnover, and polishing a company's public image. Such testimonials are legion. The Families and Work Institute presents flow charts and graphs proving that businesses with more "supportive workplaces" have more satisfied employees who are more committed to the success of their employers and more likely to remain on the job. They cite the case of the pharmaceutical giant Johnson & Johnson, where absenteeism plummeted after the introduction of a raft of family programs. Officials at Fel-Pro claim that their turnover rate dropped from between 30 and 40 percent to 10 percent after they opened a company summer camp. Merck reports that it saves three dollars for each dollar it spends on family programs because workers wind up less stressed, less likely to arrive at work late or leave before the end of the workday, to miss work to take care of sick children, or to quit to stay home with the kids. John Fernandez, a Philadelphia management consultant, posits that family-friendly programs can reduce absenteeism by as much as 19 percent and the rate of employee turnover from 8 to 3 percent.

By the time *Business Week* published the results of its first survey of family-friendly corporate America in 1996, Corporate America was in full swoon. "Disbelievers, skeptics, working stiffs, take note," proclaimed the magazine. "Work-family strategies haven't just hit the corporate mainstream—they've become a competitive advantage. . . . It is a phenomenon, in other words, that executives deny at their own risk."

The numbers, however, don't add up, given the demographics of the American workforce. How can turnover and absenteeism drop so precipitously in response to childcare assistance, family leaves, and scholarships for employees' kids when, according to the Bureau of Labor Statistics, only one-third of the workforce has children at home under the age of eighteen? How can daycare centers account for 50 percent reductions in turnover when only 8 percent of women workers have kids under the age of six? How can a company like Chase Manhattan Bank spend seven hundred thousand dollars a year to run a daycare center in Brooklyn for 110 children and justify the expenditures by citing "return-on-investment" analyses showing savings of $1.5 million in avoided absenteeism alone? Were the parents of those 110 children missing that much work?

Since there are 13 million more working women without kids at home than with kids—38 million to 25 million—how can corporate America's obsession with family-friendliness possibly be improving morale? Adoption allowances, maternity and paternity leave, childcare, sick kid care, afterschool care, and summer camps are entirely irrelevant to them. Those benefits don't do all that much for workers who do have kids, since the vast majority don't adopt, don't seem not to want institutional daycare, and can't take long parental leaves because they can't afford six months without income.

Rather than boosting morale, in fact, the programs are having an opposite effect—and for logical reasons. How would you feel if you had no children and worked at Fel-Pro, where employees have access to child-centric benefits worth thousands of dollars more than the benefits you can use? Imagine what it is like to work at *The New York Times,* where parents can claim long unpaid leaves to bond with their children as a right while those without children who ask for unpaid leave to pursue *their* interests, which usually involve writing books, are subject to management whimsy, which often means that their requests are denied.

Consider what state your morale would be in if you, as a nonparent, heard endlessly about your company's concern for employee morale and the balance in their lives, then discovered that the office charged with both was called Work/Family and spent most of its resources referring parents to daycare centers and planning luncheon workshops on parenting. Would you not ask how the morale of the other two-thirds of the workforce was being tended? And think what it would feel like to be on the staff at NationsBank and hear the chief executive officer call the bank a "meritocracy" when you know that the flexible schedule of the man sitting next to you, or the five thousand dollars in extra benefits of the woman behind you, aren't rewards for meritorious work, but for reproduction.

In today's workplace, childless employees are well-versed in the Ten Commandments of workplace etiquette in family-friendly America. They're not yet included in employee handbooks, or posted prominently on bulletin boards alongside flyers about safety or workers' compensation. But they are etched into the experience of virtually every nonparent who works alongside parents.

1. Thou shalt volunteer to work late so that mothers can leave at 2:00 P.M. to watch their sons play soccer, for a mother's time is more valuable than thine.

2. Thou shalt never complain when important meetings are broken up at 2:30 by phone calls from children reporting in after school lest thou be considered indifferent to the importance of parental bonding.

3. Thou shalt take thy vacations when no one else wants time off so parents can take theirs during the summer, over Christmas, or on any other school or "family" holiday.

4. Thou shalt not apply the phrase "equal pay for equal work" to thy company's benefits plan, although it offers mothers and fathers thousands of dollars in perks thou can't use.

5. Thou shalt willingly do two jobs for the price of one while mothers are on six-month maternity and parental leaves.

6. Thou shalt never ask for a long leave to write a book, travel, or fulfill thy heart's desire because no desire other than children could possibly be worth thy company's inconvenience.

7. Thou shalt volunteer to take frequent business trips to places like Abilene, Kansas, or Cleveland, Ohio, so that parents can spend their evenings watching *ER* after they put the kids to bed.

8. Thou shalt promote thy "family-friendly" company as a firm that cherishes women because everyone knows that women equals mothers.

9. Thou shalt never utter the words "but that's not my problem" when a parent rushes out the door during the final negotiations of a corporate merger, explaining that he has promised to take the children to the movies.

10. Thou shalt smile graciously when thy coworker brings her three-year-old to the office and allows him to turn the papers on thy desk into airplanes.

But the number of apostates is skyrocketing in inverse proportion to the success of the apostles of more family-friendly workplaces. "There's a brand new uprising nationally," says Jane Yallum, mother of two, who runs a consulting company that helps corporations deal with work/family issues. "Single and childless employees feel discriminated against because they can't take advantage of benefits created for the family."

The more parent-friendly workplaces become, the less comfortable they are for nonparents, which is pushing many into overt hostility. Listen to Sandy Graf, a thirty-seven-year-old designer, who is married but childless by choice. "People seem to think a professional office can double as a petting zoo, so they bring [children] in all the time. They are very disruptive—running all over the place and making noise . . . it is a huge distraction for those that are actually trying to work." That's not Sandy's only gripe. "Breeders get *so* much time off to tend to the emergency sicknesses or the accidents or the school this and that. Who covers for them, who works more hours? The non-breeders, that's who. *And no one notices.* We are punished for not squirting out spawn."

Erin Galvin seethes almost daily about the treatment of childless employees at the small midwestern bank where she works. The working conditions there are terrific, especially the almost universal availability of flextime. But Erin is rankled by the value of the benefits designed to help working mothers that turn her compensation package into a mockery of the principle of equal pay. And she remains openly irritated that one of her childless coworkers was forced to give up the four-day schedule she had long enjoyed in order to accommodate the desires of a new team member who was a mother.

A childless woman who works in a hospital laboratory, and prefers not to be named, says this: "In our laboratory everybody likes to work the early morning shifts. Well, my shift has been 6:00 A.M. to 2:00 P.M. for ten years now. However, as the breeder's rugrats have been growing these years, more and more breeders have been whining that they need to work such and such hours to pick Johnny up from daycare or to drop Susie off at school, etc., etc. Over the ten years that I have worked at this hospital, my schedule has been adjusted to fit the needs of the breeders, which I think is totally discriminatory."

Like most childless workers, John Kiriacon, a health educator at the University of Miami who is gay and childless, is less perturbed by the extra hours he spends covering for parental coworkers than by the fact that his benefits package is so much skimpier than theirs. The university is not a notably family-friendly employer. But, like most institutions of higher education, it offers parents one employee benefit that is worth tens of thousands of dollars: free tuition for their families. Tuition, which tops nineteen thousand dollars per year, is waived for their children to pursue both undergraduate work and master's degrees. So a staff member whose two children take full advantage of this perk enjoys a bonus worth about $250,000.

At the nation's most prestigious universities, the deal is sweeter still. Parents who work at the University of Chicago, for example, can send their children, tuition-free, to any university in the nation, for the full range of undergraduate and graduate work. Nonparents, of course, have no equivalent benefit. "I would never begrudge my colleagues that benefit," says Dr. David Tracy, Andrew Thomas Greeley and Grace McNichols Greeley Distinguished Service Professor in the Divinity School. Tracy has helped pay for the college educations of his nieces and nephews, with no assistance from the university. "But would it not be more just for the university to extend that benefit to all staff, at least in some measure, so that those of us without offspring could use it to help out nieces or cousins, or even donate scholarships to poor children?"

The breadth and depth of the resentment has been disguised by the reluctance of childless employees to complain publicly about their paltry benefits packages or the extra time they spend at work that forces them to miss the latest play, or another Christmas with friends. "Who wants to be labeled a childhater?" says Ilene Bilenky, a childless nurse in Boston. John Kiriacon of the University of Miami says he would never consider griping about the routine disappearances of his coworkers with family responsibilities. "They're my friends," he says, "I don't want to hurt them." Then he lowers his voice and adds, almost shyly, "But I wish someone felt the same way about me."

When childless workers reach the boiling point, they rarely explode or complain; they simply quit—contributing to the very retention problem family-friendly programs are allegedly designed to prevent. One legal secretary applied for flex-time and was told that benefit was available only to parents. She didn't file a grievance. She found another job.

But gradually, as employers and consultants use confidential surveys to test the impact of their family-friendly initiatives, the dimensions of the anger are becoming apparent. When *Personnel Journal* asked readers, "With all the work/family programs being introduced today, are employees without children being left out?" 80 percent responded yes. To "Do single employees end up carrying more of the burden than married employees?" 81 percent answered yes. And to "Will Corporate America see a backlash from single employees?" 69 percent responded in the affirmative.

That backlash is inevitable since every study, every survey suggests that the complaints of the childless aren't idle whining. By every measure, they are working more and reaping less than their parental counterparts. When the Conference Board surveyed seventy-eight companies with extensive parental benefits, not only did 57 percent admit that the nonparents in their workforce harbored some resentment toward colleagues with children, but 42 percent acknowledged that childless employees were subsidizing the health care of workers with children.

Furthermore, among the thirteen benefits covered in the Conference Board survey, the only ones used more frequently by childless employees were tuition assistance, domestic partner health insurance for gay and unmarried couples, and wellness programs such as fitness centers. Even seemingly "neutral" perks, such as financial planning, home mortgage assistance, eldercare assistance, legal assistance, and personal days, are used far more by workers with children.

The lament of nonparents that they are carrying a heavier workload than their colleagues with kids has also been borne out in repeated studies—most produced, ironically, to bolster the demand for more parental benefits. In a survey conducted for *Fortune* magazine, 46 percent of parents said they missed work one or more times during the previous three-month period because of family responsibilities. Another survey of twenty thousand employees at thirty-three companies in Portland, Oregon, revealed that women with children under the age of twelve were absent almost 25 percent more than women without children at home.

"It has created something of a hornet's nest," said Mary B. Young, a Boston-based consultant and author of "What's Behind Work/Family Backlash," a report issued in 1997 for the William Olsten Center for Workforce Strategies. Trying to gauge whether a backlash had set in against family-friendly benefits, Mary organized focus groups divided by parental status at various corporations. Her fear that no one would mention their anger was quickly dispelled. It came up in every group very early.

"A good society acknowledges the needs of all its members and supports those needs," she continues. "What drives me and other childless people crazy is the assumption that only parents have needs. They act as if what parents do is better, more important, as if raising children were a holy calling that lifts them up in terms of entitlement above the rest of us mere mortals. As a society we have to recognize that work time is a major social problem for all of us. If we only respond to parents because we've bought into the romanticization and idealization of family as the most exalted form of life, blood begins to boil."

For the most part, business executives haven't taken such warnings seriously. They are too busy keeping up with the corporate Joneses who are riding the "family-friendly" bandwagon and vying for the approval of *Working Mother* magazine. They know, or should know, that single and childless workers are the fastest-growing group in today's workforce. Nonetheless, they treat childlessness as a temporary condition that women will outgrow, so they assume that, in the end, everybody will "get theirs."

Few understand, or perhaps care, that the *assumption* that policies and benefits packages built around the needs of parents are fair because everyone has children is intrinsically insulting to many nonparents. Being ignored, after all—as if your interests, your commitments, aren't even a blip on the corporate radar screen—is degrading. But human resource professionals continue to design employee benefits packages, for example, around that very assumption. It's not just the daycare centers and parental leaves. It is life insurance policies, which most of the unmarried childless would love to trade for something relevant to their lives. It is company picnics organized around games for kids, flex-time limited to those with "family" responsibilities, scholarships, camps, and adoption benefits. American Express Financial Advisors, in Minneapolis, for example, offers eleven benefits designed specifically for parents, from quarterly seminars to reimbursement for childcare expenses when an employee with kids travels. The only perk used primarily by those without young children is the annual company holiday party. "This needs to be talked about," says Paul Demke, a securities broker there. Demke isn't asking that parents' benefits be canceled. A former high-school teacher, he is hardly hostile to the children of the mothers and fathers who work with him. But he wants equity—and few managers running the corporate show are listening to that plea.

Ironically, those managers are behaving exactly as their predecessors behaved before the passage of the Equal Pay Act in 1963, singling out "heads of household" for greater benefits and perquisites than those offered to other employees. Only the gender composition of the privileged has changed, so that today women, too, are enjoying such benefits. Unlike the early 1960s, however, today's secretary of labor is not railing against such unequal treatment, as did Kennedy's, who insisted, "Pay is for work done, rather than for the number of dependents of the workers." In fact, Clinton has thrown the full weight of the federal government behind "family-friendly" programs that directly violate this principle.

When asked directly about this contradiction, about the fairness of awarding superior perks and schedules based on parental status rather than the quality of an employee's work, most corporate executives wave their hands dismissively, or parrot such consultants as John Fernandez, who misses the point entirely. "Corporate America is not an egalitarian organization," he responds to the question of equity between parents and the childless. "The higher one's position the more perks one gets. No one has argued that this unequal treatment should be abolished."

Even those who have direct evidence of the anger and frustration of their own childless workers—from surveys, notes in suggestion boxes, and direct complaints—have proven unable to break out of the mind-set created by a decade of fierce lobbying by family-friendly workplace activists and consultants indifferent to the inequities they have forged. Confusing generosity or friendship with satisfaction, they point to reports from managers and to survey results indicating that nonparents routinely pitch in when parents have daycare problems or sick children as proof that tales of discontent have been drastically overstated. But the childless aren't heartless monsters. When a school nurse calls a coworker to report that her child has a fever, most freely offer to help out. And few are willing to risk the harsh scowl of their regular lunchmate by hesitating to stay an extra hour or so to allow a parent to catch a glimpse of her child in the championship soccer game. That does not mean they are happy about the continuing demands on their time, employer indifference to the inequities, or the lack of reciprocity. "It never comes back to you," a married, childless construction supervisor in Baltimore said. "Every time you are happy to cover for a friend, but when you add it all up, your turn never comes."

The problem is clear, whether or not corporate America wants to accept it: All that family-friendliness is provoking a crisis in morale. Jeff Guiler, a professor of management at Robert Morris College in Pittsburgh, sums it up succinctly. "What's happening out there now is that childless and single people are feeling they're getting the shaft."

The parents who reap the fruits of these inequities seem blithely unaware of the inequities they are breeding. When confronted directly about them, they obfuscate. They change the topic. They mount their moral high horse, turning a serious matter into a pissing match about who has more stress or makes the greater contribution to society. No one gives up hard-won privileges without a fight, and most parents aren't ceding a millimeter. It is hard to eavesdrop on the sort of conversations in which parents and nonparents tangle over these issues, since most occur spontaneously over the coffeepot or in the parking lot after work. But listen to what happened in April 1997, when *The Wall Street Journal* sponsored an interactive discussion on family issues in the workplace, staged as a sort of intellectual faceoff between Mike Mesko, who worked in forecasting and analysis at Patagonia, the sporting goods manufacturer, and Ann Price, who owned a small consulting company and was a member of the Childfree Network, one of the semiorganized groups representing nonparents.

Patagonia is the kind of company that *Working Mother* magazine promotes relentlessly. It maintains a high-quality, and heavily subsidized, onsite infant and childcare center, grants paid maternity and paternity leave for eight weeks, and gives adoptive parents a twenty-five-hundred-dollar check to help out with the expenses. Organized to facilitate breastfeeding, the company not only maintains a lactation room with breast pumps, refrigerators, and rocking chairs, but, if a nursing mother is at a meeting during feeding time, one of the caregivers from the center brings the baby to the conference room so she can breastfeed without skipping a professional beat.

When Mesko described those benefits, Ann Price asked, "What kind of child-free employee benefits are comparable to this?" Mesko seemed stunned and stammered out his insistence that the childless of Patagonia didn't mind the reduced benefits. Price countered, "I think there are a lot of child-free employees who keep their complaints to themselves because of the culture around them. Take the example of our bookkeeper. At her previous job, she says she always felt she had to pick up the slack for her counterpart, who took an administrative position instead of a more demanding job so that she could have more time for her children. It would be day number thirty-six that her counterpart was asking, 'Would it be OK if you stayed late or covered the phones for me even though you really should be going home now? Because my child is sick.' Or, 'Nobody came to pick my kid up,' or, 'There is a problem with the nanny,' etc., etc.

"The bookkeeper felt that it was really abusive. What's more, she felt that there was no opportunity for reciprocity. She couldn't say, 'I have a private errand to run, would it be OK if I left?' There would be a hundred questions: 'What kind of private errand? Is it the dentist? Is there a medical problem? Is it going to impact your work somehow?'"

Mesko was not moved. "The question of equality is a confusing one. No one here is sitting down and saying you have used 'X' amount of your benefits. It's a foreign thought to me even to be comparing it, dollar for dollar," he said, apparently unaware that those who receive more rarely make such calculations.

Price pressed her case. "If you're going to set aside money for benefits, at least give employees a list they can choose from. Say, 'Here's ten thousand dollars, and you can use it to take maternity leave, you can get fertility treatments, you can adopt, get a boob job, buy a breast pump, get your teeth whitened, take a course in the university, go traveling somewhere and find yourself,' or whatever list of things your company feels it can support. I'm just trying to say that there are people who are not in this equation. My issue is only that all employees—whether they are women or men, or are pregnant, or in a wheelchair—all employees should get the same benefits."

Nothing Price said made a dent in Mesko's thinking. "It's just the family-friendly culture of our company. Nobody says you have to work here." Price hesitated before answering, "You're telling me child-free people aren't wanted here?"

A similar exchange occurred in August 1994, when readers without kids lashed out at Richard Louv, a columnist at the *San Diego Union-Tribune,* for a piece he'd written about the importance of making the workplace more compatible with parenting. "Because I have no 'family,' it would be perceived that I have no 'life' and therefore could be exploited and imposed upon by my employer without restraint," one reader responded. Other workers need time off to care for children, or attend parent-teacher meetings or a child's performance? No problem: Just shunt their work onto people like me who have nothing in their lives except work anyway. We'll take up the slack."

Stung by the criticism, Louv penned a follow-up column in which he backed off a smidgen, laying down five principles that would provide parents with the flexibility they need without running roughshod over their coworkers. But he just didn't get it. "The first principle of a family-friendly workplace should be to define family as broadly as possible," he wrote. "Perhaps not today, perhaps tomorrow, a worker with no children may need workplace flexibility to visit or care for aging parents or an ailing spouse. Many employees may not have children of their own, but they're still child-connected; for example, they have nieces and nephews to whom they feel responsible, or they volunteer as a Big Brother or Big Sister." Further on, he noted, "The third principle of a family-friendly company should be: Flexible time and leave policies for all employees with family needs (and in some cases, family could be defined as the broader community). A study of Johnson & Johnson's flex time and leave policies found that parents did not abuse them, nor was there a rise in absenteeism and tardiness. Parents who took advantage of the program were less stressed, more satisfied with their jobs and more likely to recommend Johnson & Johnson as a place to work. A company would similarly benefit if such policies were extended to nonparents."

Louv's "more enlightened" plan fell like a dud bomb into the childless on-line community. "What about people without parents and without spouses?" asked one man. "Do we just forget about them? Is this guy dense? Can he see no value to any pursuit but family and children?" Most posters, however, reserved their deepest derision for Louv's easy resolution of the problem, the addition of care for ailing spouses and parents to the family-friendly mix. That had become a popular sop to nonparents—in employee benefits packages and in the Family and Medical Leave Act—long before it was suggested by Louv, a pretense of inclusiveness that sways few, who react as did the male on-line poster who wrote, "Come on, how many hours a year do most people take off to care for sick parents or an ailing spouse compared to the time taken by parents?"

It's not merely that parents seem willfully clueless about the inequities they are creating. Buoyed by the same boundless sense of entitlement as men in the pre–Equal Pay Act era—an abiding sense that nothing, no principle or purpose, could possibly be as noble as their parenting pursuits—they are utterly indifferent to counterarguments and counterclaims. Motherhood has, once again, become America's highest ideal, and no cause or person is too lofty to sacrifice to a mother's wants. And want they do. Despite the childcare, the maternity and parenting leave, flex-time, and corporate sensitivity training, the moms who are driving this train claim that society owes them still more—not more wants, in their argot, but more *rights,* as they call them. And they are finding lawyers all too willing to make their case in court.

In July 1998, for example, Alicia Martinez, a former producer at MSNBC, filed a lawsuit against the network claiming that she had a federally protected right to a comfortable and secure place to pump breast milk at work and a schedule designed around her childcare arrangements. According to court documents and her attorney, when the tiny, dark-haired thirty-two-year-old returned to the network in March 1997 after a three-month maternity leave, her supervisor agreed to allow her the use of a spare editing room so that she could pump breast milk in privacy. That arrangement went smoothly for five months—until male coworkers began bursting in on her. It wasn't voyeurism. The need for editing rooms had increased and MSNBC needed the space.

The personnel director offered Alicia a choice of two other locations—the women's locker room or the women's bathroom. She rejected them both. The former was too far from her office and insufficiently private, Alicia said. The latter had no chair. When they promised to bring her one, Alicia then refused the bathroom as unsuitable. Instead, Alicia tried to commandeer the office of one of the female human resources directors, assuming that any woman would understand her needs. When such sympathy did not translate into carte blanche to evict the woman from her own workspace, Alicia hit the roof. She grew angrier still when her supervisor assigned her to work weekends, a not uncommon schedule change in the news business. Alicia resisted, insisting that she did not have suitable childcare for hours other than Monday through Friday from 7:00 A.M. to 7:00 P.M. MSNBC promised to help her make new arrangements. Alicia held her ground, refusing to change her schedule. Ultimately, she was allowed to maintain her old hours, but they came with a demotion.

MSNBC's actions constituted discrimination on the basis of gender and "disability," Martinez alleges in a suit filed in federal court in Manhattan. She contends that the Civil Rights Act of 1964 and the Americans with Disabilities Act guarantee nursing mothers their choice of pumping rooms and parents work schedules that suit their preferred childcare arrangements. How these statutes apply is murky, at best, although it appears that Martinez is asserting that wanting to breastfeed is a disability under the ADA and that failure to give a woman her desired work schedule constitutes sex discrimination. Her attorney, however, declines to discuss such legal niceties. "If MSNBC doesn't settle, we'll have to figure that out," says Robert Swetnick, unfazed at revealing his lawyerly, bluffing tactics.

Alicia's colleagues at MSNBC were shocked by her actions. *They* thought of the network as a pretty parent-friendly place, the kind of informal worksite where anchors tended to bring their children onto the set. Network brass will say only that Martinez's case "is without merit. We take great strides to accommodate the needs of new mothers and are sensitive to all the issues surrounding new mothers returning to work."

Alicia Martinez isn't some hothead out on a limb all alone. The issue of accommodations for breastfeeding, in fact, has become a hotbed for litigation. The most notorious case involves Lieutenant Emma Cuevas and her husband, Lieutenant Jeff Blaney, both West Point graduates, who filed suit in federal district court in Washington, D.C., asserting that the U.S. Army was denying their nine-month-old daughter Isabella her "constitutional right to breast-feed by having her mother impounded by the government."

Emma Cuevas graduated from the West Point in 1993 and married Blaney the following year. After being trained, at her request, as a helicopter pilot, Emma was posted to Panama, where her job entailed flying a mammoth ten-ton Black Hawk helicopter filled with American troops over and through the jungles of the Darien Peninsula. Emma, who did not use birth control, gave birth to Isabella in the summer of 1996 and was given a routine six weeks of maternity leave. When she was rotated back to work, she formally requested to be relieved of duty and transferred to the reserves, contending that the difficult schedule of a helicopter pilot made it impossible for her to breastfeed properly. The army, short of helicopter pilots, denied her request and reminded Emma that she'd made a deal when she entered West Point. In return for a free education, including pilot training, that cost taxpayers more than five hundred thousand dollars, she had pledged to stay in uniform until May 2000. "Breast-feeding is the healthiest way to feed a baby," Emma responded. "Isabella's not in the military, so why should the Army deny her this?" She and her husband promptly sought relief through the courts.

Emma's suit provoked a storm of criticism from other women in the military, who caustically suggested that Emma should have considered the realities of a pilot's life when she decided not to use birth control. "Her selfishness is a disgrace to women in the military," Major Mary Finch, also an Army helicopter pilot, told *Time*. Finch, the mother of two girls, breastfed them during her maternity leave and then switched to formula. "This is playing right into the hands of those who believe there is a natural conflict between motherhood and military service."

No one has yet asked Cuevas's attorney precisely where in the Constitution the right to breastfeed is mentioned, but that question will become moot if H.R. 3531, first introduced into Congress on March 24, 1998, by Representative Carolyn Maloney of New York, becomes law. Her New Mothers' Breastfeeding Promotion and Protection Act would make it illegal for companies, and, presumably, the army, to fire, discriminate against, or single out women who choose to breastfeed or express milk when they return to work. It would further guarantee them the time to do so.

The controversy and legal maneuvering isn't confined to efforts to bolster a working woman's right to breastfeed at work. Joanna Upton of Boston asked state courts in Massachusetts to require employers to give single mothers their desired work schedules because neglecting children is "in contravention of public policy." When Upton, the divorced mother of a young son, was hired in 1991 to be the product manager at a JWP Businessland computer store, she was told that her work hours would be 8:15 A.M. to 5:30 P.M. daily. Several months later, however, her supervisor announced that because of an upcoming merger, all managerial staff would temporarily have to work until 9:00 or 10:00 each night. Unmoved by the problems she would create not only for the company, but for her coworkers, Upton refused, citing her need to be with her son. She was fired two weeks later.

Upton filed suit in Dedham Superior Court, charging discrimination based on her status as a single mother, which allegedly made her unable to work longer hours. She also maintained that her former employer's actions—assigning her to work extremely long days—violated Massachusetts's public policy of protecting families and children. When the superior court judge, unable to find any element of discrimination in a schedule applied to all managerial personnel, threw out her case, Upton appealed to the Supreme Judicial Court. "People are being forced to choose between their children or families or their jobs, which is a violation of Massachusetts public policy," argued Harvey Schwartz, her appellate attorney. In August 1997, the court ruled against Upton, finding that employees in positions like hers can be fired for refusing to work over-time—no matter if they wanted that extra time to spend with their children or families. "We sympathize with the difficulties of persons in the position of the plaintiff who have faced the challenge of reconciling parental responsibilities with the demands of employment," the decision read. "However, employer liability under common-law principles is not an appropriate means of addressing the problem."

The legal possibilities have recently attracted the attention of the far right, which senses political potential in an area of law that has been, to this point, guided by liberal feminist thinking. In 1998, an attorney affili-ated with the Rutherford Institute, which handled the Paula Jones sexual harassment suit against Bill Clinton, sued the *Spartanburg Herald-Journal* on behalf of Andrew Friedlander, a sports reporter, and his wife, Glenda, a stay-at-home mom, as part of the institute's "Fighting for Family" cam-paign.

In the spring of 1995, Glenda, who was pregnant, was rushed to the hospital bleeding and told to remain in bed until delivery, which was esti-mated for the first week in June. Andrew took off several days to care for his wife and then asked his editor if he could work half-days at home. The editor denied Andrew's request, and, after a series of disagreements, pulled Andrew off the football beat for the duration of Glenda's preg-nancy. That treatment was so harsh, the Friedlanders allege, that Glenda, who had been told by her doctor to avoid stress, had "spent the night wor-ried and in tears." Things did not improve after the birth of their son. An-drew felt that his star had fallen as a result of the time constraints he'd suffered, and his relationship with his editor remained tense. According to the suit filed in federal court in South Carolina, one sign of the continu-ing harassment Andrew was forced to endure was his editor's insistence that he remain at the paper until the final scores were reported from a track championship he was covering, although he knew that Andrew and Glenda had tickets to see *Sesame Street Live.*

Andrew was ultimately fired for violating the paper's policy against freelancing without permission, an action he alleges to be a simple ruse. After seeking satisfaction from the Department of Labor and the Equal Employment Opportunity Commission, Andrew and Glenda filed suit contending that by refusing to "properly accommodate" the Friedlanders' pregnancy, "management went out of its way to interfere with [their] right to have their baby," and that the newspaper had violated the Americans with Disabilities Act, the Family and Medical Leave Act, the Civil Rights Act of 1964, and the Fair Labor Standards Act, as well as a host of state laws.

Thus far, the courts have not been overly kind to the Alicia Martinez's, Joanna Uptons, and Andrew Friedlanders. But in his 1999 State of the Union address, Bill Clinton promised to remedy that oversight. "Parents should never face discrimination in the workplace," he intoned, offering middle-class parents the psychic rewards of victimhood, and its attendant federal civil rights protections, that Martinez et al. had claimed. No cheers followed this plea for equal rights for parents. In the press gallery, puzzlement shadowed the faces of hundreds of reporters. "I will ask Congress to prohibit companies from refusing to hire or promote workers simply because they have children," the president continued.

At the time, few noticed the president's odd harangue. No commentator returned to the statement during the endless hours of postspeech analysis. No Republican either criticized or claimed credit for the new civil rights initiative. Even *The New York Times* managed to avoid putting any mention of the comment onto the record. But four months later, word crept out on Capitol Hill that the president was serious about that promise and would, with the cooperation of Senator Chris Dodd of Connecticut, ask Congress to make "parents" a protected class, like classes based on race, sex, age, or religion. The proposal provoked puzzlement in the press because reporters found themselves unable to find evidence of rampant discrimination against parents. Most, in fact, found a pervasive pattern of workplace discrimination against nonparents, whose plight the president seemed disinclined to address.

Family advocates, however, gleefully declared that the Messiah had taken yet another step forward and that the bill would protect employees who refused to work overtime or work weekends because of parenting obligations. "I get calls every day from people who've worked 10, 20, 30 years and think they are putting their job on the line if they go to their child's hockey game," wrote Harvey Schwartz, Upton's attorney, in a letter to Al Gore applauding the initiative.

Meanwhile, Roger Clegg of the *Legal Times* dubbed the new law PAN-DER (Parents Act for Non-Discrimination in Employment Relations) and declared it constitutionally questionable and discriminatory against non-parents. The *National Journal* called it "The Stupidest Law of All." Timothy Noah, the father of two small children who writes the Chatterbox column for the on-line magazine *Slate,* concluded, "If you don't want your work to suffer at all, your best options are either not to become a parent or to resolve to be a really bad parent who spends little or no time with your kids." And *The Boston Globe* called the notion of making "parent" a protected class "an overdose of legal Prozac."

But those cautions were irrelevant. "After all," Clegg wrote, "PANDER polls well."

Running against this tide, even just trying to inject some perspective into this mania of family-friendliness, is a risky business. If you don't believe me, ask Joyce Purnick of *The New York Times.* Purnick should be something of an icon for young women in journalism, especially those at the *Times.* In more than two decades at the paper, she has risen steadily through the ranks, from reporter to city hall bureau chief and, finally, to metropolitan editor, the first woman to run the *Times*'s largest news division. But Purnick, who is now a metro columnist, managed to enrage female reporters with young kids within weeks of taking over that editing job.

The long July fourth weekend was coming up, and reporters were dreading publication of the list of who would be tapped to work on the holiday. They knew who wouldn't be tapped: Under Purnick's predecessor, Mike Oreskes, reporters like Debbie Sontag, Celia Dugger, and Esther Fein had long been off-limits on such occasions, by some combination of their stardom and motherhood status—the weight of each a matter of endless speculation in a newsroom rife with gossip. But they had forgotten that the torch had been passed from Oreskes to Purnick since the last holiday roster had been posted, and that Purnick was a stickler for equal treatment. As the weekend neared, oblivious to the tradition established by Oreskes, she asked a clerk to draw up the schedule for the long weekend and to assign only those who had not worked a holiday during the prior two years. The long faces in the room that afternoon, then, did not belong to the usual crowd of "un-familied" reporters. Sontag, Dugger, and the other mothers who had long been protected from such assignments sat simmering in their cubicles.

That turnabout provoked satisfied delight among reporters who resented the privileged status granted many reporter-mothers. Playing the kiddie card, they were protected from the daily grind, leaving the pool of reporters available to cover routine water main breaks or late-breaking stories woefully small. They argued family responsibilities and turned off their beepers at night, on weekends, and on holidays, forcing the remaining reporters to pull that much more of the weight. While the parental benefits at the paper are not of the caliber of a place like SAS or IBM, mothers were being offered job and leave flexibility that was the envy of their peers at other newspapers. When Melinda Henneberger returned to the Washington office from maternity leave, her schedule and assignments were repeatedly adjusted and readjusted in accordance with the balance she wanted to strike between family and professional success at any given moment.

And parents seemed to be the only members of the reporting staff who could command unpaid leave or flexible schedules without a hassle. When Jan Hoffman, who covered legal affairs for metro, adopted a baby girl, for example, she asked for and was granted maternity leave and family medical leave, then permitted to extend that leave well beyond the federally mandated twelve weeks. But when Linda Lee, an editor in the culture section, requested unpaid leave to pursue a project that was important to her—a new book—her request was denied. Celia Dugger, Esther Fein and Mirta Ojito, all reporters on the metropolitan desk, were granted four-day schedules without hesitation.

The newsroom mothers seemed blithely indifferent to the bitterness their demands for special treatment were fostering. So when the July Fourth schedule was posted, all they saw was their ruined weekend plans. Nonetheless, their hard feelings toward Purnick might well have faded, in time, had Purnick not managed to ignite the mothers again within less than a year. The following spring, she was asked to deliver the graduation speech at her alma mater, Barnard College. Flummoxed as to what she should talk about, Purnick combed through the remarks delivered by other speakers over the past five years for guidance and found herself disconcerted by a single recurring theme. The young women had been told, again and again, that they could have it all: rich, rewarding family lives and fast-track, high-powered careers. Purnick didn't believe it for a minute. She herself was not only childless, but had married late, having thrown her considerable energies into mastering the politics of both New York City and *The New York Times.* She couldn't imagine how she could possibly have climbed the newsroom ladder if her attention had been divided between those efforts and children.

In planning her remarks, then, Purnick decided to take the new graduates for a quick stroll down her personal memory lane, carefully extracting the relevant object lessons for young women all too likely to view the difficult choices they faced through the rose-colored lenses popular with postfeminist Pollyannas. She knew that few graduation speeches were filled with such straight talk. But Purnick has always thought of journalists as "truth-tellers."

When she rose before the crowd gathered at the ivied campus on the Upper West Side of Manhattan, Purnick began by explaining that, unlike most women of her generation, she'd grown up believing that she could do "absolutely anything," the legacy of a mother determined to protect her daughter from the limitations imposed on her own life. That self-confidence, bolstered by workaholism and considerable talent, moved her steadily through the ranks of journalism—from clerk to reporter, from columnist to editor, and from *The New York Post* to *New York* magazine and, finally, to the pinnacle, *The New York Times.* "Along the way, without realizing what I was doing to myself until it was too late, I forfeited the chance to have childen, but found love when I was forty and got married at forty-two to a wonderful man who understands driven women—at least this one—and the demands of journalism," she explained. Then she struck to the heart of the matter. "So, what can you learn from this?" she asked the graduates. "One thing is this: you *cannot* have it all. . . . Having it all is a phrase for books and speeches by political cheerleaders . . . you can have a lot of it, in ways that women could not just a few decades ago. You have choices my mother did not have, and that is so much a given today that you are probably sitting there puzzled, wondering why I am wasting time on the obvious."

But those new professional choices, she said, carry steep personal, familial prices. "I made a choice there too, albeit a passive one, and I confess I will always regret it. I wish I'd thought earlier about having a family because then I probably would have done something about it. . . . The flip side of my experience is that I am absolutely convinced I would not be the metro editor of the *Times* if I had had a family. . . . [T]his is where 'having it all' comes in. With rare exceptions—in nearly all competitive professions—women who have children get off the track and lose ground. I see it all the time in my business. There is no way in an all-consuming profession like journalism that a woman with children can devote as much time and energy as a man can. . . .

"If I had left the *Times* to have children, and then come back to work a four-day week the way some women reporters on my staff now do, or if I had taken long vacations and leaves to be with my family, or left the office at six o'clock instead of eight or nine, I wouldn't be the metro editor. I wouldn't be out on the street. I'd be a reporter, or a lower-level editor. I might even be happier. But I doubt I would be able to work twelve-hour days, sometimes seven-day weeks."

Leaving no room for the young women to dismiss her as anomalous, Purnick punctuated her remarks with the stories of friends and colleagues, other high-profile women who had tried to have it all. One, a well-known—unnamed—magazine editor, had managed the feat of raising children and becoming one of the powerhouses of American journalism, but only with the help of a personal trainer, a personal hairdresser, a housekeeper, cook, chauffeur, and two nannies. Another woman she mentioned, the only woman with children whose name appears on the masthead of the *Times,* had succeeded because, when her children were young, her husband had the flexibility to take on the lion's share of the childcare.

But most women, she warned, aren't that lucky. They have to make choices that have consequences all too few women want to accept. "I remember a case when fourteen women turned down a top editing job, citing family obligations," she recalled. "A man finally got the position. Another woman just recently rejected a top job and took a less powerful one because she didn't want to be away from her young children for so long. When her children get older, she says, she will be willing to devote more time to her job. But won't others who have been working the twelve-hour days—mostly men—be rungs ahead of her? Shouldn't they be?

"*Should* women and men who have taken the detour of the Mommy/Daddy track be as far along as those who haven't? Would that be fair? I reluctantly have to say that it would *not* be fair."

Purnick's was a thoughtful, reflective speech, the musings of a fifty-two-year-old woman who'd risen to a summit and could see clearly what she had left behind. Regret tinged her rhetoric. It never occurred to her that anyone beyond the most earnest young women in the audience would pay much attention to her entreaties. It also never occurred to her that those entreaties would land her in the worst maelstrom of her life. After all, what had she done? Expressed her remorse at not having children? Told a group of young women that life isn't a fantasy novel?

But that's not how a group of female reporters and editors—mothers and mothers-to-be—read her speech. They discerned in it a warning to women that they can't have it all, that they shouldn't—and a dire warning to women at *The New York Times* that motherhood could put their careers on the line. These were, for the most part, acolytes of the Susan Chira school of balance in women's lives, which is the gospel of "you can have it all and if you do, you will do all your jobs better and be happier." Chira, who'd given up life as a foreign correspondent to be the *Times*'s deputy foreign editor, had just written a book called *A Mother's Place* in which she waxed long and poetic about the rewards of juggling a career with kids. Purnick, then, had committed a countercultural crime.

Nothing raises the dander of successful professional women more than being told that they can't have what they are convinced they want and deserve—and this group of powerful female journalists shed dander all over the newsroom. No matter that Purnick had said nothing that many of the *Times*'s leading mothers had not said to one another and to their friends, about the stress, about having to pass up juicy assignments or neglecting their children. Debbie Sontag, for example, had turned down a promotion to the national desk several years before because of family obligations and had resisted the paper's implorings that she accept the position as deputy metro editor for the same reason. Celia Dugger and Esther Fein had both cut back to four-day workweeks.

And Chira, who'd spent much of her career flying around the globe chasing stories, had slowed down when her kids were born and ultimately taken a desk job in New York—a job she admitted she could handle only because other editors covered for her when she took off for school meetings or appointments with the pediatrician. In her book, Chira had candidly acknowledged much of what Purnick suggested. "A newspaper's rhythms are hard on families. The very hours when most people are leaving the office, when children are ready for dinner and bed, are the hours when the deadlines loom and the heart of a newspaper begins to pound. . . . There are moments when I feel depleted, guilty, distracted and deprived of time with my children."

But truth made little impact on women with top-flight careers intent on feeling threatened, or at least aggrieved, by Purnick's message. As their anger coursed through the newsroom of the Grey Lady, where every detail of the paper's life is chewed over by one hundred aspiring columnists, the ranks divided. Some reporters wrote off Purnick's speech as the bitter rantings of a woman who belonged to a generation that had been forced to choose between family and professional advancement and was wracked with envy of the younger generation who did not face such stark alternatives.

That was a convenient take on the situation at a moment when the press had become enamored of the concept of a cat fight between the older "trailblazers" and the younger "want-it-all-nows." And the seeds of such dissension have been firmly planted. In an interview with *Forbes* magazine, an ethics professor at Arizona State University summed up the attitude of many of the "trailblazers" with telling candor. "We came in with the attitude of making good and paving the way, so we were diligent," said Marianne Jennings, forty-five. "Now that we've paved the road and equality has spoken, women have the right to goof off, I guess." Needless to say, younger women blanch at that withering characterization.

In some workplaces, the tensions between older and younger women have become so intense that mediators have been called in to resolve the squabbling. "Different generations of women in the workplace have very different value systems—which leads to a lot of conflicts between them," says Albert Bernstein, clinical psychologist and management consultant in Vancouver, Washington, who recently mediated such a dispute at a major law firm on the West Coast.

But while generational value clashes might have played some role at the *Times,* Purnick's supporters and detractors didn't fall into such easy categories. Although few dared to express it publicly, many reporters—male and female, old and young, childless and parents—congratulated Purnick on what they found to be thoughtful, important remarks. But the rage of the mothers was too swift, too overwhelming, and the reporters who seconded Purnick's thinking too timid in the face of motherhood-as-political-correctness to stem the tide. Purnick was bad-mouthed from the *Times* building to the furthest nook and cranny of American journalism, as seven irate female reporters and editors, convinced they had grabbed the moral high ground, stormed into the office of Bill Keller, the managing editor, calling for her head.

The invasion of Keller's stark office put the managing editor in a political bind. No group of *Times* women can raise their voices in collective complaint without shooting a chill through the spines of the senior managers who run the news empire that dominates a quiet block of Manhattan real estate just off Times Square. Memories of the *Times*'s humiliation at being sued for sex discrimination by its most revered female reporters remain too fresh, despite the fifteen years that have passed. The paper's vanity about its own moral and intellectual superiority is as deep, and often as accurate, as its front-page promise, "All the News That's Fit to Print."

Times executives never acknowledged the validity of the allegations of those original plaintiffs in the lawsuit filed in 1974, such women as Betsy Wade, Grace Glueck, and Eileen Shanahan—although the record of disparities in salaries, preference in promotions, and openly humiliating treatment was striking. When the paper reached a settlement with the women four years later, executives contended that they had admitted to no discriminatory employment practices, past or present, although they conceded that they had put in place a new affirmative action plan. That public posture, wrote Nan Robertson in *The Girls in the Balcony,* a lively account of the acrimonious dispute, boiled down to, "We didn't do it, and we won't ever do it anymore."

With that settlement, the paper of record had gotten off lightly financially, and still more lightly in the eyes of the public, since the denouement occurred smack in the middle of the second-longest newspaper blackout in New York's history, the result of an eighty-eight-day newspaper strike. But the *Times*'s notoriously brittle pride had been badly damaged by what the newspaper's lead attorney called an attack on its "institutional credibility."

Keller, then, an affable man with intense blue eyes, needed to tread carefully lest he set off the women in his office—many of them stars at the paper with their own direct channels to the editor-in-chief if not the publisher. They were complaining as *women,* after all, alleging that Purnick's offense had been an offense against their gender—although gender could be a relevant issue only if you consider that mother is synonymous with woman. Women, in fact, were soaring at the *Times* as never before. The names of women unrelated to the publisher of the news empire appeared on the paper's masthead, the only professional real estate that counts. Women ran two departments in the news division, Maureen Dowd's wit dominated the editorial page, and few female reporters could even remember the bad old days when women were isolated in low-paying jobs and the women's pages. But the specter of the accusation hung heavily over the newsroom.

So Keller was in a tight squeeze because the women before him had never complained about Purnick's behavior as manager. And they had no real complaint other than their dissatisfaction with her free speech, which he could scarcely deny. Coddling the mommies, as some *Times* reporters call the mothers who come in late, leave well before deadline, and never find themselves assigned to an unwanted story, was one thing. Punishing an editor for questioning the consequences of doing so was another.

Keller's options were also constrained by the fact that word of the latest scandal at the *Times* had spread like oil from the Exxon *Valdez* through the insular world of New York and national journalists, whose penchant for being gossips is an actual career advantage. A few lonely voices spoke out in Purnick's public defense, although most of them were well out in the heartland. Sara Eckel, a syndicated freelance writer, penned a piece that ran in the *Macomb* (Illinois) *Journal* declaring that "Purnick was only telling the truth," and accused the *Times* editor of "shooting the messenger." Mickey Kaus, *Slate* magazine's Chatterbox, issued a half-hearted defense of a "fine, provocative, heartfelt speech in the 'you-can't-have-it-all' school of realism," but felt compelled to rebuke Purnick for her failure to bemoan the unlevel playing field between working dads and working moms.

Although Purnick's speech had been greeted with deafening applause by the Barnard students and nearly all of the mail she received in the wake of the flap congratulated her for her remarks, in the nation's most august media outlets she was branded an enemy of the people, at least of those people who happened to be mothers. Writing in the New York *Daily News,* Cokie and Steve Roberts responded to the incident by branding Purnick "hateful" for spreading a "demoralizing message to many young women who are already tormented by the conflicting demands of work and family." They declared that the *Times* would be a lot better off if it did have mothers running the metro section. A reporter for the *Philadelphia Inquirer* seized on the incident to condemn as mother-haters women "who have chosen to put their careers before or in place of family." Sue Shellenbarger of *The Wall Street Journal* wagged her finger at Purnick for assuming that women of the younger generation would have to make the sacrifices she herself had been forced to make. "Those sacrifices turn toxic when projected on others as the road to success."

So Keller walked a careful line. Ultimately, he gave the women a careful and polite hearing, reiterating the reassurances already delivered to them by Joseph Lelyveld, the paper's executive editor, and Arthur Sulzberger, Jr., its publisher, that Purnick's remarks were not a backhanded institutional message of discouragement to female employees. Then he broke out of role, or at least the role that most male executive in major corporations play these days. They have learned, from their attorneys, how legally critical kid gloves treatment of mothers can be when companies are sued for sex discrimination. Even when such legal challenges have nothing to do with motherhood, the law firms representing American business want to be able to extol the generosity of maternal benefits to sway judges in these complex cases.

Keller, however, seemed not to be guided by legal strategy or a fear of lawsuits so much as by the patent unfairness of a gang of women descending on his office to belittle his metropolitan editor for speaking her mind. In doing so, he earned hero's status in a world where few dare challenge the glories of family-friendliness, in the workplace or in public policy, and where those few are summarily slapped down. "Much as I cherish the fact that you feel free to speak your minds," he wrote in an e-mail to the seven women involved, "the group response had a faint whiff of the lynch mob about it."

2

Pregnant Payoffs

On a gray, gloomy morning in 1991, they began filtering into room 2212 of the Rayburn House Office Building across from the Capitol: Dave Sarpalius of Texas, a Democrat who was swept out of office by a Republican freshman three years later; Bill Barrett, a freshman who bragged that he represented sixty-three thousand square miles of Nebraska; Dennis Hastert, now Speaker of the House of Representatives, then just another congressman from Illinois most Americans had never heard of. Patricia Schroeder of Colorado, the senior Democratic woman in the House of Representatives, nodded as they took their traditional chairs. The hearing of the House Select Committee on Children, Youth, and Families was her show—and Pat Schroeder knew how to run a show.

This wasn't one of those televised hearings jammed with reporters, witnesses, and lobbyists lined up against the walls and spilling out into the halls. The committee with the grand title had no legislative power. It didn't even merit its own meeting room. And the media weren't camped out in the hallway, poised for one of those obligatory group gropes that erupt when journalists smell news in the making. American troops were pouring out of Iraq after their temporary defeat of Saddam Hussein in Desert Storm, and Cal Ripken was slugging a record number of runs for the Orioles, so editors didn't have much space in the news hole for yet another meeting of yet another congressional committee.

Besides, it was April 15, a day most Americans had better things to worry about.

A hearing about reclaiming tax law for America's families—which meant parents with children—then, wasn't very high on the national radar screen. But you could not have guessed that from the high-powered oratory.

"By the time we get done today, we certainly hope that America's families are 'seeing red' about what has happened to them in the tax code," said Schroeder. "I think economic equity for families is going to be one of our great rallying cries.' . . . Today is tax day—the day our federal taxes are due to the federal government and the opening day of a revolution by American families to reclaim the tax code." No bugles trumpeted that declaration of war. No shots were fired. Just two hours and nineteen minutes of political posturing that no one but a handful of obsessive-compulsive personalities who read the transcripts of congressional committees would ever take note of.

"The purpose of all of this is to help moms and dads to spend more time with their families," said Frank Wolf of Virginia, the ranking Republican in the room. "If we look for the most efficient Department of Health and Human Services in this country we will find that it is run by the thousands of 'domestic engineers' who go by the title of 'Mom and Dad.' In comparison to government programs, families require much less overhead and oversight to perform effectively and should be provided the resources to do so. We should begin to reinvest in this department through tax relief targeted to families."

Unlike many congressional hearings, this one was not held to consider any specific bill. Dozens of plans for "family" relief were floating around Capitol Hill, so the group scheduled a legislative free-for-all, where anyone could press any agenda that purported to decrease taxes on "the family."

It was still the early 1990s, so even the most liberal Democratic members of the committee felt no need to define what a "family" was, at least for purposes of taxation. The political correctness police weren't yet breathing down their throats, so no one bothered to state the obvious: a family meant a least one parent, biological or adoptive, preferably two, and of different genders, living in a household with at least one child.

While the specific proposals made by witnesses and congressmen alike ranged all over the map, the mantra of the morning was unanimous: families were paying too much in taxes because the tax burden had been shifting onto their shoulders since 1948. The family-tax crowd had begun to obsess on that date because in that year the personal exemption used by the nation's taxpayers for filing their federal income tax returns was $600. Adjusted for inflation, that exemption would have been worth $12,000 for a family of four in 1990, rather than the $2,050 the Internal Revenue Service allowed, or so the chairwoman said. Wolf used the figure $7,800, while Gary Bauer, then president of the Family Research Council, offered the number $8,000.

Republicans and Democrats on the panel, and among the witnesses, competed openly to prove their allegiance to the American family with overwrought rhetoric about families staggering under the weight of a crushing tax burden, and with notions for how to alleviate some of the attendant pain. The Democrats were upstaged by Frank Wolf, who was sponsoring a Tax Fairness for Families Act to increase the dependent deduction to $3,500, although only for children. For some reason he chose not to articulate, adults would have remained valued at just $2,050. "American families haven't had any lobbyists working for them in Gucci Gulch—the halls outside the tax-writing committee rooms," he said during his opening remarks.

Not to be outdone, Schroeder, the mistress of the bon mot, quipped that "families feel like hamsters on a wheel," then threw her support to Wolf's bill. She couldn't resist suggesting a twist of her own, however, one that no one ever picked up on, perhaps because it seemed utterly inexplicable. "I studied tax law at Harvard Law School, and I always wanted to tax families the way we do corporations," she said, seemingly advocating that couples be allowed to deduct three-martini lunches as "family" expenses as long as the children were being discussed. "If you gave everybody the proper personal exemption they should have, it's probably $8,000 or $9,000, maybe more. Any family that had more exemptions than income, allow them to sell them. You wouldn't need welfare."

Most of the witnesses submitted ideas of their own, of course. Gene Steurele, a senior fellow at the Urban Institute and the architect of the Tax Reform Act of 1986, advocated a plan that would shield poor families moving from welfare to the workforce from the IRS, although few in the room seemed overly concerned about the poor. Robert Shapiro from the

Progressive Policy Institute recommended a $40 billion tax cut for families with children or, as a first step, a $10 billion tax reduction packages for those with kids under the age of four.

Gary Bauer could not contain his delight at the spectacle of so many prominent liberals agreeing with him at what turned into a bipartisan love-in. "Madam Chairwoman, I have been in Washington now for about twenty years, and during that time we have both been in Washington, I have had a hard time recalling an issue where you and I agreed," he said. Ironically, perhaps, it was Bauer, one of the nation's leading conservatives, who offered a word of caution about the danger of creating yet another program that purported to help the poor but wound up easing the lives of the upper middle class. But he then ignored his own warning by throwing onto the table a plan to offer a per-child tax credit worth $1,800 for preschool children and $1,200 for children ages six and above, no matter the wealth or poverty of their parents.

As the hearing droned on, university professors handed out cross-cultural comparisons. Pollsters—modern-day wizards who can divine the most subtle shift in the putative national pulse—submitted proof, to the surprise of absolutely no one, that Americans hated taxes. The head of a stay-at-home-moms group decried the childcare tax credit as an anti-mother boondoggle, followed by an attorney from the National Women's Law Center, who decried all efforts to cap that credit for workers making above $70,000. Congressmen asked profound questions, "And have you any suggestions for paying the bill?" being a perfect example. Witnesses responded with sage answers— "No." And the hearing was adjourned at precisely 12:20 P.M., leaving everyone involved plenty of time for a long lunch.

During the 139 minutes the members of Congress were gathered to brainstorm, not a single person in that august hearing room bothered to address the most salient issue of the day: Who was going to pay for tax cuts for parents? Everyone lamented the fact that the tax burden had shifted onto families in the forty-two years since 1948, but no one bothered to ask who it was shifted from, or even acknowledged that a burden shifted onto someone has to have been taken off someone else. So no one was forced to talk about who it would be shifted back onto.

It was a convenient omission that allowed everyone to leave the room feeling sure that someone—clearly some group they didn't like—would be forced to carry the costs.

Hugging Baltimore's northern edge, Towson, Maryland, was the city's first modern suburb, a collection of mini-neighborhoods divided by broad, store-lined thoroughfares, shopping centers, and enough parks, trees, and open space to feed the illusions of ex-urbanites. The old farm village that grew up around Ezekiel Towson's tavern had become home to upper-middle-class retirees who bought homes there as young couples, when they could finally afford to move beyond urban rowhouses or the slapdash, cookie-cutter communities built in the postwar frenzy. In recent years, they have been joined in growing numbers by their children's generation, who once swore they would never be like their parents, then followed them to the same peaceful enclaves, where the classrooms are pristine and the high school teaches courses in ornithology.

Towsonites are the voters every candidate for office seeks with almost reckless abandon. Maryland, traditionally a Democratic party stronghold, sends Congress some of its most vociferous liberals, from Barbara Mikulski in the Senate to Kweisi Mfume in the House. But the idealism of Towson's dwellers has been burnished by age and affluence. For more than a decade, they have been wooed with increasing success by moderate Republicans.

Lisa and Richard Doe—a, er, hypothetical couple, of course—make their home midway down on a winding road on what was farmland a generation ago. The deck off the back of their two-story home provides them a perch from which to watch Sara, eleven, and Jason, twelve, play on the swings and mini–jungle gym. Before she left for college, Jamie, eighteen, had taken over the upstairs den that had been their private retreat. In the year since she moved away from home, they have left her tangle of clothes, posters, and books undisturbed.

When the Does graduated from the University of Maryland, in 1977, they rented a small apartment in the city and, after a lifetime in suburbia, threw themselves into urban life. They hung out at the Great American Melting Pot among the artsy crowd of Mount Vernon, mingled with the masses at the newly built Inner Harbor, and worried their parents no end.

Richard, who had a degree in accounting, worked in an executive training program at a major bank, while Lisa finished her M.S.W. at the University of Maryland campus in town.

By 1980, the young couple were beginning their upward rise in earnest. Richard was promoted regularly, and Lisa slaved away in the tangle of social service agencies that pretended to meet the city's needs. Those were the golden years when they still played rugby with their friends on weekends, drank pitchers of beer on Saturday nights, and shared a summer house at the beach at Rehobeth. But when Jamie appeared in Lisa's womb, unexpectedly, they buckled down to some serious saving, cutting back on spending sprees in the antique stores of Ellicott City and fifty-dollar Saturday nights at the tavern in Mount Washington.

"It's time to grow up," they quickly agreed, and growing up meant buying a house. The best they could manage was one of those brand-new townhouses springing up just beyond the beltways of so many cities. The streets weren't leafy, as they would have liked, and their new home looked out onto a parking lot. "It's just a starter house," they told their parents and each other. "We'll move up when our daughter gets older."

After Jamie was born, Lisa kept working, juggling daycare between her mother and the center at the hospital where she worked. The recession still hadn't eased into the boom, and Lisa and Richard were determined to beat the economic odds. Saving became their obsession. By the time Jamie was ready for school and Jason was growing in Lisa's belly, they were ready for the big move. With the twenty thousand dollars they'd put away, a ten-thousand-dollar gift from Lisa's parents, and Richard's mounting salary, they began looking for a house that would really be a home, a house on a street with other young couples who would want to swap daycare, organize play dates and form mixed-sex Little League teams.

Jason's arrival was followed by the birth of Sara one year later, and Lisa couldn't cope with getting Jamie up and off to school, dropping the little ones at daycare, working, cooking, and cleaning and still have enough energy to be a civilized, modern woman. She and Richard calculated their monthly expenses carefully and decided that it was time for her to quit. The plan was simple: With her M.S.W. and a decade of experience, she needed only some practical, supervised experience to become a psychotherapist. So she hired a baby-sitter for a few hours each week, arranged for supervision by a local therapist, and carved out her version of the much-maligned Mommy Track.

By the time Bill Clinton was reelected, the Does' climb into the upper middle class was proceeding steadily, if not as quickly as they would have liked. Jamie was headed for their alma mater, where tuition was just four thousand dollars, but dorm fees, books, and spending money added up. Even with her private practice bringing in almost twenty thousand dollars a year, Lisa didn't see how their stock portfolio could keep growing.

Then came their windfall, the winning ticket in the political lottery. In preparing their 1996 tax returns, they had squeezed every possible credit and deduction from Washington's offerings. But their federal tax bill was still $10,592, which meant they'd paid almost 12 percent of their income to Uncle Sam. The Taxpayers' Relief Act of 1997, however, presented Lisa and Richard with an enormous bonus, in the form of a four-hundred-dollar tax credit for each of their younger children, and another fifteen-hundred-dollar credit for Jamie's tuition. When Richard finished calculating their return for 1997, he had his annual savings in hand: the $3,260 difference between what he'd paid the year before (which he'd planned to pay that year) and what he actually owed. His tax rate had fallen to just above 9 percent.

His neighbors, Frank and Adele Jones, had no such reason to be happy with the Beltway Insiders that year. Unlike the Does, they were among the taxpayers the relief act had forgotten, although the incomes of the two couples were identical. Adele, with a degree in accounting from Frostburg State University, earned thirty-five thousand dollars a year, and Frank brought in another forty-five thousand dollars from his job as a high-school English teacher in Howard County.

The difference was that Frank and Adele were childless.

They hadn't planned it that way. The problem was that they hadn't planned it at all. But money was tight during those first years after they got out of school. Then Adele's mother got sick, and Frank needed to keep up with night school to maintain his certification. When they finally got around to making a concerted effort to get pregnant, nothing happened. Keep trying, it's too soon to panic, Adele's doctor reassured her. So they did, with no result. They both went through the predictable rounds of tests, which didn't show much of anything. For a while they talked desultorily about trying in vitro fertilization, since, under Maryland law, it would have been covered by Adele's health insurance. But conceiving a child artificially felt, well . . . too weird.

Anyway, they didn't feel deprived by their lives as childless adults. The sons and daughters of their siblings raced around their yard on weekends and during family picnics. And Frank had his students at school. So they invested their savings in a house in Towson, where they figured its value would grow and protect them for retirement. And they focused on the freedom they had to travel, the extra money they could send Adele's father every month, the extravagant gifts that delighted their nieces and nephews.

Frank was never any good with taxes. English was his subject, not math. So, year after year, his neighbor Richard volunteered his expertise. When they sat down in Frank's study to tot up the numbers for 1997, Frank was excited. He'd read dozens of stories in the *Baltimore Sun* about the middle-class tax break and about the tax cuts given to wealthy investors, and he knew all about Richard's windfall. Frank wasn't the kind of high-roller who could cash in on the investment tax break, but he was surely as middle class as his friend, and he was hungrily eyeing a new car. But when Richard finished adding up the numbers, his heart sank. His windfall totaled $376. His federal tax bill was $5,528 higher than Richard's on the exact same income.

No matter which way the political winds blow, toward the elephant or the donkey, Frank will remain the loser in the federal income tax sweepstakes. Following the momentum created by hearings like Schroeder's, leaders of both parties vowed to decrease Richard's taxes. They passed the first round of cuts in 1997, and they aren't done yet. Proposals for how to do so pour out of think tanks, campaign headquarters, the White House, and congressional offices: tax credits for stay-at-home moms, increased daycare subsidies for working moms, IRAs that would allow parents to use pretax dollars to save money for private school tuition, federal rebates on local school taxes for parents who send their children to private institutions, increased child tax credits, higher dependent exemptions for children—and the list goes on, all in the name of providing tax relief to the beleaguered American family, which is shouldering more of the burden now than it did in 1948.

So, let's talk about the much-heralded year of 1948 that Pat Schroeder and her committee referred to so glibly. By every measure, that was an anomalous time in modern American tax history, the watershed between the tax system of the war years and that of peacetime. Between 1913, when Woodrow Wilson signed the income tax legislation into law, and the entry of the United States into World War II, the federal income tax wasn't a fly in the ointment of most Americans. It had been created as a "bilk the rich" scheme and was designed with such high personal exemptions that in 1914, only 0.5 percent of the population was required to pay anything at all. By 1939, that number had risen to less than 7 percent.

And that was enough because the federal government wasn't sending millions of dollars to states for education, cushioning the poor, or subsidizing daycare. With the advent of the war, however, the *class* tax was turned into a *mass* tax. Exemptions were lowered, and suddenly 34 percent of the population was sending a check to Washington, D.C., to fund the war effort. Tax revenues, which had been just 1 percent of the Gross Domestic Product (the dollar value of the good and services produced by the nation) skyrocketed to 8 percent of the GDP.

For a moment—a mere moment—after the war, those numbers were poised to drop back toward prewar levels. And 1948 was that moment. Not only had the federal thirst for taxes declined precipitously, but Americans who chose to marry and bear children received record tax breaks. Before the war, the dependent exemption for a child was less than half of the exemption given for an adult dependent. The 1948 Revenue Act equalized the tax value of children and adults. And it imposed a sort of "singles penalty," which gave married couples an actual tax bonus and forced the unmarried and childless to pay 40 percent more in taxes than parents with the same income.

But neither the overall demand for tax dollars nor the bias toward the family could last long if the federal government was going to hand out millions of dollars to veterans for college tuition, to buy houses, and to take care of their health. The federal treasury needed money to pay for those programs, and there simply weren't enough childless working adults to fill the federal coffers. Families didn't grouse about the consequent increases because their paychecks were growing right along with the economy, jobs were plentiful, and life looked pretty good, at least for the people who counted—the white, middle-class folks who read their daily newspaper and cast their ballots without interference.

And then came the war in Vietnam and the Great Society, both mighty expensive propositions, so politicians were forced to muck around with the tax rates. John F. Kennedy did manage to swing a modest tax cut, which he doled out by increasing the standard deduction, which was a rel-atively even-handed measure. No one complained much at the time, al-though, in retrospect, Sylvia Ann Hewlett and Cornel West—who believe that any tax cut that fails to give parents special consideration is antifam-ily—single out that moment as an insidious omen of an antiparent bias creeping into the tax code. As Hewlett and West, authors of *The War Against Parents* and major figures in the parents' rights movement, see it, JFK was but a minor enemy of the family. The real villain in their history book was Richard Nixon, who ended the postwar singles penalty in 1969, when it became obvious that married couples were receiving such huge tax breaks for licensing their relationships that the unmarried were at a dramatic disadvantage. Nixon's other crime was to permit the Federal Housing Authority and the Veterans Administration to permit more loans and benefits to be awarded to singles and to childless couples, rather than maintaining strict preferences for married couples with kids. What those singles and childless couples saw as equity, then, Hewlett and West inter-pret as a plot to pull the rug out from underneath the family, an escalation in the war against parents.

Until the 1990s, however, Americans griped about taxes collectively. Everyone hated paying them. Everyone wanted a tax break. But no one outside Corporate America was clamoring for "special interest" tax cuts. But as the political winds shifted—which is the topic of the next chap-ter—"family values" came to include a bottom-line component, a real cash value. Conservatives called for special tax breaks for parents in order to save the American family from death by taxation strangulation, blam-ing taxes for divorce, out-of-wedlock births, infidelity, lack of commit-ment, and a host of other social ills. Liberals, ironically, embraced eerily similar plans, although on behalf of children floundering in hopeless squalor and single mothers slaving in pink-collar jobs as clerks and secre-taries and hairdressers, yet still unable to put enough food on the table, to buy the extra book for school, or to pay for a special outing—all because of taxes. The $110,000, even $150,000 income caps on their tax cuts suggest how broadly they defined squalor.

That bipartisan movement culminated in the passage of child tax credits in 1997, the first victory of a populist special interest tax cut in decades. Those tax cuts will cost the U.S. Treasury roughly $100 billion over a five-year period, and someone has to make up for that shortfall. That someone is Frank and Adele, since, if all the Richard and Lisas pay less, the Frank and Adeles, perforce, pay more. That's Tax Policy 101, which Representative Pete Stark of California boils down to the simple adage, "There is no tax fairy who is going to put this money under our pillow."

Tax analysts and gurus justify this sort of tax shift in the name of horizontal equity. Now don't stop reading just because I threw in some Washington Wonkspeak. Stick with me. I promise you'll learn something that is relevant to your life. You don't need to remember any statistics or economics to understand horizontal equity. The concept is simple: that the tax system should be designed so that taxpayers with the same means—with the same ability to pay—are treated roughly equally. Or, put another way, people of the same means should make sacrifices that are equally painful.

That's easier said than done, because folks with identical incomes don't necessarily have the same ability to pay taxes. Some have bigger mortgages than others, more children, higher medical expenses and commuting costs or a greater need for nice work clothes. So we try to forge horizontal equity in order to hold everyone "harmless" from things that would make them less able to pay than others in the same economic position. The question is: How do we level the playing field between all these people? And when should we try, since we can't hold everyone harmless for everything?

Some things are simple. If you have two taxpayers who both earn fifty thousand dollars, but one suffers a terrible accident and has thirty thousand dollars in medical bills, shouldn't the latter guy get some break on his taxes? It's not his fault that New York Presbyterian Hospital or San Francisco General wiped out his paycheck. He didn't *choose* to get hit by a truck. So while the government doesn't reimburse him for the cost of the accident, the IRS doesn't treat him as if the accident didn't happen. They let him itemize his deductions and adjust his income accordingly.

And it's just as straightforward at the other end of the spectrum, with economic circumstances that we don't hold taxpayers harmless from. Few would argue, for example, that we should give a taxpayer with a penchant for Giorgio Armani suits special tax breaks although his shopping patterns leave him with less disposable income than his neighbor who shops at Sears. That's a consumption decision, a choice, and we expect taxpayers to pay for their choices, or so the theory goes.

But there are dozens of situations that complicate horizontal equity. For example, we don't hold taxpayers harmless for their decision to live in Manhattan or Boston, whether or not they were raised there or transferred there by their firms. We know that a person earning, say, $50,000 in the heartland—where you can still buy a house for under $150,000—has a pretty comfortable life, while that same person living in Manhattan and paying $1,500 month rent for an apartment the size of a tool shed you can buy at The Home Depot for $789 would barely get by. But we don't factor geography into horizontal equity, which means that the hypothetical $50,000 guy in the heartland winds up with a much better deal, even from the IRS, than his income counterpart in a major city.

And we don't allow people to deduct money for nonuniform clothing they buy for work or the money they spend commuting, although these aren't entirely "consumption" decisions. The problem is that every measure we adopt to forge horizontal equity mucks up the tax system with loopholes and forms. One person's tax break is, by definition, a penalty for another, since it shifts the tax burden in his or her direction.

Which gets us back to Richard and Lisa and Frank and Adele. The tax code holds Richard and Lisa harmless from their decision to have children, which means their tax cut becomes a penalty for Frank and Adele. How do we justify refusing to consider geography, for example, in our quest for horizontal equity while factoring in family size? Well, we don't. Defenders of the current tax system dismiss geography as an unmanageable factor. They turn around and calculate that a family of three needs an income of at least 125 percent of the income of a family of two, and that they should thus be taxed as if they earned several thousand dollars less than they really do.

How do we defend doing this, treating childbearing, which is a choice, like a medical catastrophe, which is not? Read how Joel Slemrod and Jon

Bakija, economists at the University of Michigan and authors of *Taxing Ourselves,* explain it: "Having children is largely a voluntary choice, and may even be viewed as a matter of personal consumption preference from the point of view of the parents. Some adults prefer to save up and spend their money for a round-the-world trip, while others prefer the joy of children with the attendant costs of food, diapers, Nintendo, and possible college. Is it fair to reward adults who prefer to have children, at the expense of adults who prefer other ways of spending their money?

Congress has never held a hearing on that question. Indeed, the question has never entered our social discourse. Reducing the taxes of parents in accordance with the number of children they support is simply assumed to be a good and just social policy. It is assumed to be fair. After all, it's expensive to raise children, children are our future, and a tax break is a minor compensation for parental investment, or so the mantra goes.

In the world of taxes, however, fairness is in the eyes of the payer. Those who prefer or are forced to rent homes believe it is unfair to give homeowners a tax break for mortgage interest. Factory workers consider it is unfair that corporate executives can deduct two-hundred-dollar lunches as business expenses. These are, after all, consumption decisions, and why is it fair to reward consumption, which penalizes nonconsumption?

Residents of the Northeast cry foul about taxes on home heating oil, on which their lives depend. And Montanans, who can't help but drive long distances, complain about gasoline taxes that hike up the price of each trip to the supermarket. The rich gripe about carrying the lion's share of the system. The middle class grumbles that the rich get off cheap. And the poor—or at least those who pretend to advocate on their behalf—wonder where all the money is going.

So arguments about fairness don't advance the discussion very far, especially when, in the end, the issues are resolved not by reason or discourse but by elections and votes and campaign contributions.

Okay. So let's agree for a moment—although many childless would take issue with such an agreement—that we cannot treat children the way we treat trips around the world, and that it is only fair for parents to receive tax deductions for their offspring, the same exemptions they receive for themselves or for aging parents that they are supporting. The question remains: How many *additional* tax breaks should parents receive? When do the expenses involved in raising kids cross the line into consumption or personal preference, like Armani suits, and thus lose their horizontal equity protection?

Consider public schools and the swelling outcry to give parents more control over the education of their kids through vouchers or tax breaks for private education. Sure, what parent doesn't want as much power as possible over what his children learn, how they are taught, and how far they will go? No one can quarrel with that instinct, even with that right. But the question is: Should everyone else be expected to pay for that right? Is that what public education is about?

Hardly. Public education was never intended to provide individual parents with the educations they wanted for their kids. It was designed around what society needed. In the late nineteenth century, as America grew into a full concept of itself as a democracy, and as the implications of that word took root, the ideals that Horace Mann had espoused in Massachusetts captured what passed for the public imagination. Mann, the first secretary of education in Massachusetts, was convinced that democracy could not thrive unless the common school system, which had sprung up to teach the children of the poor, was transformed into a nationwide system of free public schools. In the 1840s and 1850s, Mann's was a revolutionary vision of a society that had never existed in human history, one in which the next generation of doctors and lawyers would be trained in the same classroom as future carpenters and farmers, in which the children of the humble would have access to the education and culture that the elite had long monopolized.

Americans opted to tax themselves to create and support that kind of system not so that parents could send their kids to school for free, or so they could control what they learned, but because universal, compulsory education is essential to a democracy—to educate a new generation of skilled workers and to provide children of all social classes with the chance to break out into the American dream. So, although they have no children themselves, Adele and Frank are expected to contribute to the cost of public education—by paying more than three thousand dollars a year in school property taxes. They are forced to do so not to make their neighbors happy, or to relieve them of the financial burden of educating their own kids, but because public education plays a vital role in the nation's future.

That ante has been rising exponentially, well beyond inflation or the cost of books, teachers, and school buildings. Every year between 1975 and 1997, the budgets of the nation's elementary and secondary schools rose, on average, 2 percent faster than the Gross National Product, personal income, or educational expenditures—at an average of 9.4 percent. And, for the most part, property owners without children in the schools paid the attendant rise in school tax bills without complaint.

But, recently, the childless seem to be the only taxpayers keeping their eyes on Horace Mann's communal vision. For at least fifteen years, parents disgruntled with the public school system have been demanding more control over their kids' futures in the form of wider "school choice," a catchphrase that includes a melange of schemes to wrest control away from the public school system: school vouchers that would allow parents to withdraw their kids from public schools and apply their pieces of the educational pie toward tuition at private ones; federal tax credits for all or part of the school property taxes paid by parents who send their kids to private schools; educational savings accounts that allow parents to use pretax dollars to save for private school tuition.

That catchphrase is disingenuous, at best, since parents already have the right to choose where their children study, at least if they have enough money to pay private school tuition. The movement might more accurately be called "school secession," because the plea is for the right to take your kids' share of the public school budget to spend on a private school of your choosing. The school secessionists have pressed their case by conjuring up the plight of poor parents frustrated by inner-city academies where drugs are more common than books, or parents in rural areas dismayed that their schools lack such basics as computers. But, as with the rhetoric of so many other family-friendly initiatives, the "for the poor" tactic of the school choice crowd is little more than a ruse. Few poor people can afford to kick in the extra money required to meet private school tuition beyond the voucher they'd receive from their local school system, or to save the five hundred dollars or five thousand dollars a year for an education IRA.

The parental choice crowd are using the disastrous state of inner-city and rural schools to create a breach in the public school monopoly over public money in order to gain more choice for themselves, for a fascinating alliance of Christian fundamentalists anxious to protect their kids from "modern" ideas and upper-middle-class parents who want their kids at Andover or Exeter without paying the full freight.

Let me be clear: Individual children, perhaps substantial groups of children, might benefit from school choice. But giving those children and their parents that flexibility is at odds with Mann's vision of throwing all of American's youth together to learn as a group, to be educated with a common purpose and curriculum. It inevitably resegregates American education along the lines that Mann so decried. The only element of his concept that would remain would be the notion that everyone, even nonparents, should pay. But if we're paying for parental control over their kids' education, rather than for broad-based education for the common good, the compact has been broken and couples like Adele and Frank might legitimately ask why they should still remain bound by it. After all, should they be expected to pay tuition for children at religious schools? Or at private schools where they have no voice?

They're already doing just that for the college educations of the sons and daughters of their neighbors—funding both a public system that ensures that the poorest have access to higher education and the tuition of children whose parents prefer Harvard over Berkeley or the University of Miami over the University of Michigan. Counting the ways in which taxpayers support higher education is a journey into the Byzantine, into the caverns and crevices of the budgets of dozens of federal, state, and local agencies. But let me boil the list down into some semblance of order:

First, through their state income taxes, state residents pay for state universities and local community colleges directly and also by funding scholarships, grants, and loans for state residents who study there. Take New York as an example, where the state spends a whopping $6.7 billion on higher education. New Yorkers contribute $1 billion to support the sixty-four campuses of the State University of New York system, another $1.6 billion to the City University of New York, and $2 billion more in scholarships, loans, and grants. That doesn't begin to touch all the bases, because these figures exclude tax exemptions for tuition savings accounts, and executive branch administrative costs and oversight.

But that's not all. They also contribute heavily to the financial health of private schools, scores of them, from Columbia University to Audrey Cohen College, music schools, art schools, religious schools, fashion schools, and aeronautics schools. The state gives many of these colleges direct funding for specific programs. It awards students scholarships, grants, and loans to enroll there. Finally, it does not tax the millions of acres of property these institutions own, which costs the state an incalculable sum in lost property tax revenue.

And that's just state spending. The federal government kicks in billions more for higher education. The Department of Education hands out huge pots of money annually to individual schools, such as Howard University ($195 million in 1997), and lends money to such wealthy private institutions as Georgetown University at below market rate for universities to upgrade their physical facilities. Then add on $329 million for educational research and statistics, and another $843 million for institutional and program development. Finally, cap it off with $7.28 billion in student grants and another $30 billion in student loans.

A lot of this is money well spent if you believe that educating our young redounds to the collective good. But a hefty percentage of it finances consumption, as tax experts would call it, the decision of parents to opt for "luxury" education even where perfectly adequate, inexpensive education is readily available. Should public money—tax money collected from millions of people whose only interest in higher education is that illusive "public good"—be used for this purpose?

Furthermore, with all that public money around supporting private universities, and all those public institutions where tuition varies from virtually free to five figures, why do we need to tack on yet another subsidy for high-income parents with kids in college? That's what the Hope Scholarships established in 1997 do, providing a fifteen-hundred-dollar tax credit for the first two years of a student's higher education.

When Bill Clinton first suggested the Hope Scholarships, in a commencement address the president delivered at Princeton University in 1996, Dick Morris, who had not yet fallen from grace at the White House, compared the initiative to Horace Mann's advocacy of free public schools—seemingly unaware that virtually free public institutions of higher education already existed in every U.S. state. David Merkowitz, spokesman for the American Council on Education, however, dismissed the notion as irrelevant to the students and parents most in need of tuition assistance. "These proposals are completely aimed at middle-income families, so will we see large numbers of low-income students take advantage of these program? No," he opined. Lawrence Gladieux, executive director for policy analysis of the College Board, called the tax breaks "bad tax policy and worse education policy." David Wessel of *The Wall Street Journal* characterized the "scholarships" as "another step toward a new middle-class entitlement, a federally subsidized college education for families with incomes as high as $100,000 a year."

Which was precisely the goal. Middle- and upper-middle-class families now have the opportunity to triple-dip at the public trough. Richard and Lisa's daughter, for example, attends the University of Maryland at College Park, where tuition is $4,699 a year, thanks to the $665 million Maryland taxpayers send to the state's public university system annually. Although Richard and Lisa have plenty of money in the bank to pay that tuition, like many upper-middle-class families, they took out a student loan to cover it. That was sound financial thinking because the interest rate on the loan, partially underwritten by the federal government, was low, allowing them to keep their savings in the stock market, where they could earn considerably more money. Add in the Hope Scholarship, and their neighbors are making a three-way contribution to the education of a young woman whose parents earn ninety thousand dollars a year.

Those Hope Scholarships and the child tax credits aren't the only "middle-class" tax breaks Richard and Lisa receive on top of dependent deductions just because they have kids. Lisa works a few nights a week as a therapist, seeing clients in the private office she carved out of a room in the back of her house. That's less an economic decision than a personal one; they admit they could live comfortably on Richard's salary. But Lisa wants and needs the stimulation of work. Because Lisa is earning money, she and Richard can claim a dependent care tax credit of $960, which represents a percentage of what she pays a baby-sitter. She doesn't need that baby-sitter in order to work since Richard is home in the evening when she is in her office. But they have the right to a tax break for childcare, even if they use it primarily to go out to dinner and the movies. That's $960 the federal budget will have to do without or that Frank and Adele will have to make up for.

So, is this—to use the dreaded word—fair? Should parents receive tax credits or deductions for childcare? Under what circumstances, and with what rationale? The first time an American woman tried to write off childcare expenses, she pitched them as a cost of doing business—and the Internal Revenue Service didn't buy the argument. It was 1937, and Lillian and Henry Smith, who were both working, deducted the cost of a nanny to watch their young child. When the auditor denied the deduction, they appealed, and the Board of Tax Appeals ruling from 1939 reads, in part:

> [The Smiths] would have us apply the "but for" test. They propose that but for the nurses, the wife would not leave her child; but for the freedom so secured, she could not pursue her gainful labors, and but for them, there would be no income and no tax. This thought evokes an interesting array of possibilities. The fee to the doctor, but for whose healing service the earner of the family income could not leave his sickbed; the cost of the laborer's raiment, for how can the world proceed about its business unclothed; the very home which gives us shelter and rest and the food which provides energy, might all by an extension of the same proposition be construed as necessary to the operation of business and to the creation of income.

Until 1954, the prevailing winds stormed against women's work outside the home, and the tax code, which always reflects social sentiment, continued to offer working women no breaks for defying convention. That year, however, political hearts softened where widows and poor women were concerned and hardened toward mothers on welfare. The former had no choice but to work, and it was high time that the latter joined them, members of Congress concluded. So tax deductions for childcare to a maximum of six-hundred dollars a year were conferred on women in both of those groups.

By the 1970s, pressure was mounting for changes that would reflect the new economic realities of women's lives and also shove still more welfare mothers into the workforce. The latter, of course, necessitated direct federal spending on childcare. So Congress added more money and programs to provide free daycare for poor working mothers and fiddled with the existing tax deduction to give lower-income parents some added tax relief to offset the cost of daycare. By 1973, dual-working couples in which both worked at least thirty hours a week, or single parents earning under eighteen thousand dollars a year, were eligible for tax deductions for in-home or out-of-home childcare.

This paltry tax break has long been a major bone of contention for feminists and their supporters in Congress, who are convinced that women—not just poor women or welfare moms, but *all* women—deserve childcare as a *right*. Forget $960 tax breaks. Forget income caps. They call for public funding of universal daycare to underpin women's ability to work in a society that still charges women with responsibility for care of children. Bowing to their growing clout, in the mid-1970s, Democrats tried moving in that direction with a massive infusion of federal funds into childcare centers. Richard Nixon, however, was in the White House. While he supported some expansion of childcare benefits for the needy, he had no truck with federal subsidies for daycare expenses of parents of means. By 1980, then, all but one of the three dozen federal daycare programs was targeted exclusively to the poor and low-income workers.

Liberal legislators and women's advocates, however, haven't given up on their quest for federally funded daycare for all women, no matter their economic circumstances. To bolster their case, they paint a portrait of harried mothers forced to leave their kids alone at home or in the back of their cars because they can find no safe, affordable place to guard them. But the childcare crisis—a crisis in availability, affordability and quality—has been wildly overstated. In half the homes in America, parents don't use any paid childcare beyond the occasional teenage baby-sitter. Their children are cared for by one of their parents, by both of them working split shifts, or by a relative. And survey after survey indicates that American parents of all races, income levels, and political persuasions believe that children do best when cared for in such settings.

Furthermore, surveys conducted by the U.S. Department of Labor and the Department of Health and Human Services show a 10 to 15 percent vacancy rate in the nation's eighty thousand daycare centers and that the cost of such care, adjusted for inflation, hasn't budged since the late 1970s. And in those same surveys, 95 percent of low-income families expressed satisfaction with their current childcare arrangements.

Once again, the poor are being used to promote the interests of middle- to upper-middle-class women in places like Towson who want the government to pay more of their daycare bills although they are perfectly able to pay them themselves. We're already paying a significant chunk: Two-thirds of the $7 billion in federal funding for daycare is delivered as tax breaks for the affluent, rather than services for the poor. But it still isn't enough. Far be it from me to suggest that the Lisas of America shouldn't work or that childcare is "woman's work." But it seems inappropriate to force the childless to underwrite Lisa's ability to work, or to compensate her for the fact that Richard is still stuck in the ninteenth century. And on what basis can we, as a society, defend requiring the childless to pay for tax credits for well-heeled families that pay for childcare? As a business expense? That's ridiculous, as the tax court pointed out so eloquently. A hardship allowance? It's hard to consider behavior for which you volunteer to be a hardship. Job development for nannies?

Trying to do so catapults us down yet another high-speed slope. Conservatives and stay-at-home moms say: If we are going to give tax credits to those who pay others to take care of their children, then we can't refuse to give tax credits to those who do the work themselves. Bill Clinton, at least, seems to have been persuaded by that logic and has opined that, in the name of equity, stay-at-home moms merit a five-hundred-dollar tax credit.

So now we're not only giving taxpayers a break for having kids, but compensating them for the time they, or a paid caretaker, spend raising them. How much further are we going to go in turning what have traditionally been considered private functions into ones that are public enough to demand financial support?

At whose expense? And are all these benefits really "for the children"?

Senators and representatives rushed into the hearing room in the Dirksen Senate Office Building shivering on the morning of April 6, 1995. By the first week of April, Washington is supposed to be in bloom, or at least in full bud. But dreams of spring had been dashed by a cold snap that had sent the cherry blossoms into below-freezing shock.

The air in the hearing room, however, was heated, as much from the political climate as from the boilers in the basement. It was the ninety-second day of the infamous hundred days of the revolution ushered in by the Republican victory in the polls the November before. Exhausted and numb from a legislative snail's pace that had turned into a sprint, members of the House of Representatives were staggering around Capitol Hill, unwashed, unkempt, unsure what they had done or what they would do next. The Senate was swamped with legislation passed by a House that planned to mark the completion of its legislative agenda the following day with a celebration on the Capitol steps.

If Republicans were jubilant, Democrats were alternately befuddled and irate, still paralyzed by the intellectual and political earthquake that had loosened their long hold over the House of Representatives. Turned into backbenchers, former committee chairs didn't know how to act like the opposition. Even in the Senate, where etiquette and rhetoric are, by tradition, more contained than that of the House, tensions and tempers were too hot for the thoroughly gentlemanly pretensions that normally govern the business of the land.

The ringmaster for that morning's round of partisan sparring by the Joint Economic Committee was Rod Grams of Minnesota, and the members were warming up for the *pièce de résistance* of the Contract With America, the Family First Act, which Grams had been trying, unsuccessfully, to get Congress to pass since he first set foot in the Capitol, in 1993, as a member of the House. Two years later, he had graduated to the Senate and political momentum was on his side. His ally in the House, Tim Hutchinson of Arkansas, had guided the legislation through the House. The ball was in Grams's court.

The legislation bore a striking resemblance to the schemes presented before Schroeder's committee four years earlier: It provided a five-hundred-dollar tax credit for every child in the land, to be deducted from the tax liability of every working parent. But nobody mentioned the similarity. These were the bold new Republicans who were going where no congressional majority had ever gone before, so they had a vested interest in pretending that the plan was earthshatteringly original. And the Democrats, who were defining themselves by what they were against, which was pretty much anything the Republicans were for, were in no mood to acknowledge that the Republicans were sponsoring a plan that many of the Democrats themselves had once endorsed.

It should have been a crowning moment for Grams, who owed his political career to the name recognition he'd garnered as a Minneapolis television news anchor and preacher of "fiscal discipline". But he had just come from the dentist and was slurring so noticeably that he felt some explanation was in order lest his fellow misinterpret his condition. "The dentist said, that's okay, you can just talk out of the other side of your mouth," Grams kidded, "And I said, well, I guess I'm used to that."

Grams kicked off the morning session with a recitation of the statistic that had compelled him on his quest for a family tax cut. "Since 1948, the Gallup organization has asked Americans what they think about the taxes they pay. That first year, 57 percent of the people said, yes, taxes are too high. Today, 67 percent of the American people say that they're handing over too much of their own money to the Federal Government."

Members of the audience traded glances. "Only 67 percent? Who would have thought that a full one-third of Americans don't want to pay lower taxes." Grams, however, put a different spin on that figure. "The mandate of November is clear and the people are demanding change. They're tired of the rhetoric. They're tired of empty promises. And they're tired of their elected representatives merely tinkering around the edges, afraid to make real changes."

The Family First Tax Credit of five hundred dollars per child was proclaimed as the goose that would lay the golden egg for millions of American parents. The credit, Republicans said, would allow families to buy health insurance for their kids, buy time with them, arrange special educational opportunities for them or purchase more peanut butter and jelly for them. Invested over the course of a child's life, it would pay for college and still channel $25 billion into the economy, thus stimulating economic growth and new jobs.

Show-and-Tell for the session—and there's nothing that members of Congress like better than Show-and-Tell—was a Virginian who worked at the state Department of Alcohol Beverage Control, had three children, a wife at home to take care of them, and an income of forty-five thousand dollars. Things are pretty tight, he said. "Last year, for example, we were forced to give up our support of Young Life, a nonprofit Christian youth organization.

"I know that there are those who say that the best way for government to help children is to invent new programs like AFDC or food stamps, or to create new agencies, or to otherwise increase the size of government," he said, offering his full support to the tax credit plan on the table—which would have no impact on children eligible for AFDC or food stamps. "But a private program already exists that deals with the needs of children and it's proven its ability to deliver cost-effective care. It's not an advocacy group like the Children's Defense Fund or an orphanage like Boys Town. It's called the family."

The session might have turned into a two-hour congressional encounter group with each member raising the rhetorical volume on the myriad benefits of the bill, except for Pete Stark, who had managed to found and run a successful bank before running for Congress and still get to Washington when he was just barely forty. Stark, too, seemed utterly indifferent to the impact of the bill on the nation's nonparents. But he was in no mood for high-minded oratory about the needs of the nation's families. "This is really affirmative action for the rich, and bait-and-switch for the poor, or the lower-income families," he said, after comparing the Hundred Days to a kidney stone—painful, but temporary.

"We have been urged to support this credit because it's family-friendly, but which families this policy is supposed to be friendly to is open to some discussion," he continued. He then proceeded to have a one-man discussion about precisely which families would be helped by a five-hundred-dollar-per-child tax credit. The families of the poorest one-third of children in the nation were slated for no relief whatsoever. The next 10 percent, he explained, would not receive the full amount.

"I want to credit Senator Grams for taking care of those new children who have the misfortune of being born into families with more than $200,000 a year of income."

Stark's monologue was eerily prescient and could have been repeated again and again over the coming three years as Congress enacted a growing number of "family-friendly" programs geared toward comfortable families. As finally enacted, the child tax credits cost the federal Treasury $95 billion over a five-year period, with 41 percent of the credits going to higher-income taxpayers. As part of Clinton's 1997 middle-class tax break, a couple earning ninety thousand dollars a year, but netting another seventy-five thousand dollars from sales of stocks, received a six-thousand-dollar tax cut. Even such education breaks as the Hope scholarship, the fif-teen-hundred-dollar credit for college tuition, were maneuvers for the middle class since, as nonrefundable credits that are subtracted from taxes owed to the government, they gave no relief to taxpayers who didn't owe the government that much.

But that was all in the future, a future in which Democrats jumped on the family-friendly train with their Republican opponents. In 1995, the Republicans were, for the most part, riding that train alone. It fell to them, then, to respond to Stark. "The $500 per-child tax credit, in my mind, has unfortunately been mislabeled middle-class tax relief," responded Scott Hodge, a fellow in budgetary affairs at the Heritage Foundation. "I don't think it is. It is family tax relief, That is the crux of the issue. All families are overtaxed. All families should be treated equally."

Hodge danced a careful jig in his invocation of equality, since that tax credit was anything but equal if you considered *all* taxpayers, rather than just those who happened to be parents. Equal treatment under the law ap-plies to nonparents as well as those with kids, or at least it did the last time I checked the U.S. Constitution. But the word family had been carefully chosen to shore up adults raising children while maintaining the pretense of equality—and childless couples, both gay and straight, and single peo-ple, living together or individually, be damned. After all, who cares about equality for nonparents?

Certainly not Peter Ferrara, a senior fellow at the National Center for Policy Analysis, who picked Hodge's equality ball and ran with it to a ring-ing denunciation of discrimination against the children of the wealthy. And Marshall Wittman of the Christian Coalition went so far as to assail those who wished to cap the child tax credits at, say, incomes over sev-enty-five thousand dollars as engaging in "the politics of class conflict."

As the discussion raged around him, David Liederman, the executive director of the Child Welfare League of America, grew increasingly fran-tic. "Two weeks ago, the House of Representatives voted to cut $3 billion in funding for abused and neglected kids," he said. "Two weeks later, our representatives of the people now turn around and pander to the middle-class and upper-middle-class voters with, as Speaker Gingrich put it, a gift to America.

"So what do we have here?" he asked. "Sixty-six billion of cuts on the backs of poor kids and a gift to the American people of ten times that much mainly to take care of middle- and upper-class families.

"In essence, the House has approved shredding the safety net for poor children and families in favor of padding the wallets of upper-income Americans. . . . Tell me, how can we claim fairly to help American families to take care of their children when proposals give benefits with one hand and take them away with another?" he continued, begging the members to consider capping the credit at two hundred thousand dollars and to reconsider multi-billion-dollar cuts in welfare and food stamps. No more attuned to the question of fairness to nonparents than the Republicans, Liederman at least tried to give the child tax credit idea the kind of weighty backing of justice that would make shifting more of the burden onto the childless ethically palatable.

That year, federal, state, and local spending on low-income kids—and the average low-income child lives with parents who make under ten thousand dollars a year—worked out to about ten thousand dollars per child living below the poverty line. If the money the per-child tax credit would cost the Treasury had been divided among them, the agencies charged with helping those children would have had an extra $25 million a year to play with, an extra one thousand dollars per child.

But increases in poverty program spending weren't on the agenda of either party that spring. The welfare reform package both sides were planning would wind up denying welfare assistance to almost 75 percent of the nation's poor children within five years of its passage. They would lose $4.3 billion in food stamp benefits, and half of those receiving disability payments from Social Security would lose that assistance entirely. In the face of new political realities that were still poorly understood, Liederman looked desperate. Members listened to his entreaty with barely disguised impatience. He persevered nonetheless. "Every politician seems to be falling over themselves in order to show that they're helping the middle class. The middle class, loosely defined, is anyone earning up to $200,000 a year. I understand that this is good politics. . . . But it is lousy public policy. To cut programs for our neediest citizens in order to help mainly our most comfortable citizens is outrageous and it is bad public policy."

PART TWO

For the Children?

Hardly—
Pure Politics Are Driving This Train

For the Sake of Which Children?

On October 10, 1983, millions of American parents turned on their televisions to watch their worst nightmare unfold in a two-hour docudrama. Reve Walsh—a picture-perfect upper-middle-class housewife with a three-bedroom house in the suburbs and a husband with a good job in the hotel business—strolled through the mall in Hollywood, Florida, holding hands with her six-year-old son, Adam, who looked like a latter-day Opie in green shorts and a striped Izod shirt. As the two wandered through Sears, Adam, lit up by a grin that framed the gap between his front teeth, raced for the Star Wars video game in the toy department. Reve smiled, knowingly, and handed her son some change to indulge his passion. Then, warning him to stay put, she wandered off to the lighting department to buy a brass lamp.

When she returned ten minutes later, Adam was gone.

Frantic, Reve searched the store, grabbing strangers and shoppers and passers-by to see if they had spotted her young son. To no avail. Mall security swept through the stores and the corridors with no luck. The police force of the suburban town just north of Miami was called in and combed the community. Adam did not reappear. Two weeks later, Adam Walsh's severed head was discovered in a canal in Vero Beach, 135 miles north of the Walshes' home.

Viewers watched as Daniel J. Travanti, playing Reve's husband, John, coped with the news, crying and screaming, smashing lamps, tipping over tables, destroying whatever he could find to vent his rage and frustration. It was a numbing, terrifying scene.

As the final image of the Walshes' trauma faded, they were left watching color photographs of sixty missing children flashing across the screen while the real John Walsh read their names and begged viewers for help, "May your eyes bring them home."

In the two years between Adam's murder and the made-for-television rendition of the horror, John Walsh had launched a one-man crusade to convince Americans that their children were not safe, that their most precious possessions could vanish in an instant if they turned their backs. "This country is littered with mutilated, decapitated, raped, and strangled children," he said in testimony before Congress, reporting that 1.5 million children were reported missing each year, with the whereabouts of fifty thousand never discovered. Cold fear surged through the hearts of parents. The nation erupted in a frenzy of barely contained hysteria about child abduction, something that the agony of thirty-one sets of Atlanta parents had not succeeded in provoking in the years since their children began disappearing in 1979. Those children, of course, were black. Although middle-class white parents might have sympathized with their plight, they did not identify.

It seemed that every day another freckled or pigtailed child disappeared, snatched from a schoolyard, a playground, or a backyard by a stranger. In Des Moines, two newsboys, who lived in quiet, suburban neighborhoods eight miles apart, vanished somewhere between their homes and the corner drop-off points where they picked up the newspapers they delivered. In Palm Beach, Florida, employees and patrons at a restaurant phoned the police to report an abduction when they saw a man in a uniform grab two boys and drag them toward his car. Six officers, three detectives, and a helicopter were dispatched to comb the area for the black car patrons had described. It turned out that the uniformed man was a security guard at a nearby Zayre's who had been chasing the boys, who had tried to steal a bicycle from in front of the store. Then Laura Bradbury, a three-year-old with a Little Dutch Girl haircut who disappeared from a campsite at Joshua Tree National Monument, became the poster child whose face kept the notion of innocence at risk in the forefront of the national consciousness.

State governments responded to the mounting parental panic by establishing clearinghouses on missing children to help parents and police pool information. In the U.S. Congress, scores of senators and representatives signed on to a bill demanded by Walsh establishing a nationwide computer database of missing kids. In New Jersey, authorities began fingerprinting schoolchildren. In North Carolina, microdots were drilled into molars. Parents were encouraged to videotape their kids to give police ample identification tools in the case of a kidnapping. The federal government established a toll-free number that citizens with information about missing kids could call. And the faces of those children began appearing on grocery bags in Florida, pizza boxes in Virginia, toll booths in New York, and milk cartons in at least a dozen states.

Confronted with Walsh's continuing use of the fifty-thousand figure, newspapers tried to verify his number, or round up solid statistics on the numbers of children disappearing into thin air. The FBI was openly disdainful of Walsh's mathematics. "Impossible," said Bill Carter of their Public Information Office. "More than fifty thousand soldiers died in the Vietnam War. Almost everyone in America knows someone who was killed there. Do you know a child who has been abducted? That should tell you something right there." He offered the bureau's annual count, only sixty-eight cases of unexplained disappearances in 1984, for example. Of the 12,150 abduction cases reported to the National Center for Missing and Exploited Children in its first two and one-half years in existence, more than half were runaways. Most of the remainder were kidnappings by fathers or mothers or grandparents in disintegrating families. Only 393 were abductions by strangers.

That message gradually cut through the frenzy. But the panic did not end—it just mutated.

By the mid-1980s, the alarm was being sounded about latchkey kids, children left at home alone after school by working mothers. Officials with the Detroit police department reported that one-sixth of the fires in the city were caused by unsupervised children. Antidrug and alcohol crusaders cautioned that kids were getting into their parents' liquor cabinets or trying marijuana because no one was there to stop them. As Americans were assailed with images of young children coming home day after day to empty houses, newspapers scrambled for statistics on precisely how many children were imperiled by the possibility of fire or the incursion of sexual molesters, drug addiction, or alcoholism. Few bothered to mention that most of those "latchkey kids" were over the age of fourteen.

Then came the chemical scares, as a nation suddenly bereft of the Red Menace found new targets for its disquiet. Suddenly parents noticed mysterious odors inside their children's classrooms, soil of strange color in their playgrounds—and besieged school officials proved helpless to calm their fears even with the best laboratory results and pediatricians to guide them. Every bottle, appliance, dry-cleaning bag, tool, and toy became a potential hazard to kids, and federal regulatory bureaucrats worked overtime writing regulations requiring the labeling of products like five-gallon buckets and all-terrain vehicles for parents unable to assess the dangers themselves. Dolls and miniature cars were redesigned to guarantee that no part could come loose and lodge itself in the throat of a helpless child.

When a Boston infant died under mysterious circumstances and the blame was laid on his nanny, Louise Woodward, Americans affluent enough to have nannies—even those who could afford only the occasional neighborhood teenager as a baby-sitter—panicked, a panic fed by companies selling hidden video camera systems to monitor the behavior of their children's caretakers and whipped up by television news magazines that could not find enough dangers to kids to fill all their available air time.

Entirely ignored in those endless reports was the reality that one in ten of the nation's children was being fed on thirty-five cents per day.

In 1998, thanks to the reportorial endeavors of *20/20,* Americans learned that the new menace was phthalates, a chemical found in the plastic used in toys and teething rings. The message to parents was blunt and terrifying: Children chewing on toys designed to be chewed on might suffer liver or kidney damage. Mothers and fathers scurried to banish such items from their homes, unaware that in order to ingest enough phthalates to damage their organs, children would have to eat the entire toy or teething ring, an act that would be far more dangerous than the chemicals contained in them.

By the fall of that year, peanut butter panic had broken out, thanks to the efforts of the Food Allergy Network of Fairfax, Virginia, which sent a chill down the spine of school administrators with alarming statistics about the number of children suffering death by peanut butter. Although the Centers for Disease Control reports only eighty-eight deaths among Americans of all ages from food allergies, including peanut allergies, from 1979 through 1995, the network warned that 125 Americans die from food allergies annually, most from allergies to peanuts. Public schools in New York and Connecticut, Massachusetts and California raced to set up committees to investigate the new peril and responded with peanut-free zones or a total ban on peanut products in their cafeterias. Such private schools as Horace Mann, in Riverdale, New York, avoided such drastic action by keeping peanut butter under wraps—in the form of premade sandwiches snugly enclosed in plastic and available only in designated areas.

A year later, when shots rang out at Columbine High School and killed twelve students, parental panic rested on solid, blood-soaked, ground. But, again, the response was utterly out of proportion even to that horror. A second-grader in Alexandria, Louisiana, was suspended and sent to the local Redirection Academy because she brought her grandfather's pocket watch to show-and-tell, with a one-inch knife hanging off the fob. Near Harrisburg, Pennsylvania, a fourteen-year-old girl was strip-searched and suspended because during a class discussion of the Littleton shooting she admitted that she understood how unpopular kids could be pushed into violence by their peers.

As promoters of wider agendas sensed the potential in the mounting kid-hysteria, the fears fragmented into dozens of nightmares, both real and imagined. In 1998, the crusaders for cleaner air and water, lobbying for passage of the Children's Environmental Protection Act introduced by Senator Barbara Boxer of California, warned that the safety standards used by the federal government were inadequate to protect the tender lungs and skin of kids. The public face of the movement was Nancy and Jim Chuda of Malibu, California, whose daughter Colette died of cancer at age five, a death they attributed to unknown pollutants.

Religious conservatives jumped onto the speeding train, proffering their own brand of fuel. They publicized cases of good, decent, inevitably Christian parents whose children had been seized by heinous agents of the dread "Nanny State." They ratcheted up their attacks on Hollywood for making movies like *Honey, I Shrunk the Kids* and *Home Alone,* which depict parents as blithering idiots and ineffectual fools. In February 1999, in his *National Liberty Journal,* Jerry Falwell warned parents about the perils of an animated television character who might be giving their kids positive images of gay people. "Parents Alert . . . Parents Alert" read the headline of the story explaining that the children's television character Tinky Winky of the Teletubbies, with his red purse and purple triangular antenna, was an intentional Trojan Horse entering their homes.

Every possible danger to middle-class children was reported in bold headlines and earnest tones. No mention was made of the study released by a Berkeley biologist suggesting that almost half of the nation's black children were at risk for cancers because they were suffering from broken chromosomes due to the absence of folic acid in their diets.

In retrospect, the hysteria was predictable as the first members of a generation that had come of age during the greatest economic boom in American history crossed the great divide into parenthood. Baby boomers were America's golden children, the best educated, most amply fed, and most coddled generation of kids in the history of the world. Watching the passage of their parents from cookie-cutter homes in postwar Levittowns to sprawling suburban ranchers with manicured lawns, they expected that progress would be, as GE taught them, their most important product—in the form of bigger houses, extra vehicles, and more exotic vacations.

Few realized that they were measuring the trajectory of their lives against an anomalous postwar moment. Had they done so, fewer still probably would have cared. Their expectations were woven into every fiber of their beings. Confidence was their legacy. They would grow up to end war, eradicate poverty, colonize the moon, and erase racism from the heart of America. By the late 1970s, however, the unease and discontent of recession had eroded that cocky self-assurance. Wages eroded. Homes seemed smaller, vacations more infrequent, and careers in jeopardy. Dashed expectations created fertile ground for fear, and those fears were played out as apprehension for the future of their children, whose lives were supposed to be more golden than theirs had been.

A decade earlier, middle-class parents wouldn't have been caught dead demanding government assistance for their children. The "dole" was a place for losers who couldn't compete. And at a time when images of children with distended bellies, from Biafra or Mississippi, were vivid in the national imagination, parents with refrigerators filled with milk and juice, and pantries stuffed with everything from bread to Twinkies, would have felt humiliated to declare their kids needy.

But as the drumbeat grew louder with every report, every rumor, every nighttime fear turned to daytime concern, and so it began. Children are being kidnapped; the government has to do something—pass laws, design prevention programs, create computerized databases. *Emergency, emergency.* Children are being raped and mutilated; the government has to do something—castrate the offenders, keep them in jail for life, spread the word about where they live and work and dine. *Emergency, emergency.* Children are dying in fires because they are alone after school; the government has to do something—hire more policemen, lengthen the school day, sponsor after-school programs.

Like their parents caught up in the thrall of the Red Scare and the image of Nikita Khrushchev vowing to bury them beneath the hammer and sickle, they brooked no counterargument nor any reassurance. At the end of the Year of the Child in 1979, a survey of the state of America's youth had reported that no better moment had existed in human history for children to be born healthy and to stay that way. Polio had been conquered. Leukemia was being cured. The greatest danger to kids—to the children of newspaper editors and reporters who sounded the alarms, of the politicians who responded to every report, no matter how unnuanced, of the stockbrokers and consultants, lawyers and analysts whose self-interest drove the nation's self-awareness—was the way their parents drove on the roads.

A few hesitant voices like Marian Wright Edelman's suggested that everyone was worrying about the wrong kids. But when Americans talk about "for the children," they tend to see only the faces of their own progeny. Others suggested that the government was powerless to protect middle-class children in the face not only of grinding recession, but also of massive social change that meant that few were living like Wally and the Beaver. But stressed-out and overwrought parents didn't want to hear those voices. They couldn't imagine not having it all, having to make choices or sacrifices, having to scale back the wildest dreams, for themselves and their children, that they'd imagined as reality.

So the drums beat faster and louder, at first with modest suggestions for clearinghouses on child abuse, more funding for public education, more programs to shore up the American family, and later, with bolder schemes for a utopia for the nation's youth—until the images of Biafra and Mississippi, the Sudan and Navajo reservations dissolved in the crescendo of middle-class want.

Conservatives, caught up in the "World We Have Lost" syndrome, advocated new divorce laws to keep families together, prayer in schools, and the mandatory education of schoolgirls in traditional female roles, all in the belief that turning the clock back would give today's children their fantasies of the youth they had enjoyed. Liberals convinced that children's lives would be improved most by shoring up their mothers' equality and ability to have both progeny and power insisted that the concept of equal pay for equal work be modified to apply to comparable work, that more federal money be channeled into daycare and programs to safeguard six-year-old girls from the taunts of the six-year-old boys who sat behind them in elementary school—taunts that were all too easily labeled sexual harassment.

Taken on their own, each plan and concept was driven by some internal logic, although few addressed the problems they were designed to remedy. But as the fears became more extreme—that allowing children to exchange Valentine's Day cards at school would scar those who didn't receive many, that applauding valedictorians at graduation might damage the self-esteem of young men and women who had not excelled—so too did the solutions, crescendoing, like Ronald Reagan's answer to the threat of the Evil Empire, into the parental equivalent of Star Wars.

The first comprehensive parental defense scheme was designed by the National Commission on Children in 1991. Chaired by Senator John D. Rockefeller IV, the commission counted among its members luminaries from politics, medicine, and a dozen activist groups and think tanks. Marian Wright Edelman, founder of the Children's Defense Fund, sat alongside her political nemesis Wade Horn, a Reagan appointee at the Department of Health and Human Services. Then-governor Bill Clinton traded thoughts and ideas with Kay Cole James, the Virginia secretary of health and human services who went on to work for Ronald Reagan.

The commission's report and blueprint were an odd contradiction. After two and a half years of research and interviews across the nation, the group concluded that "most American children are healthy, happy, and secure." Then they turned around and argued that American children—including those who were healthy and had good, stable and loving parents—were in danger. So, despite all the good news, the thirty-four-member group declared a national youth emergency to blunt the "harshness" of children's lives and designed a blueprint for a radical restructuring of every aspect of public life, from the tax system to health care, from the media to the schools, the family, and the courts. Concluding that the middle class needed every bit as much help as the poor, they designed a $40.3-billion-per-year tax break for parents, universal health coverage for pregnant women and children under the age of eighteen, and a works program of the sort launched to create jobs during the Depression. This one, however, would guarantee paid employment only to parents.

How did they expect to pay for such generosity? Their plan robbed Peter, Paul, and anyone else they could find to tax more or to shelter less. They suggested modest increases in the tax rates for the wealthiest Americans and corporations, and a more substantial increase on taxation of Social Security benefits for households earning over thirty-two thousand dollars. They recommended doing away with the personal income tax exemption, reducing home energy assistance, canceling the manned space station, and cashing out food stamps, since they would not be necessary to feed children whose parents would receive other federal assistance. It was a revolutionary scheme that would have dramatically redistributed the nation's spending and tax burden to increase programs for kids of all backgrounds and reduce the taxes of parents of all incomes. But it was not the last.

By the mid-1990s, conservative think tanks, realizing that catchphrases like "for the children" or "beleaguered parents" hefted more political cachet than "for the family," rejiggered their "profamily" agenda accordingly. It's not completely crazy to invoke "traditional family values" on behalf of kids, despite the disgust it engendered in liberals. By every measure, the children of "traditional" families are thriving, while kids living in one-parent households are in trouble. As a group, those kids are more likely to commit suicide, suffer from serious physical problems, or be caught up in violence or drug use. And the reason is apparent: Even after factoring in government assistance—housing, food stamps, direct cash payments—38 percent of single-mother families live below the poverty rate, while only 6 percent of two-parent families do so. Three out of four children growing up in single-parent households spend part of their first ten years in poverty. Only one in five of their counterparts in two-parent homes join them there.

The new conservative thinking about children and their parents has been laid out in dozens of volumes, but the most succinct overview, *The Assault on Parenthood: How Our Culture Undermines the Family,* was penned by Dana Mack, an affiliate scholar with the Institute for American Values, a family policy research organization. In Mack's view, the root of all problems—familial, children's, stress, you name it—is the demise of the two-parent family and the public scorn for what is loosely, and sloppily, called "family values." But instead of blaming a litany of rock stars, movie producers, and television shows for undermining those values, she hones in on the *real* enemy: an incompetent—nay, evil—government. The "nanny state," she says, routinely and purposefully thwarts parental efforts to raise their kids well. Rather than teach them to read and write, schools spend hours teaching sex education and "life-skills that separate children from their parents' culture." Rather than bolster parental authority, lawyers and courts defend children's rights. Rather than enforcing the marriage contract like any other contract, society treats that commitment as expendable and breakable.

Her solution? Well, like most conservatives, Mack says that her solution is to return parenting to the parents. But, in the end, the savior she turns to as rescuer of the endangered family, and its attendant children, is the same evil government she spends more than three hundred pages assailing. Her seven specific suggestions include tax relief for parents, which would be granted by the government; three months of paid maternity leave for working mothers, which would be mandated by the government; raising the retirement age to allow parents to take reduced work schedules while they are young, which would be instituted by the government; an "obscenity" tax on broadcasters who don't air enough PG programming, which would be levied by the government; and charter schools and school choice, which would be paid for by the government.

Liberals, of course, have countered with their own "family-friendly" government programs, a helter-skelter collection of do-good, or at least sound-good, programs only tangentially linked to the problems they are allegedly designed to address. For the most part they have restrained themselves from voicing the ideas they discuss privately, European-style schemes that pay parents to raise their kids. The implications of paid parenting, after all, might create unease in a society wed to the familial free market.

Rather, they have thrown their weight behind the Family and Medical Leave Act, which sounds parent- and child-friendly, but offers nothing to those parents who cannot afford to take the twelve weeks of unpaid leave their employers are now required to give them. And they have fused women's and children's programs, arguing that increasing women's wages and providing daycare for working women cannot but redound to the benefit of their kids.

The most startling approach—as much for the credentials of at least one of its authors as for its content—was unveiled in *The War Against Parents,* a vitriolic jeremiad against an allegedly "parent-hurting" society by two prominent liberals, Sylvia Ann Hewlett and Cornel West. Their book is a parental *sturm und drang* about the state of the nation's young and "the agony of the impossible pressures and choices our society thrusts upon moms and dads." Stringing together every possible dark statistic in what one reviewer called "the droning apocalyptic litany of what's wrong with American capitalism," they beat the alarmist drum about child poverty, declining SAT scores, juvenile crime, and child obesity, to prove that "the whole world is pitted against them."

No one is spared the blame for this dire state of affairs: greedy corporate moguls, indifferent politicians, self-interested feminists, salacious TV executives, liberals who worship individualism at the expense of family, conservatives who venerate the marketplace, school administrators indifferent to the schedules of working mothers and fathers, the writer of the stunning Australian movie *Shine,* who blamed the on-screen demanding dad for his son's mental illness, the authors of the book *Toxic Parents* for spreading seditious lies about parents, celebrity single moms like Rosie for being bad role models, the heavy metal group Megadeth for singing that parents are "dickheads"—and the list goes on.

The only relevant group excused from responsibility are mothers and fathers themselves, 62 million hapless men and women whom West and Hewlett paint as powerless to resist the antiparenting assaults of a society in which they are a demographic plurality.

The involvement in the project of Hewlett, a Welsh economist who has been living in the United States since taking her doctorate at Harvard, was not surprising, since she has spent more than a decade lamenting the plight of America's children. In her 1987 volume *When the Bough Breaks,* she had invited Americans to emulate England, France, and Sweden, which spend two to three times as much of their federal budgets on children—although she managed to avoid mentioning anything about those countries' tax rates. And, in speech after speech, article after article, she had copiously lamented the fact that divorce, abandonment, and work had left American children with ten to fifteen hours less per week of parental interaction time than they had in 1960.

The arrival of West on the "profamily" scene, however, was something near breathtaking. A Harvard professor of African-American Studies and the Philosophy of Religion, West, one of the nation's most incisive public intellectuals, is best known for his fiercely astute and passionately eloquent contributions to the national debate on race. A "prophetic Marxist," as he calls himself, West would have seemed the least likely American thinker to let affluent parents get away with seeing themselves as ill-fated victims.

But both Hewlett and West acknowledge with surprising candor that their concern for the state of parenthood was provoked less by scholarly endeavors than by traumatic personal experiences. Hewlett's epiphany occurred when she lost twin fetuses to a miscarriage, a tragedy she blames on Barnard College, where was working full-time and struggling to get tenure during her pregnancy. And West was moved to concern about the state of parenthood because his wife divorced him and moved away to Atlanta with his two-year-old son, despite his best efforts to block the move. Hewlett might have dealt with her tragic loss by warning other women of the dangers of trying to do everything simultaneously, of the importance of planning pregnancies to occur during relatively unstressful times at work, or at least not when you're in the middle of a tenure struggle. Likewise, West might have used the experience of losing regular contact with his son by reflecting on what had gone wrong with his marriage, or by looking for a job in Atlanta, which a man of his stature certainly could have found.

Alas, neither followed any course that would have included accepting a modicum of responsibility for their own difficulties. Rather, the lessons they took away from those experiences was that someone—in the form of the government or that elusive body called "society"—should not have allowed those difficulties to arise in the first place. Someone should have forced Barnard College to be more sensitive to the needs of a pregnant woman. Someone should have guaranteed a father like West more rights over his son—although those rights would inevitably have restricted those of his ex-wife.

West and Hewlett openly long for what are clearly romanticized views of their own childhood eras—when the government allegedly supported families, children watched Ed Sullivan and the Mouseketeers, Mom walked the kids to school, and Dad handed out some serious discipline. And their prescription for recapturing that past is laid out in a detailed Parents' Bill of Rights that would guarantee mothers and fathers everything from more time with their kids to more clout at the ballot box. In West and Hewlett's family-friendly utopia, parents would receive twenty-four weeks of paid parenting leave funded—believe it or not—by the teetering Social Security system. Fathers and mothers could divide this leave as they saw fit, but dads would also be required to take a ten-day fathering leave. Companies offering parents benefits like flex-time or childcare would receive tax breaks, parents with children under six would receive a government allowance, and sales tax would be eliminated on diapers and car seats. Most important, to give parents the political power to force the nation onto the straight-and-narrow, the vote would be extended to children, whose parents would exercise it in their behalf until they reached the age of eighteen.

Why, in the West-and-Hewlett view, should the nation confer these rights on parents? It's a simple question of justice, they opined. "We expect parents to expend extraordinary amounts of money and energy on raising their children when it is society at large that reaps the rewards." Amazingly, nobody laughed, at least not in public—not even at proposals that would destroy the Social Security system or reduce payments to the elderly or disabled in order to bolster the bank accounts of boomer parents, or at the blithe dismissal of the concept of one adult, one vote. No one noticed that their parental entitlements would have left nonparents staggering under an almost unimaginable tax and work burden. No one mentioned that virtually every parent in the nation had volunteered for that job. No one commented on the odd contradiction at the heart of their treatise: that the very forces being blamed for undermining parents—the government, the media, and industry—were led by parents themselves, turning their War Against Parents into a schizophrenic struggle requiring psychotherapy rather than political action.

Quite the opposite. Ted Kennedy branded their Parents' Bill of Rights "both workable and inspired." Maya Angelou called the work a "brave, wonderful effort." Jonathan Kozol declared that the polemic provided "an eloquent agenda for the future of the family and the dignity of parents."

Is the child- and parent-friendly fad in America about the dignity of parents? Sylvia Ann Hewlett might scoff at the implication of that question, but it is a serious one. Are we rewriting the nation's tax code and reshaping workplaces from Maine to Missoula because our kids are in trouble? Or have middle- and upper-middle-class adults, bored with the poor, found a politically and morally acceptable justification for diverting a hefty share of the public pie in their own direction with such a demand for dignity? Those questions are not popular. Neither are the answers.

By almost every measure, the average American kid has never had it so good. His chances of dying in the first years of life are half what they would have been in the 1960s, one-third what they were in the highly overrated 1950s. And the probability that his mother will survive childbirth to raise him has more than doubled. The birth rate has fallen dramatically since his grandparents' day, from an average of 3.7 children per family to 1.8, so he is born into a small family where he is less likely to get caught in the crowd, more likely to get the food and attention he craves. His parents belong to the most educated generation in American history, with over 80 percent holding high-school diplomas and almost one-quarter degrees from colleges or universities. They waited to have him until they were established at work and had money in the bank, so they are older, theoretically wiser. They are decidedly more affluent, earning almost 50 percent more than their parents did in the 1960s, even adjusting for inflation. And they are lavishing that money on kids like him—$200 billion a year—and giving him and his friends another $20 billion for movies, toys, and baggy shorts. Life feels more expensive to them because inflation has raised prices dramatically. But while they spend a greater percentage of their paychecks on health insurance, Social Security, and college tuition than their parents did forty years ago, almost everything else costs less, from housing to food, clothing, and travel.

The health of today's kids is terrific, at least according to their folks: More than 80 percent report that their children are thriving. They should be, since they have almost all been immunized against measles, mumps, rubella, diphtheria, and polio. Car seats, seat belts, and smoke detectors help protect them from harm. Regulation of dangerous chemicals that used to be sprayed onto our foods or ooze into the water supply have given them the cleanest water and freshest food of any American kids since industrialization. And diseases that once would have killed them—from leukemia to polio—have been conquered or tamed.

The average American kid's Mom and Dad are crazily busy: They both work long hours, spend time at the gym, and have active social lives. But he does not come home to an empty house after school. Either one of his parents is waiting for him, or he spends those hours with other adults. Most nights—five out of seven—he will sit down to a family dinner with his parents and siblings. Ironically, while his parents aren't around as much as their parents were, he spends about as much time with them, one on one—doing homework, watching TV, talking, fishing, or having what author Deborah Fallows calls "all-out, undisturbed, down-on-the-floor-with-the-blocks time"—as they did with their folks.

The public schools in his neighborhood or town have never had more money to prepare him for the future. Their budgets have increased an average of 2 percent faster than the rise in the cost of educational expenditures for the past fifteen years. His teachers are not paid anywhere near as well as, say, his pediatricians. But they are catching up. Over the past fifteen years, their annual salary raises have been 2 percent higher each year than the increases of working people nationwide.

If he is born unable to walk, he will not suffer the isolation of the handicapped of previous generations because schools and museums, offices, restaurants, shops, and bathrooms are open and accessible to him. If he cannot hear, he will find out what is happening in the world by watching close-captioned news and will stay in touch with his friends and family thanks to a TTY. No matter what his physical limitations and challenges, he will study with his peers and have legal recourse if denied a job.

Not everything in his life will be rosy. His parents will nag and complain because he and his friends aren't doing as well in school as they did. And it hurts the national pride that their scores on competitive tests in math and science aren't as good as those of children in France, or England, or even in Thailand. But he needs to know the secret flaw hidden in those statistics: Not nearly as broad a group of students in those other countries ever has the chance to take the test. So the comparison is a little shaky.

His parents are always panicked that he will be harmed by a stranger, or fall in with the wrong crowd and get into serious trouble. But, despite the high-profile cases where kids bring guns into school and shoot up their friends, that violence is unlikely to come nearer to him than his television screen. The rate of juvenile violent crime has been falling; fewer than 0.5 percent of kids commit such offenses. If his friends are arrested, it is likely to be for the kinds of crimes kids have always committed—shoplifting and drinking and bothering the neighbors.

His mom and dad worry, too, about his mental health because they can't open a women's or parenting magazine without reading about the startling, almost epidemiclike increase in attention deficit disorder, hyperactivity, and obsessive compulsive disorder. Those articles are true—at least literally. But since little attention was paid to ADD, hyperactivity, and OCD in earlier eras, even one hundred cases nationwide would be a dramatic increase. And the statistics bandied about by mental health professionals, that one in five American children suffers from mental health problems, throws momentary depression over a romantic breakup, or anxiety over a pimple that popped out just before the prom, in with schizophrenia and mania.

He does face dangers and temptations against which his parents have no easy vaccine. Kids around him are drinking, and some are trying drugs. They are risking potentially fatal illnesses by having sex before they know how to protect themselves. But kids have been drinking since parents began having liquor cabinets. And they know more about sex, and its attendant risks, than most of their parents knew when they were already adults. And they are decidedly less likely to be guzzling booze, smoking cigarettes, or trying illegal drugs than their parents were twenty years ago.

The National Commission on Children put it succinctly: Most children "belong to warm, loving families. . . . The majority of young people emerge from adolescence healthy, hopeful, and able to meet the challenges of adult life. . . . They are progressing in school, they are not sexually active, they do not commit delinquent acts, and they do not use drugs or alcohol." Middle class parents don't *feel* that their kids are doing all that well. "For families raising children, the gap between economic expectations and achievement has widened," the National Commission on Children reported. Almost two-thirds of the nation's parents worry that they won't be able to give their children the kind of lives they would like, according to a survey done by pollster Celinda Lake. And virtually all of the parents report that they live in a miasma of stress.

But what's new in that? How many nonparents feel that they have been as economically successful as they had expected? Is this a crisis in bread-and-butter, or a crisis in expectations? And how many parents, whatever their circumstances, *don't* worry that they won't be able to give their children the kind of lives they would like? "I worry about it constantly," one mother I know recently told me. "But that doesn't mean the worry is realistic. I know that, but that doesn't change anything. Worrying. It's a standard parent thing." And who doesn't have stress, especially when we are bombarded twenty-four hours a day with messages about our stress level?

This hardly sounds like the kind of national crisis that necessitates a massive redistribution of resources from nonparents to parents. And it's not—for the *average* kid. For children unlucky enough not to be average, however, the picture is inarguably grim, and that picture is painted by poverty. Certainly there are children born in affluent homes who are in danger. Some are among the estimated three million children abused or neglected each year. Others are raped by their peers, or shot by their friends. But those cases, while attracting enormous attention, are anomalous. We are obsessed with them because the children involved are from the kind of middle-class families with which most Americans identify.

But our inability to make any meaningful dent in the poverty rate, which endangers millions of children, *does,* or at least *should,* constitute a national emergency. And perhaps it would if the patience and attention of Americans for such endemic disasters weren't so woefully limited. But these days, we only tolerate wars that are short and finite, and we seem to have developed the same national boredom for domestic difficulties that defy easy fixes.

Nonetheless, if our cries about the plight of our children are to have any meaning, they need to conjure up the faces and lives of the one out of five American children who live below the poverty line, a line that all too frequently becomes a ceiling. All too many of those children die before they can walk, or get shot before they can drive. Nine out of ten of them are born weighing too little. They are twice as likely to repeat a grade, drop out of high school, or be single mothers before the age of twenty-four than their peers in the suburbs. Their schools are too often cruel parodies of educational institutions. They are the only kids likely to benefit from increased spending on education, yet they are the least likely to receive it.

Bill Clinton, Dana Mack, Cornel West, and all the other family-obsessed thinkers are right: Children and their families are in trouble. But what does giving 25 percent tax breaks to affluent parents have to do with saving 20 million children living in squalor?

Today's new and suggested programs "for the children" and "for the family" are the equivalent of giving emergency aid to all the residents of Florida just because a hurricane decimates portions of South Miami—and with woefully little left for those who actually lost their houses. Measure the schemes against the problem: The National Commission on Children concluded that middle-class families needed help as much as the poor and anchored their plan to assist both poor and middle-class parents on a $40.3 million nonrefundable tax break. Such largesse would have done nothing for the poor, since few poor people pay any taxes that could be refunded. Their planned universal health coverage for pregnant women and for children under the age of eighteen, a plan which has been instituted under President Clinton, gives some concrete assistance to the needy, but only to a point—and to the point of absurdity. That coverage suggests that women deserve health care only when they are pregnant, which would move the nation backward to the days when women's value was measured by the activity in their uteruses. The moment they complete that exalted duty, who cares if they get sick? Sure, their children might suffer neglect if their mother is laid up with pneumonia or a broken leg she cannot afford to get treated. But so what, as long as the child has medical insurance? Is that really enlightened public policy?

Take Dana Mack's suggestion that we return parenting to the parents. Which parents? Should we leave children in the hands of mothers who are too stoned to remember to feed them? To fathers who would rape them? And what about the idea of guaranteeing parents the right to work reduced schedules while their children are young? Well, that sounds great if you have enough money to feed them on reduced-schedule wages. But the bank balance of the parents of America's neediest children would never stretch that far.

And what of Cornel West and Sylvia Ann Hewlett? What do they recommend that might solve the crisis among kids trapped in poverty? Twenty-four weeks of paid parenting leave means that for the first four months of their lives, those kids would have close supervision and, one would hope, loving attention. But what then? Their parents might relish the memories of that time, but are we to believe that having Mom or Dad home caring for a kid until he's twenty-four weeks old is going to improve the trajectory of a life spent in substandard housing, eating starchy food, and hearing gunshots in the streets?

Is this what passes for progressive social policy designed to give poor kids a chance in life?

How will Clinton's five-hundred-dollar tax break for stay-at-home moms save children born on the meanest streets in South Central Los Angeles, or in the most miserable hollows of West Virginia, from violence, illiteracy, drugs, or even the disintegration of his family? Will it begin to make up for the loss of welfare benefits, food stamps, or Social Security disability payments, all of which Clinton has cut?

Either the designers of these programs can't add, or they have some other agenda—and no one would accuse West, Hewlett, Mack, the National Commission on Children, Bill Clinton, and his attendant lackeys of being mathematically challenged. The bottom line is that all of the endless hand-wringing and angst about the state of the nation's children isn't being directed toward kids at the greatest risk. It's a charade designed by and for parents who aren't thrilled with the consequences of their own choices, who feel *guilty* that they don't spend enough time with their children—and who, after decades of funding welfare for the poor, no matter how parsimonious, are demanding theirs.

Okay, they say: So the average kid isn't all that bad off. But it's still tough, and expensive, to be a parent today, and that should count for something. But the problem is that the portrait limned of American parents is streaked with melodrama and short on facts. Listen to William Rasberry, the columnist, describe their plight:

> Picture a desperate parent reaching up from an earthen pit, barely able to touch the child she loves, feels responsible for and yearns to take care of. Now picture a society that offers this deal: We'll lower down to you a basket of money with which to meet your parental obligations, but you must send up a basket of dirt in exchange. This, I think, is a fair analogy of the trap in which more parents find themselves. They know they need to spend more time nurturing their children. And yet they don't see how they can; the providing-for takes so much of their time, energy and emotional resources they can't quite manage the nurturing. But suppose the dilemma is not their fault—not the result of bad choices, unaffordable lifestyles or false priorities but of forces beyond their individual power to resist.

The problem is that it is difficult to pinpoint precisely what those irresistible forces are. Family income has risen, in real dollars, by 50 percent in less than a generation, and while some things are comparatively more expensive, everything from food to housing is relatively cheaper. Most Americans have fewer children, more access to transportation, and every possible time-saving convenience, from take-out food to meals that can be prepared in a microwave minute.

So, do parents—as a group, with no consideration of their income—really *need* social welfare programs of the sort being bandied about by the left, right, and center? Need, of course, is a relative judgment. Ask parents earning $150,000 if they need fifteen-hundred-dollar or three-thousand-dollar tax breaks. Very few, if any, are going to say no. No matter how comfortable you are, there's always something else you feel you need, a new car, an extra vacation, an upgraded computer. The more money you earn, the higher your expectations rise, after all. But does need, the kind of need that constitutes a moral demand for help, include more than what is necessary for proper shelter, clean clothing, adequate food, and access to a decent education?

By that standard, of course, most of those deriving the greatest benefit from these new forms of parental welfare aren't suffering from need. They are suffering from terminal want, that most modern of American diseases. The line between need and want, after all, isn't carved in stone. It's fuzzy. One person making sixty thousand dollars feels deprived while another feels comfortable. And, certainly, an income of sixty thousand dollars doesn't mean the same thing in rural Kansas as it does in metropolitan New York or Boston. But if you're talking about diverting public money in some new kind of welfare scheme, the bar can't be set by want—by what we wish we could have, or thought we would have. That spreads public money so thin as to leave too little for those who really, honestly, and truly need help.

The family programs instituted over the past three years that put the bar of assistance at adjusted gross incomes of $110,000, $80,000, or $60,000 mock the concept of need. It's hard to imagine that a couple with an adjusted gross income of $110,000 is needy. It strains credibility to even include the $60,000 crowd, who—unless they live in places like New York City or San Francisco—might feel cramped by credit card debts, or have to work a part-time second job to keep two new cars in the driveway. In most towns and cities in the country, from Detroit to Baltimore or Portland, $60,000 for a family of four won't buy much luxury, but it does not constitute need, especially considering that the average poor family with children lived on $8,632 in 1996.

If the issue, then, is want, not bedrock need, the focus of the national conversation changes dramatically. Want isn't a sound basis for determining who gets tax credits and tax reductions and other more direct government largesse—which is why parents rarely acknowledge want as the basis of their demands. Instead, when they harp on the need for kids to be protected, and then on the financial strain of raising them, they eschew any mention of want and take refuge in the final rhetorical device left to them: *deserve.*

Michelle Gaboury is convinced that she deserves every tax credit, every tax cut, every student loan, childcare deduction, and dollar of funding for her children's education that she can wring out of the system. Michelle and her husband, Paul, raise their two children in Acton, Massachusetts, a leafy suburban town west of Boston. They live at the end of a cul-de-sac in a stately new home—the kind of upscale, oversized cookie-cutter house that is the standard McMansion of suburbia. Driveways there overflow with minivans and Subaru Outbacks, the neighbors are friendly enough to gather for the occasional community potluck supper, but the lawns are wide enough to make good fences.

Acton is Soccer Mom Heaven. The public schools offer pick-your-own pedagogy, from open classroom to traditional education. The Children's Discovery Museum, whose mascot is a climbable dinosaur named Bessie, teaches kids how to make their own flagstones and how to test which gum blows the biggest bubbles. The K.S. Elite Academy allows parents with extra cash to enroll their children in programs "to encourage self-esteem through the development of individual talents using non-competitive, play & learn approach," which means golf, roller hockey, soccer, or lacrosse. Children can call a publicly funded storyphone when they need company, and mothers with kids under two can drive up to the supermarket and pull into parking reserved exclusively for them.

It's the kind of place that inspired some of Francis X. Clines's most eloquent prose.

> There was a time, and a good time it was, when someone else's kids could be handily deplored, if only because families were larger and reproduction seemed so much less an extension of individual egos. W. C. Fields could say things like: "I like children. If they're properly cooked." No opinion-page monographs followed from specialists in juvenilia or parents sensitized to parenting. Just vindictive belly laughs.
>
> Things are different nowadays as the boomers' offspring are carted aloft and in glorious display in sedan-chair backpacks and imported,

safety-steeped strollers encased in screening like little Popemobiles. They bear the terrible burden of being designer clones of the parents, displayed for genealogical appreciation.

The Gabourys' lifestyle—which includes vacations in France and winter ski weekends—is buoyed by the largesse of the public. They can claim a five-hundred-dollar tax credit for their son Jesse (in addition to the dependent exemption parents have claimed for decades), fifteen hundred dollars in tax credits because their daughter Jillian is in college, and, since Michelle works part-time as a psychotherapist, a tax deduction for childcare even though Jesse is in school.

Paul, a kind of moderate Republican, derides these gifts as "affirmative action for parents," favors that the affluent should most decidedly *not* be given. But Michelle has never considered the possibility that it should not be so. Indeed, it has never occurred to her that anyone would challenge either these benefits or the preeminent right of parents to be compensated by society for their unique contribution. "I think we need to look at the social value of families, value propagation within that context and make some sacrifices along the way," she says, sitting in the kitchen at the back of her home, the sliding glass door overlooking a heavily wooded lot. Her home is precisely planned and decorated, with a heavy emphasis on antique oak. But tiny sneakers and the occasional toy strewn across the floor suggest how thoroughly seven-year-olds undermine the designs of their parents.

"Children are an investment in the future," she says. "There are a lot of risks for people who have kids. Having a family is outrageously expensive. Maybe the childless take the brunt in some ways, but this isn't about justice. This is about living in a community. I agree with Hillary, it takes a village and we have to support members of society who are at a disadvantage."

Michelle readily concedes that she is not needy, no matter how far you stretch the definition of that word. So what does it mean when the owner of a house worth almost a half-million dollars refers to herself using the word "disadvantage"? Quite simply, it means that by bearing and rearing children, she is losing both time and money. And, like a growing number of parents, she feels in her gut an almost unconscious sense of entitlement springing from a deep-seated belief that since she is preparing the next generation, society should compensate her for that loss.

It is a strikingly nineties attitude, at odds with every belief and tradition Americans have historically held about parenting. Even a generation ago, parents wouldn't have engaged in this type of economic calculus of parenting. They didn't demand, as does Michelle, that propagation be valued for its social worth: They were convinced of its individual value. They had children because they thought they should, because they wanted children, because they dreamed of perpetuating family name and traditions. They didn't think of what they were doing in terms of loss—lost potential wages, lost money, lost time. They weren't looking for a return on their investment. For most Americans, that return had disappeared decades before, when children ceased being workers who brought money into the family. They were focused too narrowly on the gain, on the sheer joy of holding their first-born, of watching her take her first step or throw his first football. Parents might have talked about the hard work of childrearing. They might even have talked about the "sacrifices" they made, but not grudgingly. Children, they believed, were their own reward, and hard work and sacrifice were part of the package.

What has changed, other than virtually everything? Most important, women started working outside the home and started placing value, *market* value, on their time. For centuries, women had lived without the concept that their time had economic worth. It surely did, whether they were taking care of the house, sewing clothes, or plowing the fields. But until the turn of the century, comparatively few ever received money in exchange for work. Most women, then, couldn't conceive of the time they spent taking care of their families in economic terms.

Today, however, virtually the entire female population works for wages before having children. They have grown accustomed to thinking of their time as having economic worth, worth that comes in a tangible form, preferably green. Staying home to raise children, then, even taking a break during the first months after childbirth, represents an economic loss. And putting in a "double day" of wage work and childrearing feels like unpaid overtime. Even for such women as Michelle, for whom lost wages represent no diminution of their lifestyle, devoting themselves full-time, even part-time, to their children represents giving up something concrete. It feels like deprivation. It feels like "disadvantage," to use Michelle's word.

Women like Michelle are not suffering merely from the decline in the social respect that full-time mothers are accorded, as conservatives would have us believe. If so, they'd be seeking the parental equivalent of, say, the Navy Cross or, for really good parents, the Congressional Medal of Honor. This is the age of materialism. Medals are nice, but cash is the current medium of honorific exchanges.

Don't get me wrong: I'm not blaming women for putting a monetary value on their time. Most men, after all, have been thinking that way for more than a century. But putting the gander into the same mind-set as the goose made it inevitable that the vocabulary of the economic calculus of parenting would creep into social and political conversation. Today, social scientists meticulously compute the costs of childrearing and lay out cost-benefit analyses of how much value each dollar spent on children's education or health is worth to the national economy. Politicians take those costs and pledge to offset some of them to compensate parents for their economic contribution. And, recently, an economist from Florida A&M went even further by suggesting that we need to correct the "family balance sheet" by declaring a parental dividend, a tax on the incomes of grown children that would be given directly to their parents.

Read this, from the first page of Shirley P. Burggraf's book, *The Feminine Economy and Economic Man:*

> WANTED: Parents willing to bear, rear, and educate children for the next generation of Social Security taxpayers and to carry on the modern culture of learning and progress. Quality parenting preferred. Large commitments of time and money required. At least one parent must be willing to work a double shift and/or sacrifice tenure and upward mobility in the labor market. Salary: 0. Pension benefits: 0. Profits and dividends: 0.

"Will anyone be answering this ad in the twenty-first century?" she asks, the assumption being that without direct economic gain, the human beings inhabiting the United States will simply give up on reproduction.

Her thinking would be compelling if she were talking about, say, cucumbers. Imagine that cucumbers were essential to human survival and that cucumber farmers weren't producing them in sufficient quantities. It would make sense, then, for the government to do something to increase the crop. It would behoove them to put in place incentives to farmers to switch from corn to cucumbers, to put price supports in place, to do anything and everything to make cucumber production rewarding.

Children, however, are not vegetables planted, sown, and reaped for economic gain. They have been an economic liability to their parents for as long as today's Americans have been alive, and the crop is not particularly scarce. Although few individual parents are producing them in any quantity, in 1990, the same number of children lived in America as lived here in 1960—64 million of them, which suggests that parents haven't been all that scared off by the arithmetic.

Treating kids like an agricultural commodity, like any commodity, is absurd, not just because it is more than a little crass, but because reproductive inclinations are impervious to market manipulations and interventions. In China, where the entire force of the state is brought down on those violating the "one-child" rules, women nonetheless risk loss of wages, loss of educational opportunities for their children, and public disgrace in order to bear more kids. In Western and Eastern Europe, governments have tried for decades to increase the plummeting birth rate by providing parents with child allowances, direct cash payments for each child they bear. The birth rate, however, remains stubbornly resistant.

And our own national experience speaks eloquently to the truth that reproductive decision-making defies economic logic. In contemporary America, there is an inverse correlation between wealth and family size. The reason the percentage of poor children continues to climb is not that the number of poor adults has increased. If anything, it has declined. But poor people refuse to apply the same economic logic to family decisions that they would to the purchase of a new car or the rental of an apartment. In the mathematical logic of American family life, those least able continue to have large families while the more affluent barely replace themselves.

Ultimately, converting parenting into a mathematical or market equation is simply too Orwellian for a nation built on a commitment to a parental free market. Paying citizens, directly or indirectly, to bear and bring up children—and that's what taking the edge off Michelle Gaboury's disadvantage means—is a slippery policy slope that the Michelle Gabourys of the nation—and they are legion—haven't ridden to its logical, thudlike conclusion. Paid labor, after all, inevitably entails supervision and control. Paid parenting could no more remain immune to that economic reality than double-entry bookkeeping or widget production. And it doesn't stop there: Would everyone have the *right* to the paid position of parent? Would every parent be paid equally, no matter how well or poorly he loves, guides, and nurtures kids? And what does this do to the long-held belief that families should be bastions of privacy and parents the masters of their own domains?

Parents have already propelled us halfway down that slippery slope, which is paved, perforce, with good intentions. But it is also greased, predictably, with unintended consequences.

4

Family Frenzy

In a different age with an altered sensibility, the Great American Family Tour would have been a cosmic joke instead of a footnote in modern political history. The notion of—excuse the alliteration—a politician, a pediatrician, and a producer teaming up to stump the nation on behalf of the family sounds like the kind of high concept some wet-behind-the-ears screenwriter pitches for a made-for-television movie. You know, the sort where pompous politicians are turned into "real folks" by their contact with the unwashed masses.

But Pat Schroeder, T. Berry Brazelton, and Gary Goldberg launched their swing through five states in January 1988 without a trace of irony. The trio trooped into New Hampshire just weeks before the state presidential primary, blanketing Portsmouth with bumper stickers and organizing kits jammed with the details about every "family-friendly" bill pending in Congress. Despite unusually mild weather and the NFL playoffs, six hundred people showed up for an old-fashioned pep rally at the local high school, where Schroeder played cheerleader.

Then the road show followed the presidential primary season into South Carolina. At a mass meeting at Booker T. Washington Center in Columbia, Schroeder preached the wonders of a federally mandated parental leave policy that would permit mothers and fathers—at least mothers and fathers with enough money to forgo wages—to spend time with their newborns or with sick adolescents. "There are only four other countries who have done less than the U.S. to help their families: South Africa, Sudan, Ghana and Burkina Faso," she told the audience. "What a distinguished group."

Wherever they went, Schroeder, Brazelton, and Goldberg hammered the same theme: The family is in peril and the grandees in Washington won't defend it. They're "still coming out of this Rambo syndrome," Schroeder proclaimed. "So we have a lot of people in Washington still terrified of talking about these issues for fear that people will think they have lace on their shorts."

Their political stunt was planned as the first step in the creation of a massive lobby that would allow American families to manipulate the reins of power "just like Exxon." It was a strange analogy. Exxon needs a massive lobby because, unlike the Great American Family, its corporate ranks do not include 63 million Americans who have the right to vote. And, unlike Exxon, most American families aren't spewing chemicals that foul that nation's coastlines. So they theoretically don't need to hand out large sums of cash to distract lawmakers and influence-peddlers from their production of toxic waste. But that didn't deter Schroeder, Brazelton, and Goldberg.

Schroeder was still licking her wounds after humiliating herself the September before by breaking down in tears during her announcement that she would not run for president. Goldberg lent the group star power, or at least a sprinkling of stardust. The executive producer of *Family Ties* wasn't exactly a face that stopped traffic in midtown Manhattan. But he and his wife, who was along for the ride, had founded a childcare center during their hippie days in Berkeley called the Organic Day-Care Center, and Goldberg had become a hero to the childcare set when he insisted, as part of his 1985 contract, that Paramount studios build a childcare center.

Brazelton was the real draw of the trio, the eighties version of Benjamin Spock, the pediatrician who taught Americans how to raise their children while still having enough time left over to organize against the war in Vietnam. A pediatrician and professor at Harvard, Brazelton was his own industry, spreading his theories on childrearing through books (*What Every Baby Knows*), magazine columns, and a television series broadcast on Lifetime, which did not yet admit that it was "television for women." The gospel according to Brazelton—the latest fad in childrearing advice that tends to swing wildly from generation to generation—was that the two-working-parent family was dangerous to children's self-image, sense of security, and values. The development of a child's sense of self, Brazelton teaches, demands copious quantities of parental time, a commodity Brazelton felt was in short supply. So he threw himself into the nascent parents' rights movement to organize mothers and fathers to find that time for their kids, even if they had to "cheat on the workforce."

At every stop, Schroeder, Brazelton, and Goldberg were hosted by welcoming committees carefully balanced along partisan lines. But the bipartisanship was little more than veneer. The policies and specific bills they were endorsing were the core of the Democratic party social agenda: a $2.5 billion childcare package, pay equity for women, federally funded housing, and parental leave (which would later become family leave in order to broaden its appeal). The Great American Family Tour was, in fact, a political advance marketing team designed to test consumer response to the repackaging of the party's traditional social agenda. The old bleeding-heart wrapping had earned them a reputation as liberal spendthrifts, and Schroeder, Brazelton, and Goldberg took to streets and the airwaves to check whether that same agenda would find more favor if swathed in a "family-friendly" wrapper.

Under Ronald Reagan, Republicans had turned the F-word into a potent political force, and the Democrats feared electoral disaster if they did not contest that terrain. The competition between the two parties over the family became a telling case study in supply-side politics, in which a political contest for the support of the privileged generates rather than responds to public demand. After all, no grassroots movement fueled the "Most Family-Friendly Party" pageant. Parents weren't marching down Pennsylvania Avenue protesting government indifference to their concerns or telling pollsters that children and families had replaced crime and taxes on their top-ten list of political concerns. Rather, it was raw political ambition that ignited an escalating firestorm of family-friendly rhetoric, family-friendly taxes, family-friendly legislation, and family-friendly workplaces.

The seeds of that rivalry were planted in the 1970s, with the rise of the Moral Majority, of widespread and increasingly sophisticated political activism on the part of socially conservative Christians. Where once slavery and drink had symbolized the decay of their Christian nation, abortion, working mothers, and the Equal Rights Amendment became signs of the Apocalypse, and conservative Christians who had long avoided politics entered the fray to take back the nation by shoring up traditional family values. In a nation committed to a tradition of political dualities, the new Christian politicos needed a political party, and the Republicans were clearly the more comfortable home, with fewer Jews, fewer atheists, and fewer wanton women vying for control. These new troops became the grassroots of a Republican resurgence, energizing a Republican fold that had long been too busy fighting the Cold War and defending the interests of business in the name of country club ladies and corporate chairmen to worry overmuch about the Christian social agenda. In Ronald Reagan, this coalition found its voice. Given his personal history, Reagan himself might well have preferred ranting about the Evil Empire. But "family values" was the war cry that energized the new party masses. Republican candidates stumped the nation warning of threats to children and the decline in values—and emerged victorious in the polls.

Democrats, still convinced they could retain political hegemony by talking about racism, poverty, and discrimination against women, were stunned by the power of Republican rhetoric—and their early inability to turn "profamily" issues to their own political advantage. In retrospect, it was almost ludicrous for them to have tried. Democrats counted among their most fervent followers millions of women who had come of age in the 1960s, when the family was an oppressive patriarchal institution. Their educated adherents had lived together without benefits of matrimony, founded communes, and consciously and willfully thrown off the shackles of Ozzie and Harriet. The glorification and rescue of the American family would hardly have stirred their passions.

Every time the party tried to play on Republican family themes, it looked ridiculous. George Miller of California founded and chaired a House Select Committee on Children, Youth, and Family—and then held hearings on things like the reactions of children to nuclear threats. Jimmy Carter charged Vice-President Walter Mondale with organizing a White House Conference on Families to be held in the spring of 1979. Before it could get off the ground, it was postponed. Then it split into two regional conferences, before disintegrating into, well, an all-out family feud. Gay activists demanded their right to be considered families, a coterie of anti-abortionists lashed out at feminists for hypocrisy (their crime being calling themselves "profamily" while being prochoice), and every possible special interest group from the taxcutters to the Greens tried to divert the family train to its own station. Most Democratic activists gave up in despair, concluding that the government should look after the country and let the family—whatever that was—look after itself.

That strategy made total sense given the demographics of the electorate. America, after all, was becoming less of a "family" nation each year, if we mean by family adults living with children. In the span of a single generation, two-parent families with children had become a small minority of the nation's households—just 25 percent—while the number of households filled with childless couples and adults living alone had surpassed them. And the electoral clout of those childless adults and singles had become prodigious. In 1956, parents were the majority of the electorate, at 55 percent. By 1988, that number had slipped below 40 percent, and was still dropping. In every election for the past half-century, parents have been increasingly less likely to show up at the polls than nonparents, starting with a 1 percent point gap in the 1950s and ending with a 12 percent gap in 1996.

The Democrats had a strong advantage among those nonparents, a virtual lock on the electoral support of gay men and lesbians, the elderly, and all those young urban dual-career professionals who opted out of reproduction. In virtually every poll, every survey, parents with children at home showed themselves to be more conservative on issues from abortion to party preference. Demography, then, was on the side of those Democrats convinced that riding the family train was a fruitless journey.

By the late 1980s, however, the White House seemed too remote for Democrats to follow their own sound advice. They were appalled by the results of exit polls that proved that the Republicans had a lock on the nation's parents. Seizing the family initiative became an irresistible temptation. In September 1986, the Democratic Policy Commission laid out a new set of principles and emblazoned "stronger families" at the top of the list. By the winter, the word "family" had made its way into the political lexicon of every committee, meeting, and press release of the party.

Then came the annual Democratic party issues conference, held in 1988 at the elegant Greenbrier Hotel in White Sulphur Springs, West Virginia. The theme was "Our Family, Our Future," and the 131 lawmakers who rode down from Washington on a special Amtrak train signaled their new commitment to the family in the most graphic way possible, by bringing their collective 180 kids along for what turned into a virtual kiddie winter carnival. Bill Cosby gave the obligatory keynote address, and Marian Wright Edelman, founder of the Children's Defense Fund, ceded no ground in reiterating the traditional Democratic agenda pitched in the most traditional terms. "We treat the well-to-do dead better than we do the poor who are alive," she said.

But the first glimmerings of a new Democratic strategy for taking back the family from the Republicans shot through the conference: children. More than a decade before, Edelman had acknowledged to the *New Republic* that she had founded the Children's Defense Fund, in part, because focusing on the young was a politically viable tactic for garnering funding for the needy. And pollster Stanley Greenberg had divined that the electorate felt secure about their own lives, but uneasy about their children. The needs of children, then, would be the Democrats' answer to Republican cant about family values.

Governor Bill Clinton, on hand with his wife, a member of Edelman's board, cautioned that appeals on behalf of the poor were outdated. Democrats would be better served by taking advantage of the country's "obsession with economic issues" and finessing their platform as children's programs that are a sound investment in the future, he said. George Miller, who'd been Edelman's congressional point man, proclaimed that the key to Democratic victory would be to talk "about these issues in hard, political terms, not just bleeding heart terms. The language has changed. What it really sends is the message of the real cost of neglecting these programs. . . . You can sell this at the Chamber of Commerce." Even Ted Kennedy, the quintessential old liberal warhorse, conceded that if the party was to end the Republican monopoly on family symbols, it had to become "more creative in reclaiming those issues."

David Liederman, director of the Child Welfare League of America, was in seventh heaven. "This is the first time the candidates will be asked to present a specific agenda for children," he said "There's enormous sup-

port for doing things for children. . . . It crosses all party lines, all philoso-
phies, all economic lines."

The Democrats' specific proposals suggested that that support wasn't
focused where Liederman or Edelman might have hoped. The cutting
edge of the party were practitioners of liberal *realpolitik,* which means
that they knew that the poor didn't vote, and that millions of affluent
baby boomers who were becoming parents did. So the old liberal family
lobby, which had preached "in bleeding heart terms," as Miller put it, and
lost ground to the profamily lobby of the right, began to crumble. If
Ronald Reagan could win the hearts of middle-class Americans on their
family values, Democrats would win those hearts back on their children
and the dent those kids made in the family pocketbooks. They would ride
back into the White House waving a banner emblazoned with "for the
children" that would eclipse the mighty power of "family values."

Smelling possibility after eight grueling and humiliating years of
Ronald Reagan's popularity, even the most unlikely party supporters
jumped on the bandwagon with abandon. Organizers of the Women's
Agenda Conference in Des Moines—which pretends to bipartisanship but
is always dominated by liberal feminists—took pains to explain that their
concerns were "family issues, not just women's issues," and shied away
from all discussion of the Equal Rights Amendment and abortion. Their
themes were childcare, comprehensive health care, and affordable housing, which they called "kitchen-table issues" at the center of the lives of
the New American Family in which both parents worked outside the
home, or in which a woman was the sole support of her kids.

Candidates in the presidential primaries fell over themselves to prove
their allegiance to this new family and their new issues. Dick Gephardt
tapped as his official advisor on family issues Ethel Klein, a Columbia
University political scientist who gushed that family issues "transcend the
gender gap." Bruce Babbitt announced his candidacy for the Democratic
presidential nomination in a daycare center and vowed to make his first
priority as president the creation of a voucher program to help "every
working parent in America" find a safe, affordable place to care for his or
her kid.

In July 1988, the Democratic National Convention in Atlanta was
awash with children. Keynote speaker Ann Richards of Texas allowed her

granddaughter Lily to upstage her. Jesse Jackson's five children introduced their dad, one by one. Lynn Cutler, vice-chair of the event, began the political circus by talking about children. And the candidate-in-waiting, Michael Dukakis, used that moment of high political drama to announce that his daughter-in-law Lisa and son John were expecting right around Inauguration Day. In his contest for the hearts, minds, and electoral support of working women, Dukakis declared it "time to see that young families are never again forced to choose between the jobs they need and the children they love" and threw his support to the Act for Better Child Care, with its $2.5 billion price tag for its first year of funding daycare for all families up to the median income. For those still unconvinced of his dedication to parents and kids, Dukakis invoked his support for family leave, a Democratic bill that would require employers to give parents time off from work without pay to bond with their newborns or care for their sick children.

George Bush was not about to be left behind all alone with the grownups. Once on the actual campaign trail, like Dukakis he seemed unable to resist reading a book to the three-year-olds in a daycare center for the benefit of news photographers, or the filming of a commercial with the candidate singing with the four-year-olds. "Mark this down in your memory book," wrote Ellen Goodman in her August 6, 1988, column. "One day in the summer of 1988, both candidates for president of the United States were found campaigning in day-care centers. The eldest of the citizens in these centers was 6, ineligible to vote until the 21st century. Nevertheless, a cameo appearance by the would-be presidents was considered a sure-fire vote-getter."

Bush, however, proved restrained when it came to translating that cuddly concern into legislation. He opposed the Democrats' childcare bill because it was not narrowly targeted to the poor, who were then receiving just 1 percent of the nation's childcare budget. And he opposed family leave legislation as yet another unnecessary regulation of the nation's businesses.

Democrats predicted that such lukewarm support for "the family" would destroy Bush's candidacy, since the tea leaves they were reading suggested that daycare and family leave would be a make-or-break issue. After all, their pollsters and campaign managers argued, 57 percent of mothers with preschool children were working, and a goodly percentage of them were those infamous Reagan Democrats whom they had to seduce. Those tea leaves, however, told only part of the story, since only 34 percent of mothers with preschoolers worked full-time, and many of them for only part of the year. Indeed, the 8.3 million working mothers with children under the age of six constituted only 7 percent of the labor force and a smaller percentage yet of registered voters.

Ignoring those portents, the Democrats' political swamis made a politically fatal miscalculation. The prize, a free four-year stay on Pennsylvania Avenue, did not go to the candidate willing to give free daycare to the greatest number of children, or federally mandated job-protected parenting leave. George Bush moved down the street, and Democrats went back to the drawing boards to figure out how to make "family-friendly" play for them. It took four years, until a rube governor from Arkansas came riding into town and taught them a lesson about making the other side's thunder clap for you by seeding it with cold, hard cash.

Supply-side politics, like supply-side economics, is a tricky beast. Even with a legion of pollsters, political analysts, anthropologists, and focus groups, it is easier to exploit people's existing needs and wants than to create a new "will of the people." It demands the convergence of media and marketers, politicians, business, and nonprofits all feeding off one another, all beating the same drum in a synchronized rhythm to an audience predisposed to dance to that beat. Like the whipping up of a market for any new product, it must be charged by the power of nonstop news reports and sophisticated advertising, both political and commercial, that barrage us with pictures and slogans that ignite our fears and tap into our pity. Real needs are irrelevant; potential is the only reality.

As the number of children born in the nation soars during America's current "baby boomlet"—to 70.2 million in 1998, topping the 1996 record of 69.9 million—the plight of children and the family has reared as the ideal nineties supply-side hook. It offers something to everyone, from the handwringers and feel-gooders glued to *Oprah* to the entrepreneurs on the lookout for ways to make a better buck and politicians desperate to be at the forefront of the latest fad. Like the Red Scare of the 1950s—

which kept government agencies bloated, the defense industry gloating, and scores of red-baiting politicians in office—it is sheer opportunity.

That demand has been created, image by image. A milk carton carries the photograph of a freckle-faced five-year-old in pigtails. The broken body of an infant shaken to death by his nanny dominates the front page of the newspaper. Bloodstains are seen on the floor of the library at Columbine High School. Harried mothers speak out on the radio and television about the stress and exhaustion of double-duty. Parents are at the end of their ropes. Politicians tour dilapidated homes where low-income women leave their children for the day to wallow in their own feces and suck on sugar-laden lollipops. There is a daycare crisis.

Children in peril and parental angst have been a media dreamworld of heartwrenching stories with unlimited front-page, or top-of-the-news, potential. Think JonBenet Ramsey or Susan Smith, who provided earnest reporters with endless fodder for a public hungry for secondhand emotion. Or NBC's regular features on the angst of working women struggling to balance career and family. Forget hard fact or statistics. Forget subtleties about which kids are in danger or how many families are teetering on seesaws they built, board by board. The alternative view is too juicy, furnishing too much fodder for the ratings wars during the hiatus between OJ and Monica.

Corporate America—that amorphous conglomeration of serious business and wide-eyed sleazeballs ready to jump on any economic opportunity—has picked up the same scent and ridden it to soaring profits. With each news report about abusive nannies, security firms and camcorder manufacturers whip up the volume of terror to sell in-home spy camera systems to wary parents. With every movie about a crazed babysitter, detective agencies prick at the panic and pick off their share of the "for the children" pie by advertising their services for thorough investigations of daycare centers or childcare workers because, as they say, "Where your kids are concerned, you can never be too careful."

Marketers are having a field day selling parents everything no one ever thought anyone needed to raise a child, from gourmet baby food to two-speed battery-operated infant swings so that junior can rock without Mommy straining her back. The name of the chain Buy, Buy Baby says it all before you walk through the front door. Gilt cradles at one thousand dollars a pop, Eddie Bauer suede car seats, infant swim shoes and penny loafers, almost three hundred different kinds of bibs, stuffed tigers with twelve-hundred-dollar price tags, and $375 portable breast pumps that plug into automobile cigarette lighters so that you express milk on the highway. No physical danger to a child exists for which Buy, Buy Baby doesn't display a remedy on its shelves—usually at $39.95 or above. Stove top covers, stove knob covers, cabinet safety locks, electrical outlet shields, safety harnesses, video monitors, table edge safety guards, and radio walkie-talkies. And a desk at which expectant mothers can register to ease the shopping trauma of those invited to their baby showers.

Bookstores are replete not only with books for children, but with a growing number of parenting guides that only neglectful parents would ignore, or at least so advertisers claim. In 1998, Amazon's best-sellers included books on how to cope with the "spirited" child, the child with attention deficit disorder, the out-of-synch child, and the rude child. In 1999, the lead offerings are volumes like *Beyond Jennifer and Jason, Madison and Montana: What to Name Your Baby Now, Baby Signs: How to Talk with Your Baby Before Your Baby Can Talk,* and *The Womanly Art of Breastfeeding.*

Corporate America has discovered that kids are more than a market: They are the nation's best marketers, influencing the spending of $500 billion a year in everything from cars to building supplies. Why do they have so much power over parental purchases? "Guilt!" says Michael Kitei, president of Small Talk, a consulting firm that teaches companies how to sway parents through their kids. "Our rule for a new product is that it has to get an A or B from kids. We can get a C or D from Mom and it's no problem. An F is a problem. But if it's a C or a D from Mom and the kids love it, Mom's going to buy it."

Daycare center operators are flourishing in this kid-centric America, especially those that feed off the high-end corporate fringe benefit market. And their hype is as unsavory as that of the video camera hucksters and detective agencies. "Personnel problems?" one such company asked in a newspaper advertisement. "Convert boring, low-pay jobs into positions people want to get and keep! Reduce turnover and absenteeism! Improve morale and productivity!—Add childcare to your fringe benefits package."

Most companies aren't quite so shameless as to suggest that factory workers or telephone operators will turn into cheerful worker bees if they only have daycare as a fringe benefit. But even the most "reputable" for-profit childcare providers have learned how to exploit the current "more is better for your kids—and more expensive is better still" mania to bolster their bottom lines. Take Bright Horizons Family Solutions, the nation's "leading provider of work-site child care, early education, and worklife consulting services," as the company describes itself.

Founded in Boston in 1986, Bright Horizons, the first half of the company, which was formed by a merger in July 1998, has achieved truly spectacular growth. Carving out a niche by convincing corporations of the benefits of providing on-site daycare, it reported revenues of $92 million in 1992. By the end of 1998, it operated 260 "family centers" in thirty-six states, serving Boeing and DuPont, Johnson & Johnson, Merck, Motorola, and Universal Studios. Its quarterly revenues had topped $55 million and its shares were traded actively on the stock exchange.

"We are fairly expensive and we are not ashamed of that," Roger Brown, the CEO, told the *Charlotte Observer.* "We think everyone needs to get used to the fact that good child care is expensive." The reason for that expense remains unclear, since Bright Horizons workers earned only five to eight dollars an hour when Brown made that statement. But, in the current climate, that expense is a major part of Bright Horizons' attractiveness.

Since the company pitches itself as offering the kind of upscale facilities that keep the most finicky professional workers loyal to the corporation, corporate profits depend on the willingness of potential clients to buy that line. And Bright Horizons hasn't left that matter to chance. Its consultants gloss over the fact that despite the baby boomlet, working mothers with preschool children constitute only 7 percent of the labor force. Rather, it regularly churns out studies like the Survey of Work/Life Initiatives that it commissioned, coconducted, and lauded as a "benchmark study" proving—surprise, surprise—that "companies need to be competitive in the work/life policies they offer to attract and retain employees in a talent-scarce labor market."

Avarice isn't the only danger to truth in the building of children and families into a political and commercial market niche. Advocacy and special interest groups have contributed mightily to the hyperbole that provides the "for the family" movement with steam. The problem with special interest groups—on all issues, on all ends of the political spectrum—is that nuance, balance, and subtlety aren't the stuff of successful membership drives. If an environmental lobby, for example, wants to raise money for its work, it is likely to have more success with a mailing warning, "Contribute now or the Republicans will cut down every tree in North America," than with a carefully worded report about the impact of deforestation on, say, a rural county in Oregon.

To use another example, no fundamentalist Christian group is likely to succeed in whipping up the troops and contributions by saying, "Look, most homosexuals are perfectly decent people who just want to be left alone to live their lives." Their coffers fill up when they send out screeds forewarning of a homosexual takeover of the nation—which can be stopped only with massive infusions of cash.

Child advocacy groups are no different. The Florida Children's Campaign *has* to fill its website with grave statements like, "With Florida ranking 44th among states in how we take care of our children, it's no wonder they're dying at alarming rates." How else can it punch its message, "Pity won't save them. Put your money where your heart is"? Nancy and Jim Chuda, who lost their daughter, Colette, to a rare form of cancer in 1991, might not have succeeded in pulling Olivia Newton-John, Bette Midler, Norman Lear, and Alan Ladd, Jr., into helping them raise funds for the Children's Health Environmental Coalition Network with nothing more than photographs of sweet Colette and tales of her horrible death. But scientifically shaky alarmist research about the special risks to children of parental exposure to pesticides or the chemical dangers of bottled baby foods has struck a real chord.

Consider the surveys and polls that child and parent activists have summoned to pique the interest of politicians. "Voters have moved children from their private agenda to the public agenda, especially baby boomers and parents of young children, who have decided there is a public role, as well as a private role, for making things better for children," concluded Elizabeth Schrayer of Schrayer and Associates, a Washington grassroots organizing firm, when hired by the Children's Partnership to assess the state of interest in children's issues.

Celinda Lake, Alysia Snell, and Dave Sackett went even further in demonstrating the potential of kid power in their "Great Expectations: How American Voters View Children's Issues" poll, commissioned by the Coalition for America's Children. More than 80 percent of voters identified children's issues as being important in their 1996 voting decision and 64 percent believed government should play a large role in solving the problems facing children, they reported. Deborah Wadsworth, executive director of Public Agenda, confirmed the same trend: 52 percent of Americans say that helping kids get a good start in life ranks higher on their list of priorities than protecting citizens from crime (18 percent), creating more jobs (16 percent) or helping the poor and homeless (10 percent).

Sounds like a pretty good argument for keeping the word "children" in every paragraph of a campaign, right? Well, wrong, because the results are more subtle than the pollsters and the groups that have hired them suggest. When asked if they would support a candidate who disagreed with them on children's issues, two-thirds of those polled by the Lake group answered yes. And Glen Bolger of Public Opinion Strategies provides a succinct read on the public mood: People say they care about kids, but they "are simply not willing to pay higher taxes for kids programs."

While those polled by Lake et al. showed great concern for the quality of American education, 94 percent believed that progress would "only come with greater *parental* involvement." Elizabeth Schrayer, in fact, never suggested that concern for children meant that Americans wanted the Family and Medical Leave Act, tax credits, or any other specific program. What she said was, "Most voters, those with and without children, express concern about declining moral values and the increasing number of children being raised in non-traditional households."

More than anyone else, Deborah Wadsworth has put her finger on the mood of the public about family and children's issues. "The data show that Americans are seriously concerned about the nation's youngsters. They believe kids are in trouble. But it's not the usual suspects—poor health, poverty, or inadequate nutrition—that concern them; rather, it's the fear that America's youth are growing up with serious deficits in character and morals and are lacking in such values as honesty, tolerance, and respect for others.

"They think America's young people are disrespectful, undisciplined, and downright scary. 'Rude,' 'irresponsible,' and 'wild' are the words that come to mind for two in three Americans when asked about today's teenagers. Moreover, as we probed more deeply, we were surprised to hear people say they are troubled by children, too—whom they think of as spoiled, unfriendly, unhelpful, and routinely out of control. And although they acknowledge that it is much harder to be a parent these days than in past times, most Americans—including parents themselves—believe parents are failing to teach youngsters right from wrong and failing to pass on the values children need to learn in order to become productive citizens."

The concern pollsters find for children, then, is anxiety about the quality of parenting America's kids receive, not about government action or inaction. Parental rights activists conveniently gloss over these aspects of their own surveys. Indeed, they take active umbrage at the portrait researchers paint, which child advocates like Marian Wright Edelman, Sylvia Ann Hewlett, and Cornel West decry as "parent blaming."

The penchant of activists and politicians to latch onto "the children" and make them proxies for a dozen social issues that have lost their adult oomph has upped the volume, and political potential, of the kiddie crusade still further. Gun control used to be necessary because guns killed *people;* now gun control is urgent because guns kill *children.* Stricter regulation of HMOs was originally essential because female breast cancer patients were being denied access to potentially life-saving experimental therapies; suddenly, in the summer of 1999, the regulations became mandatory because HMO policies were threatening our young. Air pollution controls, once deemed critical to protect all Americans from toxic fumes, lost their political sheen in the 1980s. But they regained their political panache in the nineties because bad air endangers kids. Another prime example is the crusade against tobacco, which had been languishing for more than three decades, despite the warnings of several surgeons general. It regained its political and social panache when the focus narrowed to the dangers of smoking for children. The president blasted Joe Camel, and the nation's anger against the tobacco industry rose exponentially. Rob Reiner, the movie director, linked it to funding for daycare in his California Children and Families First Initiative and turned another flaky California proposition into a moral jihad.

Ultimately, however, the media, the greedy, and the advocates are amateurs in twisting concern for children and families out of all proportion. Contemporary politicians have raised the type to a high art. A cartoonist for *The New Yorker* summed it up perfectly with a drawing of a candidate haranguing an audience, "Vote for me, a man with over three dozen family values."

The mythic, and much-derided, American tradition of politicians kissing babies to win votes is back—with a vengeance. Gubernatorial wannabes not only nuzzle every baby in sight, but drag out their own kids, their grandkids, the kids of their neighbors. We all know the picture, just as we know that it is designed to suggest that the candidate is stable and trustworthy, as if the candidate *sans* offspring might somehow merit suspicion.

In the 1998 elections, one candidate in Florida did more than suggest that. She said it straight out, and treated voters to a bravura performance of kiddie political oneupsmanship. Running for re-election to represent West Tampa in the state legislature, Deborah Tamargo actually sent out a mailing claiming that her opponent, Bob Henriquez, couldn't understand issues like child abuse because he had no children of his own. Henriquez crafted his response with consummate skill. "The Lord has not seen fit to bless our marriage with any children yet," he told the local newspaper, suggesting, of course, that Tamargo was heartlessly attacking an infertile couple. At first, Tamargo stumbled in her comeback, saying, "It's not my fault they can't have kids." But she quickly recovered and softened the negative reaction to her statement by taking refuge in her son Raymond, who she said had been taunted mercilessly by his classmates as a result of the controversy. "My child has a heart condition that his dad died from," she said, "and I'm very protective of my child."

Tamargo's sin was her directness in an era when politicians are supposed to be discreet in playing on their parenthood and concern for the young. But few shun the strategy entirely. When Governor Jane Dee Hull ran for re-election in 1998, her ads read, "Wife, parent, grandparent—isn't it nice to have a real person running Arizona"—as if those of us without kids, spouses, or grandchildren weren't real people. When George Pataki made his bid to succeed himself as governor of New York, he harped on quality health care for every child in the state as a major campaign theme—as if adults don't need quality health care. Is it fine to let adults languish in emergency rooms or unscrupulous HMOs simply because they are old enough to vote?

Just after Memorial Day 1998, Senator Barbara Boxer pushed child-centric campaigning to a new limit. Hillary Clinton, whose brother is married to Boxer's daughter, was stumping with the California senator during her re-election campaign. After a joint appearance at a school in San Francisco, the women hosted donors willing to fork over one thousand dollars for baked chicken and a rendition of "I Believe I Can Fly" sung by a children's chorus. When Boxer rose to deliver her remarks, her cheeks were still stained with tears from the children's performance, and she shared with the audience the conversation she had just had with Hillary. "How come everyone I support gets teary-eyed around children?" Hillary Clinton asked her. "That's why you support them." Boxer replied.

Just before 9:00 P.M. on Tuesday, January 26, 1999, at an hour when Americans were accustomed to exercising the agonizing choice between *Spin City* and *Just Shoot Me*, 43.5 million Americans tuned in to watch Bill Clinton enter the lion's den where he had been impeached just thirty days earlier. They knew that the angels in this postmodern version of the Old Testament tale—in the guise of 373 Democratic members of the House and Senate and the weight of history—would keep the feline Republicans at bay for at least the duration of the annual State of the Union address. The cliffhanger was whether the president would manage to declaw the cats permanently.

Biting his lip to punctuate his sincerity, the president turned out an Oscar-level performance in the highest political drama of the late twentieth century, serving up a veritable tsunami of initiatives carefully crafted to prove that the First Bubba knew precisely how many interest groups the nation had fractured into. There was something for virtually everyone, from Medicare recipients hungering for prescription coverage to middle-aged workers anxious to buy into Medicare; from citizens tending to elderly parents to Gen-Xers worried about how they would support aging Boomers, antitobacco hysterics, would-be policemen, minimum-wage workers, the Greens and the gays, the computer nerds, family farmers, environmentalists, manufacturers, and servicemen. Over the course of seventy-seven minutes, the president managed to submit eighty-one proposals—an astonishing one per thirty seconds of actual speaking time.

After more than an hour, the nation still remained riveted, either by the feat of rhetoric or by the sheer chutzpah of the rhetorician. Congressional naysayers, who had controlled their venom with ritual opprobrium during the speech, followed a triumphant Clinton out of the door of the chamber into the waiting cameras, where they scoffed piously, dismissing the president's annual wish list as political poppycock. The next day, a wide swath of experts seconded their skepticism. But the criticism dissolved into the white noise of CNN, MSNBC, and C-SPAN. Clinton's stellar performance sent his already gravity-defying approval ratings into the stratosphere—to above 80 percent by Gallup's calculations.

That thundering wave of approval was a far cry from the lukewarm reception that had greeted Clinton's earliest ventures into State of the Uniondom. The pre-Newt Clinton had been similarly long-winded, but unable to use the bully pulpit to raise his approval ratings above 60 percent. By January 1995, when the president rose before the newly empowered congressional Republican revolutionaries, more than half the nation seemed openly disgusted with him.

But Clinton proved nothing if not flexible, and his third message to the nation was designed around the same political strategy that later made his 1999 speech a political tour de force. No more long discourses on the Clean Water Act, the outdated unemployment system, or the importance of GATT. No more healthcare reform or crime bill statistics. The president had learned a lesson about serious speeches explicating serious topics: They don't play in the mythic heartland. Giveaways, that's what Americans wanted, especially those theoretically beleaguered middle-class Americans, and Clinton offered up that fare, packaged in the most seductive, yet deceiving, wrapping of the late twentieth century: the family.

In his rambling 1995 address, Clinton designed new type of pork for those Americans the government had allegedly forgotten, "Those who are working to educate and raise their children and to educate themselves." In his New Covenant, he vowed to force citizens living on the federal dole into jobs and to redirect the federal dollars saved into tax cuts for all families with kids and into tax breaks for families whose six-digit incomes were being strained by their kids' college tuition bills. Old-style corporate welfare—entitlements for the captains of industry who punctuated their appreciation with multi-million-dollar campaign contributions—would be supplemented by family welfare, entitlements for Americans well able to support themselves, but whose love and electoral support the ambitious young president craved.

Pundits and politicians responded with something far short of enthusiasm, but the citizenry was moved by the president's message. "I think he is doing a good job," Stacey Schwartz told a reporter for the *Philadelphia Inquirer* who interviewed her the next day in Kutztown, Pennsylvania, where Clinton stumped before a giant scroll labeled "Middle-Class Bill of Rights." "He's getting better as he goes along."

Throughout that year, the president hammered home his newfound concern for hard-working families and their children, and his pollsters watched his approval ratings soar as the middle-class electorate sensed that Clinton was ready to trade social justice for victory in November 1996. "The era of big government is over," he proclaimed that January, identifying with the suburban recoil against any Big Government that did not acknowledge the primacy of the needs of middle-class boomers. He mentioned nary a word about reviving the inner cities or guaranteeing healthcare to the poor. He even staved off the attempts of conservatives to put lower income caps on his parental giveaways. Appropriating Republican catchphrases about the primacy of family, he unveiled a new scholarship program for students at the top of their high-school classes, threw his support to curbs on cigarette advertisements aimed at children, preached about the evils of out-of-wedlock pregnancy, and discovered the virtues of V-chips to help parents control what their children see on TV.

Creating his own take on the early feminist admonition that the personal is political, in the 1996 election, the president turned tens of thousands of mythic Soccer Moms into Bill Clinton groupies. No matter that under the president's reform of welfare, the children of women on the other side of town would lose welfare or disability benefits, or that the children of legal immigrants would be denied access to health care. Middle-class women showered their affection and votes on the man they were convinced would guard *their* children from evil and still leave them enough money in the bank to install granite countertops and commercial stoves in their kitchens.

The family strategy was not original to Bill Clinton. Conservatives had been bemoaning the "plight of the family" for years and had lofted dozens of plans geared to shore up the sagging institution—many of which Clinton stole, or at least coopted. And liberal "profamily" activists had long been proposing their own drastic schemes. Members of the Carnegie Council on Children suggested that since the survival of the family is dependent on parental employment, all parents with dependent kids should be guaranteed jobs. More recently, Sylvia Ann Hewlett and Cornel West suggested in all seriousness that the vote be extended to children, whose parents would cast their ballots in order to shore up the political clout of the "profamily" crowd.

But it was Bill Clinton, sensing the political potential generated by the sudden turn toward reproduction of the most solipsistic generation in American history, who managed to build a political power base around his family-friendliness by devising rhetoric that liberals could hear as enlightened feminism, the poor could interpret as concern for the needy, and conservatives could translate into traditionalism. When the president talked about struggling "working families," dual-career professionals in New York City thought he meant them, as did single moms trapped in pink-collar jobs, blue-collar workers—former Reagan Democrats furious about preferential hiring and the declining value of their union wage—and poor black families struggling in rural Mississippi.

In so doing, Clinton married the liberal suburban Soccer Moms—stalwart members of the "Me Generation" transmogrified into the "Me-And-Mine Crowd" by their ascent into parentdom—to devotees of James Dobson, *éminence grise* of Focus on the Family, and feminists like Betty Friedan, who see government "family-friendly" programs as key to the liberation of women. "Family" and "for the children"—with no clear elucidation of which families and which children merit such social concern—became the most powerful political verbiage since "Better Dead than Red."

American elections have been fought over matters both grave and frivolous, from the gold standard to jingoism, and protective tariffs to civil rights. William Jennings Bryan battled William McKinley over American imperialism, and went down to defeat. Alfred E. Smith tried to drown Herbert Hoover with Prohibition. And Stephen Douglas clashed with Abraham Lincoln over slavery.

But until Bill Clinton burst onto the scene, no election was ever won or lost on the state of the middle-class "family"—and that seemed just fine with most Americans. After all, the family has long been considered private turf in this country, an almost sacred bastion of retreat from the intrusion of the outside world. We might have invited the government into our workplaces, our communities, and our schools, but home life was sacrosanct, and parents—with a few exceptions—reigned as masters and mistresses of their own domains. In return, they didn't ask for much from the rest of us, so the deal seemed eminently fair.

Over the years, that wall between public and private has been breached repeatedly, since every major period of social uncertainty and dislocation has found its expression in mounting public fears for the stability of the family, and those fears have been transformed into panic about the plight of children. Before the Republic was established, the bold self-confidence settlers drew from the open spaces and distance from tradition struck terror into the hearts of the ruling elite. Shaken by forces they felt unable to control, they bemoaned instead "the greatest trouble and grief about the rising generation," and brooded about "the great neglect in many parents and masters in training of their children." In the first frantic decades of the nineteenth century, when a boom-and-bust financial cycle turned early manufacturing barons into paupers and workers out on the street, alarm about family stability and the impact on children again reared up across the land. Later, when family farms went bust and fathers were pushed out into jobs away from home, a national panic began over absent fathers and "family neglect."

Each assertion of family crisis has provoked a single demand: the intervention of the government. We sanctified and affirmed the privacy of the family, but when kids were in danger, we called in the feds. But that intervention has always been protective. We passed labor legislation to guard children from exploitation by their parents and factory owners. We designed welfare programs to guard children from the ravages of the inequities we tolerate for adults. And we gave states carte blanche to take kids away from abusive parents or to jail fathers who raped their daughters.

Bill Clinton, however, sensed that today's parents weren't all that interested in kids in danger. When they told pollsters they were worried about children, they were seeing the faces of their own kids, not the toddlers across town. And he discerned as well that while lofty Republicanesque rhetoric about "family values" might strike at the hearts and souls of voters while still respecting the traditional wall between the government and the family domain, most modern parents didn't care much about that old barrier. They'd trade it and every bit of verbiage about the decline of morality for a new brand of child protection—delivered to their parents in the form of cold cash.

The Clinton family doctrine was perfectly crafted for a moment in history when the economy is soaring and nobody is being drafted. And it meshed seamlessly with the zeitgeist of new generations of parents born and raised to a unique sense of entitlement. There's no use in belaboring the point about baby boomers' profound sense of their own superiority, their deep-seated faith that they are uniquely equipped to solve problems that had eluded all prior generations, a core belief that they deserve to have it all, whatever its "all" is at a given collective moment. That's been reported so heavily as to have become a cliché.

What's relevant is that the baby boomer "all" now includes having children, which has sent the boldest and brashest generation in the nation's history reeling. Remember, this is the generation that was going to smash the family, along with every other traditional social institution, and suddenly they are raising the very families they mocked for so long. This is the generation that invented the youth culture, and suddenly the parents among them are being treated as grownups forced to yell at their kids about drugs, curfews, and rock and roll. And this is the generation that agonized and rolfed in est, group therapy, and Jungian analysis about every injury their parents ever inflicted on them, and suddenly they are realizing that they can't perfect parenting any more than they could perfect race relations or American imperialism. A generation's collective illusions are shattering, and they are calling in all the king's horses and all the king's men to put them back together.

For women of this generation, who derived a special sense of strength and invincibility from breaking through scores of gender barriers, motherhood has proven an even greater challenge. They deluded themselves into believing that they could add children to lives already filled with careers and aerobics classes, regular dinners with friends, weekends in the country, and European vacations without missing a beat, as if children would be just one more exercise in logistics, carefully noted on their Franklin planners. Some have found, instead, that they are wracked with unanticipated guilt about leaving the house every morning, or staying late at work for yet another long meeting—which is a wrenching blow to their self-concepts. Others feel gypped that they have had to cut back on racquetball and long coffees with friends in order to run a shuttle service to swim meets and dance lessons. And many of the rest are so stressed-out from trying to cope that they are too numb to have any idea what they are feeling.

What these new mother-workers do is precisely what most poor and most working-class women have been doing for decades, and without benefit of take-out or nannies. But the stress of *those* women never made it into the women's magazines or onto regular segments of the nightly news. It was not until the editors of those magazines, the producers of those segments and their friends—urban, educated bankers and lawyers and consultants—began living with that undifferentiated melange of guilt, disappointment, and stress that the plight of the working mother became a national crisis.

Finally, raising children is a humbling experience, at odds with the psyche of a generation characterized by a collective aversion to humility. A different, less cocky generation might have accepted responsibility for their own problems and said, "We can't make this work. Doing and being everything just isn't a reasonable or realistic way to live." But boomers, disinclined to take no for an answer, abjure such personal responsibility. They are, then, perfect targets for politicians and pundits willing to assure them that the stress of their lives is society's fault for not adjusting its every nook and cranny to facilitate their desire to have the kinds of families they want, have full-bodied and lucrative careers, and still to have enough money left over to retire on the near side of sixty.

Bill Clinton heard their silent plea. Boomer parents were feeling the pain—and he realized, as only another boomer parent could, how desperately they craved a drug to ease it. When he rose to the podium at the Democratic Convention in Chicago in 1996, he loaded his acceptance speech with the drug today's boomers like best: money. He put on the table a series of tax cuts for parents that would be "profamily, proeducation." He called for increased spending on daycare, money to help middle-class parents with college tuition bills, and an extension of the Family and Medical Leave Act to guarantee an "America where all children are cherished and protected." Then he went further, making baby boomer parents feel noble for wanting the government to do more for them, part of a worldwide movement of concern for the next generation. Clinton called for stepped-up efforts to protect the environment because "ten million children live within just four miles of a toxic waste dump." He demanded deficit reduction "to leave our children the legacy of opportunity, not the legacy of debt." He proposed welfare reform that would move all Americans into jobs so that "every single child can look out the window in the morning and see a whole community getting up and going to work." He charted a continued United States role in Bosnia, Burundi, and Northern Ireland to stop wars that wind up "butchering children." And he advocated a renewed campaign against international terrorism because of its threat to the safety of, you guessed it, "our children."

You would have thought that children were providing the swing vote in the election—and that terrorism, pollution, the deficit, and genocide in Bosnia would be acceptable if no one under the age of eighteen were getting hurt.

None of that agenda was designed to help the American children most in need of help, of course. The Family and Medical Leave Act—which Clinton and the Democrats have bragged and crowed about as living proof of their concern for the welfare of parents and families—requires companies with more than fifty employees to give them up to twelve weeks of *unpaid*, job-protected leave to care for a newborn, adopted, or seriously ill child. But how many Americans can afford to take twelve weeks of *unpaid* leave? Tax credits for children? They do nothing for the progeny of families too poor to pay taxes. Hope Scholarships? Be serious, how can a fifteen-hundred-dollar non-refundable tax credit for college tuition change the life of a child whose parents make nine thousand dollars a year?

But no one seemed to notice the class bias woven into the rhetoric. By Clinton's January 1999 address, despite the national consensus that his ethical standards left something to be desired, devotion to the president had turned into the type of adulation normally reserved for Mother Teresa, or at least Mark McGwire. That night, Americans' favorite Soccer Dad stood before the world as the benevolent *pater* of the national *familias* who was so worried about kids when they had the sniffles or measles that he had signed into law the Family and Medical Leave Act to allow their parents to spend time at their bedsides; so concerned with their grades that he would personally reach into every school district and make sure all the teachers were qualified; so anxious that stay-at-home moms not feel slighted by massive federal aid for childcare for working moms that he was prepared to sweeten their tax bill as a reward for their domestic service; so worried that work would interfere with a parent's need to bond with her child that he pledged to design a special civil rights bill to prevent it.

That new progressive, feminist Democratic vision of village as conjured up by Clinton and his sidekick Al Gore didn't leave much room for concern about kids who didn't have enough food, or a bed to be tucked into. As Michael Kelly, Democratic apostate and editor of the *National Journal*, put it in March 1999, "My new Democratic Party doesn't waste its time or mine anymore with blather about comforting the afflicted; it cares about what the voters care about, which is comforting the comfortable. It's the party that looks out for No. 1."

The "for the family" and "for the children" movements aren't just political fads stirred up by the politically hungry, by parents convinced that *their* interests and the *national* interest must be identical, or by marketers with greedy eyes fixed on the kiddie market. This picture would not be complete without some mention of a subtler force driving the parental rights movement, a force voiced in carefully couched language about labor shortages, Social Security, and fertility rates, a force streaked with implicit racism and classism that rarely rise to the surface.

In 1987, Ben Wattenberg, a demographer at the American Enterprise Institute, then a little-known neoconservative think tank, issued the first coherent argument for tax credits for parents, parent-friendly workplaces, and the redistribution of wealth from the childless to the childed. Wattenberg wasn't worried about the wage gap between women and men, the bottom lines of businesses, the plight of the children, or the angst of boomer parents. He was obsessed about the impending doom he saw etched into the birth rate of the American population. In *The Birth Dearth,* he broadcast a dire warning: We face national catastrophe because we're going where no population has ever gone before: down. The inevitable consequence of a below-replacement birth rate of 1.8 children per two adults, Wattenberg admonished, is low growth, leading to no growth, ending in negative growth. Modern capitalism will crumble. The United States will lose its hold on world culture and politics. Western civilization as we know it will collapse.

After a generation of propaganda about the population explosion, Wattenberg's announcement of an impending population implosion came as a momentous, almost unbelievable, prediction. Ellen Goodman, one of the nation's leading newspaper columnists, denounced Wattenberg for blaming women who weren't popping out four or five babies for the pending "fall of the entire Western world." The zero population crowd poo-pooed his work, usually by citing endless statistics about overpopulation in places like India and sub-Saharan Africa. But in Washington policy circles, his augury took root.

Two years later, in *The Atlantic Monthly,* Jonathan Rauch increased the political heft of Wattenberg's prophecy by honing it to strike directly at the hearts of Americans' greatest disquiet, the Social Security system. If Americans have fewer kids, he asked, "How generously am I going to be supported in my old age?" Glossing over Wattenberg's predictions about the disintegration of everything from capitalism to Western values— which surely would make the generosity of Rauch's Social Security checks irrelevant—Rauch painted a portrait of a future promising reduced Social Security benefits, advancing retirement ages, generational warfare, and a 25 percent federal tax, all the inevitable results of the population implosion.

The possibilities for disaster in Rauch's twenty-first-century America went deeper than glitches in retirement plans. "Projections are showing that in the 1990s the U.S. labor force will grow more slowly than it has at any time since the 1930s," he wrote. "Fully a third of the new entrants into the work force between now and the turn of the century will be members of minority groups. Those future minority workers are today's minority children—among whom the rates of poverty and illiteracy are highest. On average, poor children grow up to make poor workers. Poor workers generate lower standards of living for society—and for their old parents."

That forecast grabbed the attention of business leaders, and analysts across the land picked up Rauch's tune and added their own words to the melody. "In the seventies, corporations had workers coming out of their ears, so they didn't have to worry about the quality of the work force," said Frank Levy of the University of Maryland. "They could just discard what they couldn't use. But once you have the labor force growing slowly and you start bumping into scarcity, then you have to assess the quality of the whole work force, because you can't just throw away the bottom quarter or twenty percent. Then you realize that we're all in this together."

Finally politicians began joining the public chorus, although none was quite so blunt as Rauch about acknowledging that the real concern wasn't the declining birth rate per se, but its particular shape. Probusiness Republicans disguised the true roots of their alarm in discourses about pending declines in "productivity." Liberals kept quiet for several years. Then Bill Clinton weighed in with remarks strikingly close to Rauch's own candor. "We have more and more young couples where both of them are working and having careers and deferring child-bearing, and in many cases not having children at all," he said. "That . . . is very troubling for our country: The people in the best position to build strong kids, and bring the kids up in a good way, are deciding not to do so."

The problem, then, isn't a dearth of birth. It's a dearth of upper-middle-class, educated white birth. And the mounting panic about productivity, labor shortages, and Social Security is the "polite" version of the discomfort many white Americans feel over estimates that whites have already ceased to be the majority in California, and that New Mexico, Hawaii, Nevada, Texas, Maryland and New Jersey aren't far behind.

After all, if productivity, Social Security, and labor shortages were the real anxiety, we could correct the problem almost overnight by increasing immigration. We already import many of our best brains, as a quick tour of the nation's hospitals and universities evidences. Import more of them. And if it's children we want, all we have to do is hand out visas not simply to the talented, but to families with small children, pregnant women, or the exceptionally fertile—at least that's what we would do if we weren't so worried about the fall of Western Civilization, a code phrase for the fall in hegemony of Anglo-Saxon Americans. Or, to address Rauch's angst about poor children becoming poor workers, we could actually fund creative and productive poverty program to break that cycle—if we weren't so worried about the fact that the "right" folks weren't breeding.

Since the goal doesn't seem to be to expand the population so much as to increase the population of children born to those "right" folks, we have begun to follow the formula suggested by both Wattenberg and Rauch for increasing the birth rate of what Clinton called the "people in the best position to build strong kids": giving them money.

Wattenberg admitted that the ideal way to increase the birth rate would be to keep women poor, uneducated, servile, and rural, since education, money, feminism, and urban life are the forces that pushed the birth rate down in the first place. Reversing that trend doesn't appear realistic in the current climate, he acknowledged, and since he said he didn't believe in coercion in any case (which is odd, since if the future of Western Civilization were at stake, you would think he might modify his position on coercion), Wattenberg offered Plan B, a series of direct pronatalist policies. Specifically: dramatic increases in personal tax exemptions for children under the age of sixteen, paid maternity leaves, housing allowances for families with children, national daycare, maybe special bonuses of, say, two thousand dollars for the birth of each child. "Give them money," Wattenberg exhorted. "Lots of it."

In other words, birth by bribery, and a program almost identical to the family-friendliness sweeping the nation.

More than a decade ago, Wattenberg feared that his plan would face major political obstacles. The elderly would denounce it. Radical feminists would condemn it as a smokescreen for sending women back into the kitchen, he warned. Conservatives would oppose it as another "big government" program, the Office of Management and Budget would denounce it a budget-buster, and right-to-lifers would condemn it as meaningless unless abortion were also banned.

Nonetheless, the growing interest among feminists and religious conservatives in programs of the precise sort he was advocating gave Wattenberg hope that his strategy could be "repackaged" in a politically acceptable manner. "You have half a century where the basic drive of this government—properly, in my judgment—was a redistribution of wealth from rich to poor," he told Rauch in 1989. "That isn't going to wash politically anymore. But suppose you say, instead of redistributing from rich to poor, 'Hey, I've got a pro-family program that redistributes money from the childless to the child-rearing.'" That kind of program could get liberals and conservatives on the same side, he said. "It's pro-family and it's pro-kids, and it's pro-poor-kids."

Rauch cheered him on. "Today, as we face the need to nurture our work force and safeguard our retirements, the question forcing its way onto the agenda is how much more we will pay for other people's children. More out of necessity than out of choice, a new redistributional politics is emerging—a politics of redistribution from the childless to the child-rearing."

And what of those childless, who will be forced to pay to motivate the "right" people to reproduce? Neither Rauch nor Wattenberg seemed any more worried about them than were the politicians and feminist activists advancing that same redistribution. They are "free riders," Wattenberg says. "People who have no children . . . are in a sense, cheating the system."

5

The Maternal Mystique

Betty Friedan hung up on me late one afternoon in the summer of 1998.

The rudeness wasn't personal. I'd never met the women whose 1963 *cri de coeur* had provided one of the intellectual underpinnings of the modern-day women's movement. Friedan, however, has a penchant for summarily slapping down uppity questions—questions that chip away at the edges of her carefully constructed worldview. I had dared ask an uppity question. Truthfully, I didn't manage to finish the query before Friedan began yelling at me in the same hectoring tone of disapproval that had been used so frequently against her.

I had called Friedan at her home on Long Island because Laurie Abraham, my favorite magazine editor, had suggested that an article I'd submitted to *Mirabella* magazine about the mounting culture clash between mothers and the childless could use some comment from a name-brand feminist. We'd batted around names of the obvious candidates. Gloria Steinem. No, I thought, family issues have never been her major concern. Patricia Ireland. Forget it, too much of a newcomer. Friedan seemed just right. The mother of three, she was the author of the first diatribe against consigning women to domestic nonbliss. No matter what she thought of the topic, I assumed she would at least be provocative.

So one morning I left a message on Friedan's answering machine, the kind of quick explanation reporters routinely spit out to give potential sources a chance not to return their calls. When I picked up the phone hours later and heard her familiar gravelly voice in the phone, my adrenaline surged for a meaty dialogue on a complex issue.

Friedan listened silently for the first forty-five seconds of my explication of the conflict I was attempting to decipher, then took over. "Why are you doing this?" she berated me. She was clearly not posing a question to which she would allow a response. "This is pitting women against women." My attempt to reply was cut off before ten words had flowed out of my mouth. "The great majority of women have children. Having children is a perfectly legitimate choice and most women support these things."

I tried to inject a calmer note, at least a reassurance that I believed in reproductive choice, including the choice to bear children. Friedan was not in listening mode. "The workforce used to be structured around the lives of men with wives at home. But today the great majority of women are working outside the home. Women don't have wives at home. We need structures to allow women to work." I scribbled madly and tried to contain myself. Okay, okay, I figured, she learned this tactic from the masters, from the guys who had drowned *her* out when she'd tried to challenge the notion that proper women belonged at home with their children. Let her talk herself out. When she calms down, I'll try for some dialogue.

"I don't approve of this. I don't approve of this at all," she continued, sounding exactly like Phyllis Schlafly talking about Friedan's vision of American womanhood. Calling on all my patience, I refused to rise to the bait. "Why are you doing this?" she added. I thought my moment had actually arrived and poised to speak. Before I could utter a syllable, Friedan hung up.

When I'd called Friedan, I never imagined that she might still be smarting over the beating she'd taken in the feminist wars over motherhood. After all, that plethora of family-friendly programs spreading across workplaces, federal agencies, and communities means that her side won.

By the late 1990s, the National Organization for Women, which Friedan helped found, was as much a mothers' lobby as a feminist liberation brigade. Leaders of the group still talked about the Equal Rights Amendments, sexual harassment, and abortion. But among the key issues they were pushing in Washington was a law mandating that employers provide women with time and space to pump breast milk at work and increased funding for daycare. NOW, which was also hawking its very own "Don't Assume I Don't Cook!" book, was asking members to sign a "Women-Friendly Workplace Campaign Consumer Pledge" to pressure businesses into ending "all forms of discrimination," which meant that they would guarantee mothers flex-time and childcare and extend equal benefits to domestic partners. Their platform threw an assiduously inclusive umbrella over black women, white women, and Hispanic women, young women and older women, poor women and professional women, single mothers, lesbians, pregnant women, and women on welfare. Only women without children have been left standing out in the rain without the protection of a feminist parasol.

It wasn't just NOW. The Institute for Women's Policy Research, created in 1987 by economist Heidi Hartmann to bridge the gap between the new scholarship about women and public policy, was churning out a steady stream of papers, studies, and propositions that routinely used the words "women" and "mothers" interchangeably. In testifying before Congress, the group's lobbyists promoted "improving women's status in the workforce" as "the family issue of the future," as if the former goal might be insignificant by itself. And while Hartmann never failed to hammer home the importance of "new and increasing diversity in family types," the one form of diversity never mentioned in any of her scores of proposals was childlessness.

Just after Bill Clinton's election, the institute gathered fifty women leaders in Arlington Hill, Vermont, to craft an agenda for the new president's first one hundred days. What did they demand? A childcare center at the White House, expanded childcare benefits, paid leave for the care of a new child, a reward system for companies implementing "family-friendly" policies, prenatal and well-child care, the conversion of the dependent tax exemptions to tax credits, and the strengthening of child support enforcement.

Signs of Friedan's victory were everywhere. The Women's Legal Defense Fund, which began in 1971 as a women's advocacy group, changed its name to the National Partnership for Women and Families in 1998, and dedicated itself to promoting "policies that help women and men meet the dual demands of work and family." In April 1986, Erica Jong, whose 1973 bestseller, *Fear of Flying*, had become a feminist classic of liberated sex, told *Vanity Fair* that what American women really cared about was motherhood. "Having stumped across this country in book tours for the past decade or so, I can bear witness to the fact that the women of America are ready for liberty, ready for sexual freedom, ready to embrace their own strengths and believe in their own powers—but they are most emphatically not ready for a movement which puts down the most meaningful relationship in their lives: their relationship with their children."

And, on its website, the White House Office of Women's Initiatives and Outreach bragged to the nation about what Bill Clinton and Al Gore had accomplished for *women:* the signing of the Family and Medical Leave Act; the Comprehensive Childhood Immunization Initiative; the Adoption and Safe Families Act; Megan's Law to require the registration of child molesters; increased funding for Head Start; education tax breaks; a national crusade against children's smoking; the first White House Conference on Child Care; a White House Conference on Early Child Development and Learning; increased funding for childcare; guaranteed health insurance for children; the child tax credit; a major program against teen pregnancy; and an end to drive-thru deliveries by requiring insurers to cover a minimal forty-eight-hour postpartum hospital stay. And these were their programs for *women.*

It's enough to make a girl think that Susan Faludi was right, that there is some sort of conspiracy to catapult women back into the 1950s.

Feminists have long had an ambivalent relationship to motherhood, fraught with resentment over the social prescription that childrearing is women's "natural" vocation yet tinged with a keen awareness of the potential power that prescription confers. Should they glorify women's unique role as mother and use it as leverage in the struggle for equality? Should they battle the prescriptive nature of motherhood, yet leave room for women to make their own choices? Or should they reject reproduction entirely as leaving women vulnerable to the control of men? Those questions have troubled women's politics for more than a century.

Early suffragists decried social and Freudian assumptions that women's anatomies were their destinies, which, all too often, consigned them to dreary, monotonous lives. Yet they were not above invoking motherhood for their own political gain. Knowing that antisuffragists, entrenched in the National Congress of Mothers, accused them of endangering every aspect of womanhood, especially its most sacred function of mothering, such feminists as Inez Milholland carefully staked their claim to the vote on their duties as caregivers to the next generation. "Women are the mothers of the race," declared Milholland, a lawyer and Vassar College graduate who rode a horse at the head of a suffrage parade in New York City, reminding women of the power of Joan of Arc and Helen of Troy. "As such they are admittedly more concerned than anyone else with all that goes to protect life."

Motherhood wasn't just a tactic. Most of the suffragists were ga-ga about motherhood, convinced that it elevated women above mortal men. "Women's best qualities . . . are inseparably bound up with the motherhood in her nature," wrote Ellen Key, a prominent Swedish feminist. Even Emma Goldman, the radical "free-lover" of the group, declared that "motherhood is the highest fulfillment of woman's nature." And Charlotte Perkins Gilman, the most important feminist writer of the pre–World War I era, proclaimed that women must "understand that, in the line of physical evolution, motherhood is the highest process."

Few of those first women's rights activists foresaw the conflicts that would be generated when that fervent commitment to motherhood sought to accommodate their equally ardent commitment to women's work outside the home. Elizabeth Cady Stanton brushed off any notion of such conflict by blithely suggesting that women simply bear fewer children. Elizabeth Duffey opined that women just needed to approach reproduction with more conscious planning and consideration. Gilman, however, proved prescient about how thoroughly the work/family conflict would plague the lives of "liberated" women and how thoroughly society would have to be reordered to allow them to cope with that difficulty. In her classic 1889 work, *Women and Economics,* she laid out a comprehensive plan for that reordering—the building of massive apartment complexes equipped with communal kitchens, cleaning services, and nurseries staffed by professionals to relieve women of the double burdens of work in and outside the home.

In the feminist lacuna between the world wars, women leaders increasingly grappled with that dilemma Gilman addressed. Notably, few of those asking such questions—to a woman, white professionals—thought to consider that mothers laboring in factories, textile mills, or offices had already mastered the tricks of the trade. Rather, educated women, and the men who supported their efforts, set about devising their own formulae.

The Board of Trustees of Barnard College were among the first to adopt the strategy that has become today's standard. The work/family quandary is rightfully a social, not an individual, problem, they concluded, and they took on their share of the burden by granting all faculty six months' paid maternity leave. "Neither the men nor the women of our staff should be forced into celibacy, and cut off from that great source of experience, of joy, sorrow and wisdom which marriage and parenthood offer," explained Dean Virginia Gildersleeve, who also advocated publicly funded childcare centers, housekeeping services, and emergency childcare services to ease the strain on working mothers.

That philosophy dovetailed seamlessly with the advice of the growing number of child "experts" who had begun denouncing the nation's doting mothers for smothering the nation's young. Behavioral psychologist John B. Watson insisted that overbearing mothers retarded the development of their children, who belonged to the future. Arguing that kids are better off without all that "obsessive maternal affection," he advocated bottle feeding, strict schedules, and early toilet training in order to foster individualism and independence. As they later would hang on every word spoken by Spock or Brazelton, mothers by the thousands followed his advice to the letter, weaning their children young, enrolling them in kindergarten, and sending them to summer camp.

Watson's childrearing advice brought a sigh of relief to many mothers confined to the home by domestic ideology, yet bored out of their minds. Their children were in school most of the day, the food industry canned the vegetables their own mothers had put up and baked the bread their grandmothers had made from scratch, and new appliances washed and dried the family clothes their foremothers had soaked and scrubbed and wrung out by themselves. If they weren't supposed to work because their children would suffer—which is what the experts before Watson had counseled—what on earth were they to do all day? Watson's prescription, then, opened the floodgates to offices and factories still wider for American women, and the avant garde programs of employers like Barnard held out, for the first time, the promise of a nation in which women could have it all.

The Watsonesque childrearing fad waned, however, as these exercises in psycho-fashion always do. The new guru of childrearing, Arnold Gesell, precursor to Dr. Spock, stole the limelight from Watson with long treatises on the importance of warmth, intimacy, and trust in children's development. Forget concerns about smothering your child, he preached. More is better. In practical terms, Gesell taught that breastfeeding was essential to strengthen the bond between mother and child, that mothers should jump the instant their babies cried, and that children needed almost dictatorial control over their mothers' schedules until they were at least eighteen months old. Without such undivided attention, he warned, a child would never feel emotionally secure.

Helene Deutsch and other psychologists denounced Gesell's teachings as poppycock, as a ploy to discourage mothers from working outside the home. Was it really coincidental, they inquired, that these new childrearing prescriptions had emerged at the very moment when mothers were beginning to work for wages in mass numbers? Did children really need all that undivided attention? But few women heard those dissident voices, and fewer still paid them heed. How many mothers who could afford not to work would have been willing to risk the emotional health of a child by bucking the experts? How many would have willingly coped with double duty in a nation where Barnard remained a lonely leader? The new cult of domesticity unfolded. June Cleaver was born.

As the 1960s dawned, the first challenges to June's hegemony were heard, although by few outside the confines of academic and intellectual circles. At an American Academy of Arts and Sciences conference on "The Woman in America," Alice Rossi, professor of psychology at Goucher College and mother of three, unveiled an "Immodest Proposal" about the absurdity of turning mothering into a full-time profession.

"In the past . . . women . . . were productive members of farm and craft teams along with their farmer, baker or printer husbands and other adult kin," she said. "Children either shared in the work of the household or were left to amuse themselves; their mothers did not have the time to organize their play, worry about their development, discuss their problems. There were no child specialists to tell the colonial merchant's wife or pioneer farmer's wife that her absorption in spinning, planting, churning and preserving left her children on their own too much, that how she fed her baby would shape his adult personality, or that leaving children with a variety of other adults while she worked would make them insecure."

The modern insistence on full-time motherhood, Rossi insisted, was utterly absurd in light of the change in household technology, of increased lifespans and smaller families. "The traditional mother role simply does not occupy a sufficient portion of a woman's life span to constitute any longer the exclusive adult role for which a young woman should be prepared. American girls spend more time as apprentice mothers with their dolls than they will as adult women with their own babies, and there is half a lifetime still ahead by the time the youngest child enters high school."

Full-time motherhood, she said, was nothing but make-work that bred guilt in mothers who were forced to work, trauma in educated women shut behind "the closed door of the doll's house," and a "perpetual state of intellectual and social impoverishment" both for women and for the husbands and children who lived with them. Why did women consign themselves to such misery? Rossi pointed the finger of blame squarely and directly: childrearing experts. Men like Benjamin Spock convince women that any stirring of antipathy to devoting twenty-four hours a day to their children is evidence of deep-seated psychological damage, Rossi explained. Nervous and uncomfortable with being a full-time mother? Dr. Spock diagnosed the problem as a "residue of difficult relationships in her own childhood." Unable to decompress with a brief trip or vacation? Dr. Spock suggested regular counseling or psychiatric treatment. Unsure whether you should work while your child is young? Dr. Spock prescribed consultation with a social worker.

Like Gesell, Spock and his adherents issued frightful admonitions about the emotional and physical damage women working outside the home would cause in children. And what about fathers? Rossi asked. Forget it. A dad isn't "considered to produce severe disturbances in his young children even if his work schedule reduces contact with them to the daylight hours of a weekend."

Rossi's tirade was received with disdain by opinion makers and the few "ordinary" women who heard or read it. And then came Friedan, whose book, *The Feminine Mystique,* echoed Rossi's message to every college-educated woman stuck in the suburbs with a washing machine, an electric range, a pantry full of cake mix, and a rotting brain. Like Rossi, Friedan put forward no plan for how women would manage to "do it all." She was too focused on freeing women to do something more than the laundry to consider that raising children and working full-time might present any conflict.

The National Organization for Women, founded by a disparate collection of protofeminists brought together in 1966 by their disgust over the enforcement of new civil rights laws for women, was similarly too focused on the world outside the home—on job opportunities and equal pay, educational equity, and political participation—to worry much about the marriage of the domestic and professional. At the first informal meeting that birthed the organization in June 1966—a hastily called gathering during the final luncheon at the third annual conference of Commissions on the Status of Women—the new group, founded as a woman's counterpart to the NAACP, dedicated itself "to take action to bring women into full participation in the mainstream of American society now, assuming all the rights and responsibilities thereof in truly equal partnership with men." The immediate areas of concern were jury duty, segregation of newspaper want ads by gender, and Title VII of the Civil Rights Act of 1964. The only mention of the work-family tension was a line in a memo hastily penned that afternoon. It read, "Unnecessary dichotomies between marriage and career; myths that have to be dispelled."

Unnecessary or not, those dichotomies were real, and the equal partnership between women and men in the public arena envisioned by NOW's founders was in jeopardy so long as women retained full responsibility for the kids, the laundry, and the cooking. The new movement had to offer women—the women they were talking to, who didn't think of work as the secretarial pool or the warehouse at Macy's—a vision of how life would be structured if women had responsibilities beyond roasting turkeys and shuttling the kids between school and soccer practice. Unlike Gilman, they did not set forth a revolutionary scheme. Naively, they saw no need for a revolution. None of this is rocket science, they insisted. Give women some help with childcare while their kids are young, train men to take on half the burden at home, and women will be free to compete on an equal footing in the marketplace.

On January 12, 1967, at a press conference in Washington, D.C., Friedan unveiled NOW's first work/family demand, this one for federally aided childcare centers for working mothers and a full income tax deduction for childcare costs. When the group's Bill of Rights for Women was approved by NOW's second convention, those demands were included, right up there with equal education, equal job training, and the enforcement of laws banning sex discrimination. By 1971, members of the New York chapter of the group were demonstrating for the right to deduct childcare expenses as a business expense with a "Baby Carriage Brigade."

Wild bra-burning and kitchen-busting radicals in the view of much of the public, NOW was, in fact, home to the most moderate women in the feminist movement, and few issues inspired more disgust among more militant feminists than NOW's positions on marriage, the family, and children. The radicals called theirs a women's *liberation* movement, a women's version of the Black Panthers, if you will, a movement to liberate women from the all-pervasive patriarchy. They dismissed NOW members, with their concern for work/family conflicts and their namby-pamby cooperation with the male "establishment," as the female equivalent of Uncle Toms.

In those heady days when smashing icons and challenging social convention were as central to the culture of young women as "grazing" became in the early 1980s, radical women laughed at NOW's notion that equality for women would be a simple recipe—add women wherever men have exclusive control, stir in a little childcare, and, voilà, equality springs forth full-blown. What sounded so straightforward, so simple, at NOW conventions seemed naive when the radicals recited the history of male resistance to women's rights and asked how women could be freed from the control of men if they continued to live under the roofs they built, inside the homes they paid for and with the children they helped create.

In her classic book, *The Dialectic of Sex,* Shulamith Firestone, the matriarch of the radical wing of the movement, opined that equality would remain anathema unless women obliterated every trace of male-centered ideology. On the children and family question, then, she was unambivalent in her call for drastic action. "Adults have been socialized to view biological reproduction as life's raison d'être because without this grandiose sense of missing destiny, the pains of childbearing and the burdens of childrearing have proved overwhelming," she wrote. The only alternatives to conventional childbearing that will emancipate women from male domination, she said, were in vitro fertilization, ex-utero gestation, and nonbiological mothering. "The tyranny of the biological family would be broken," she proclaimed.

Especially among intellectuals, the notion of smashing the biological family, hardly a popular concept among NOW's more genteel suburbanites, became an obsession. Kate Millet, one of the movement's leading writers, declared that women would not be free until the family was obliterated. In her weightier philosophical and historical tract, *Woman's Estate,* Juliet Mitchell detailed how the mystique of mothering had been raised to a fetish in order to enslave women in a role, reproduction, that would allow men to maintain male hegemony over the position that society valued, which was production.

Bashing male privilege and the tyranny of the family, Millet, Firestone, Mitchell, and other radicals grew increasingly influential in the movement. Their books became the mainstays of new university courses in Women's Studies. While their often dramatic, if not drastic, prescriptions for change ruffled feathers in the more "polite" circle of NOW, they rose to heroic status among young women just cutting their intellectual and activist teeth. Every plan lofted by the "liberals" was greeted with open disdain. Children? "Motherhood . . . is forced on women by men," wrote Adrienne Rich. Daycare centers? Please. "Daycare centers buy women off," said Firestone. "They ease the immediate pressure without asking why that pressure is on women."

Seeing herself as the woman at the vanguard of a legion of women organizing for increased status and respect in the "man's world," Friedan did not respond well to being written off as a sell-out. Furthermore, she sensed, probably correctly, that male-bashing and detailed exegeses on the origins of the patriarchy were unlikely to endear the women's rights movement to the gals in the heartland. After a decade or more of battling the young upstarts who had usurped her position, Friedan single-handedly proclaimed that feminism was ready to move into its Second Stage, as she titled the book she published in 1981. "Politically, for the women's movement to continue to promote issues like the ERA, abortion or child care solely in individualistic terms, abandoning the family to the Right, aborts our own moral majority," she wrote.

"The women's movement did not fail in the battle for equality. . . . Our failure was our blind spot about the family. It was our own extreme reaction against that wife-mother role: that devotional dependence on men and nurture of children and housewife service, which has been and still is the source of power and status and identity, purpose and self-worth and economic security for so many women—even if it is not that secure anymore."

Friedan urged the movement to move beyond the mystique that put work above family and to turn its energies to the creation of better child-care centers, more flexible workplaces, expanded maternity and paternity leaves, and the like—not just to give women more options, but to strengthen the family, as well as women's place in it. She bitterly lashed out at any woman who dared disagree with that vision, or suggested that shoring up the right to abortion or the continuing battle for the Equal Rights Amendment should take precedence over concerns about workplace flexibility. "The radical lesbian separatists have given much energy to the women's movement, but their own repudiation of women's relation to men, children and family has been, in part, responsible for the movement's blind spot about the family and has played into those fears the Right manipulates."

Reviewing Friedan's book for *The Nation,* Ellen Willis, who went on to write for *The New Yorker* and *The Village Voice* before taking over the directorship of the cultural reporting and criticism program at New York University, responded in kind, denouncing "pro-family feminists as no feminists at all." Pronouncing *The Second Stage* a step backward, she said that Friedan "would destroy feminism in order to save it, and beat the Moral Majority by joining it."

Friedan, however, had her finger on the pulse of American womanhood. Most women were too busy trying to figure out how to get Susi to the baby-sitter and Tommy to his baseball game the same afternoon they were scheduled to make a major presentation to the board to worry about the intricacies of feminist theory. If equal treatment didn't help women solve problems like that, said Friedan and her allies, equal treatment be damned. Nothing, not even the most enlightened principle, should stand in the way of giving women the tools they needed to liberate themselves from the kitchen.

That emerging demand for the tools of empowerment—paid maternity leave and flex-time and part-time work for mothers—set off a chain of panic in the Washington and New York feminist establishments. Every "special protection" ever conferred on women had wound up being used against them. Labor legislation designed early in this century to safeguard working women from night shifts or lifting heavy loads, for example, had become the routine excuse for denying women high-paying jobs. Pregnancy protections had turned into a new justification for firing women outright. Women's rights attorneys, in particular, implored Friedan's cohorts and their supporters in state legislatures to learn the most basic lesson of women's history, to be careful what they asked for. Refusing to look back, or beyond the ends of their noses, they did not heed the warning.

It was an old struggle, as Friedan herself knew full well. In the early twentieth century, it had pitted Alice Paul and the National Women's Party, supporters of an Equal Rights Amendment to the U.S. Constitution, against virtually every other women's group in the country, which knew that such an amendment would sweep aside the special labor protections for women for which they had fought so hard. The supporters of the amendment, however, found those "special protections" insulting. "If . . . a law is passed applying to women and not applying to men, it will discriminate against women and handicap them in competing with men in earning their livelihood," explained Jane Norman. This is a philosophy that would penalize all women because some women are morally frail and physically weak.

Alice Paul was decidedly more blunt: "If you demand equality, you must accept equality."

The original SuperGirl—the Maid of Might and Princess of Power who was faster than a speeding bullet, able to bend steel in her bare hands, yet savvy enough to match wits with the prowess of Brainiac—was invented by scientists desperate to save some vestige of the planet Argon, and by cartoonists seeking a new demographic. The flesh-and-blood feminist SuperWoman—who can whip up a coq au vin, sing the kids to sleep with a politically correct lullaby, and still have energy left to argue a case before the Supreme Court—was created as feminist lore by a band of upper-middle-class American women for similar purposes: to save womanhood from wrenching choices and to prove that Helen Reddy was right, that females can triumph in the man's world and still raise perfect children.

By the 1970s, liberal feminists had figured it out: Motherhood and housework were social constructs, not full-time jobs. So with men sharing the cooking and the government throwing in some childcare, nothing could stand in the way of women, who would take over law firms and state houses, factories, town halls, and village fire departments. Month after month, *Ms.* magazine served up the formula for achieving SuperWomanhood. In one of its first issues, writer Alix Kates Shulman shared with readers the marriage agreement she and her husband drew up. Breakfasts were divided evenly, although he was responsible for weekend morning repasts, including shopping and cleaning up. Alix cooked dinner except on Sunday night. He was responsible for the dishes on Tuesday, Thursday, and Sunday, while she stood at the sink on Monday, Wednesday, and Saturday. Friday's mess fell to whoever had slouched off most during the week. She did the laundry, including stripping the bed. But he took care of the dry-cleaning and remade the bed after the sheets were washed. See, the article suggested, it's not so hard.

In 1975, Letty Cottin Pogrebin, a founder of *Ms.*, published a how-to book for women having trouble with the nondomestic side of the equation. In *Getting Yours,* she led them through a step-by-step guide to dealing with employers skeptical about a woman's ability to work while having children. The trickiest moment, she admitted, was announcing that you were pregnant and emerging with disability leave. Don't be cowed by a man who says, "Pregnancy is voluntary and therefore different from all other ailments that count as disabilities," she explained before providing the precise language that should be used in response. "Rubbish! For millions of women whose religion prohibits the use of contraceptives, pregnancy can hardly be called voluntary. . . . Asking me to choose between my job and my child is not choice but punishment."

Men grudgingly began picking up a greater share of America's household responsibilities. Between 1965 and 1975, the time the average woman spent cleaning, cooking, and doing the laundry fell from twenty-seven hours a week to twenty-two, while men increased their domestic commitment from a paltry five hours to a slightly-less-paltry seven. Employers were forced by the Pregnancy Discrimination Act of 1978 to give pregnant women the same sort of disability leave given workers unable to work. And tax credits for daycare continued to subsidize women who paid others to guard and train their kids while they worked for wages.

Unaware that all the conflicting claims on her time that turned her day into an endless maze were mere social constructs, SuperWoman staggered under the burden of getting the kids ready for school, working a full day, shopping for groceries, cooking the meals, paying the bills, picking up the dry-cleaning, and taking out the dog. Is this really possible? women across the country asked in despair. Pogrebin's response to that question, printed in the March 1978 issue of *Ms.* with considerably less panache than she'd demonstrated three years earlier, predicted the shape of women's future. "Without equal parenting and more social responsibility for childcare, without equal responsibility and increased flexibility in the workplace and at home, there is virtually no person who can do it," she admitted. In other words, if you treat women even-handedly, holding them to the same standards as men, you won't get equality in the workplace.

That reality forced liberal feminists into what should have been a wrenching quandary, since the principle and the dream are in open conflict. But with admirable inventiveness that was deftly disingenuous, they waltzed past their own contradictions by blaming them on a sexist society. How can women possibly succeed, they asked, when every facet of America is organized around the outdated "breadwinner" mode? If the tax code, the workplaces, even the nature of work preclude women from fulfilling themselves both personally and professionally, then the tax code, the workplace, and the nature of work will have to be redesigned around the "working mother" mode. Anything less is a violation of women's rights.

The new strategy for that social remodeling is simple: If men won't do half the work, or if women still suffer too much stress when they do, push more responsibility off on society or corporations. Nancy Folbre, an economist, proclaimed that women's wage work would be less constrained if the costs of caring for children were transferred to their employers or to other taxpayers (an observation that does not require a doctorate in economics, since whose wages would not be "less con-strained" if someone else paid a chunk of their bills?) So NOW joined with Elinor Guggenheim of the Child Care Action Network and Repre-sentatives Pat Schroeder and Barbara Boxer to lobby for more federal money for daycare and more on-site, employer-run daycare centers.

"Adjust public policy to meet real-world needs," became the slogan du jour among Heidi Hartmann's crowd at the Institute for Women's Policy Research, where every study ended with yet another recitation of the con-tinuing wage gap between men and women. The women of the institute convinced themselves that that gap indicates that women were *paying* for having kids, and, in a sense, they were absolutely correct. Women paid, and pay, in the wages, promotions, and work opportunities they lose when they take leave to have babies and to bond with their newborns, when they switch to part-time work to stay home with their toddlers, or drop out of the work force entirely. "Unfair," the institute crowd cries. "Discriminatory." Men, after all, suffer no such losses. They conveniently avoid mentioning that few men make these *choices*.

Every policy adjustment concocted by women like Hartmann to "cor-rect" this perceived imbalance is subjected to a rigorous measurement of the quality of what they call "a woman's life," which means the life of a mother. No initiative meets IWPR standards if it does not decrease in-equality of income and leisure time, marginalization, male bias, exploita-tion, and poverty. Agreeing on solutions, then, isn't easy. Take child support, for example. Most people think it makes sense for the govern-ment to force deadbeat dads to help feed, clothe, house, and educate the kids they brought into the world. But not the institute, which denounces such measures as antiwoman because they increase women's dependence on men. Their alternative is for the government to collect dads' checks di-rectly and *guarantee* mothers that support whether or not dad hands over a dime. Even that approach is less than ideal, they admit, since it violates women's autonomy by requiring mothers to name the biological fathers of their kids and makes them dependent on the state. But better the state than the man who gave his genes to their kids.

The proposals that *have* met their criteria run the gamut from the fa-miliar—flex-time and paid maternity and parenting leave—to the cutting edge (which means that they will probably become familiar over the next decade). Since their goal is to ensure that no choice a woman makes about parenting puts her at a disadvantage in any way in the workplace, they demand that unemployment insurance be expanded to include women taking time off for childbirth and family care. They insist that we move to a shorter, thirty-hour workweek to ease women's time squeeze—as if time were an exclusively female dilemma. And they advocate legislation requiring that part-time workers be given the same hourly wages and fringe benefits as full-time employees because "men are able to have a family and a career, while women are more likely to pursue a career alone," and something has to change to reverse this reality.

In the midst of this frantic reshaping of society to allow women to pursue work and motherhood in tandem, feminists have twisted themselves into pretzels to avoid the accusation that they are asking for "special treatment," and thus violating at least the letter of the law on equal treatment. But it's not easy to disguise work recesses for pumping breast milk as a benefit available equally to men and women. Or to escape the reality that for every man who takes a "parenting" or "family" leave to be with the kids, twenty women stay home with the kids when they're sick. How can you forge equality of outcome in the public sector, which is the ultimate goal, when so many women freely *choose* to be the primary caretakers of their children?

Most of the women living out the struggle between work and family aren't worried about such theoretical niceties. They don't care if what they want—be it flex-time, family leave, or paid childcare—violates the principle of equal treatment. Most won't go so far as to acknowledge that those perks do. In lawsuit after lawsuit, grievance after grievance, they parse out an exercise in logic that no one dares challenge for fear of crossing some vague line of meanness, or political correctness: Mothers need scheduling flexibility, time and space to pump breast milk, and a wide range of special considerations to allow them to juggle their kids and their work responsibilities. Mothers are women. If mothers aren't given what they want, they are victims of gender discrimination.

These women were given voice by writers like Anne Roiphe, Joan Peters, and Susan Chira, all successful, affluent women, who churned out tomes bemoaning how misunderstood or ill-treated mothers like them are. In *When Mothers Work,* Peters relieves mothers of any lingering guilt they might feel for neglecting their children. If they don't have enough time and energy to mother and work well simultaneously, it isn't their fault; their husbands and social institutions that don't pick up more of the burden are to blame. In her *Fruitful,* a sort of motherhood manifesto, Roiphe, a self-styled "mother feminist," adds the feminist movement to the list of culprits. And Chira, in *A Mother's Place,* strikes out at a broad range of books, research studies, and talk shows that have taught women that they cannot be good mothers without martyrdom and self-obliteration.

A group of philosophers have gone these writers one better. Too fluent in logic to escape the inconsistency of the mainstream position, they stake their claim to mothers' rights (which they call "women's rights") not on equality, but on the innate superiority of mothering—seemingly unaware that that formulation consigns millions of women to a sort of second-class feminist limbo. Such maternal thinkers as Sara Ruddick, Carol Gilligan, and Virginia Held bemoan the fact that American society is built around "male paradigms," around the male experiences in the public world, and would have us refashion society according to a "maternal" model, discarding male concerns for hierarchy, business, and the rational in favor of such "mothering" traits as cooperation, consensus, "attentive love," and community. Forget male moral voices, which speak in the language of justice. Listen to women's moral voices and be guided by a higher principle, spoken in the language of caring, they counsel.

All this might sound like the kind of intellectual or utopian fantasies that have currency only within the ivied walls of academia. Yet the work-family folks have made remarkable progress in imposing those values on the American workplace. Giving mothers full flexibility to leave work for their kids' soccer games, or to breastfeed in the middle of business meetings, after all, sounds like someone is speaking pretty loudly in the "language of caring," at least about mothers. Permitting mothers lengthy postpartum leaves from their work in, say, law offices or consulting firms isn't rational from a business standpoint, at least not if you're the neglected client. It isn't even about cooperation or community if you consider all the others who have to pick up the work of the absent employee. But it is about "attentive love" for mothers, who, according to the maternalist philosophers, serve a higher calling, which is a beacon of light unto the rest of us poor slobs.

The feminist establishment doesn't speak the language of caring when they argue for "special consideration" for women, however. It is simply too blatant. Nor do its leaders admit that they are fighting for the empowerment of women, at any cost, even the cost of equality. Rather, they contort logic and reality to create a pretense of equal treatment. They delude themselves that they are not treating women as mommys—and, thus far, they have gotten away with it.

No challenge required more formidable intellectual gymnastics than developing an approach to pregnancy and postpartum leave that could be billed as "equal treatment." The issue first surfaced as part of the complicated mix of problems and cases that confronted the Equal Employment Opportunity Commission after the Civil Rights Act of 1964 became law. Much to the surprise—and, in many quarters, dismay—of the Washington establishment, that bill wound up including a provision banning discrimination on the basis of gender. It fell to the commission to outline precisely what that meant. Few questions were more fraught with legal or social complications than the issue of pregnancy.

Many of that era's female activists, equating women with mothers, assumed that the new law would ban discrimination against pregnant women, which, to them, meant that companies would have to treat pregnancy like any other "temporary disability," akin to a broken leg or breast cancer. But the members of the Equal Employment Opportunity Commission refused to buy that argument. Why should employers be forced to give women unpaid leave, continue fringe benefits, and hold their jobs open for a "voluntary" condition? What next, disability for cosmetic surgery? Shouldn't women be held responsible for their choices?

After waffling on those questions for years, in 1972 the commission finally bowed to Schroeder's troops, and there the matter stood until the Supreme Court threw that tidy capitulation into disarray. In 1976, in the case of *General Electric* v. *Gilbert,* the justices ruled that General Electric had not violated the Civil Rights Act when it excluded pregnancy from its disability coverage. Since the company did not impart pregnancy disability coverage to men, the justices found, their failure to extend such coverage to women could not constitute sex discrimination. Such liberal feminists as Pat Schroeder were incensed. The Court "found that discriminating against pregnancy does not constitute sex discrimination," she exclaimed in utter disbelief. "They held that pregnancy is not a sex-related condition! Had any members of the then entirely male Court been pregnant?"

The problem, of course, is that pregnancy is not a condition *intrinsic* to women, like a gynecological infection or mastitis. Women's biology creates the *possibility* of pregnancy, but biology is not destiny. Pregnancy generally occurs by design. That distinction was lost on Schroeder, a Harvard-trained lawyer, who compared pregnancy to a sport-related injury or a venereal disease, which were also, she said, "voluntary conditions."

Frustrated by the Court, mainstream feminists pressed their case in Congress, which responded in the name of "motherhood" by passing the Pregnancy Discrimination Act, which forced employers to treat pregnancy like any other temporary disability. But that was just step one. Time off for delivery and recovery from childbirth was a minor matter, since, for most women, childbirth and recuperation don't begin to use up the annual sick leave that was part of their employee benefits package. Women intent on keeping mothers in the marketplace needed to find a way for them to gain them more time off, weeks or months of leave to bond with their newborns without losing their jobs—and without claiming "special privileges" for women.

Concerned only with the first two goals—leave time and job protection—then-California Assemblyman Howard Berman (now a member of the House of Representatives) almost blew their cover in 1978, when he guided a bill through the California assembly mandating a four-month "disability leave" for new mothers. Berman knew that few women are "disabled" for sixteen weeks after childbirth. But, good liberal that he was, he believed that new mothers and their children deserved time together—and that women's jobs shouldn't suffer if they took it. The yearning to spend time with an infant, then, conveniently became a "disability."

Mothering leave, however, was not what the Washington, D.C., feminist establishment had in mind, since it undercut the "no special treatment" pretense on which they staked their honor. Attorneys interested in such legislation, especially a cadre of women from the Women's Legal Defense Fund and Georgetown University Law School, envisioned a federal "parenting leave" bill that would apply to fathers as well as mothers. No matter that when private companies offered such leaves, few fathers bothered to take it. Or that there was no grassroots outcry for an unpaid leave since few workers could afford to take one. They were intent on pushing forward the socialization of childrearing, transferring some of the burden of care from mothers to companies and to taxpayers. Turning "mother" leave into "parenting" or "family" leave was a politically correct step in the right direction.

The presidency of Ronald Reagan was not exactly a propitious moment for such an advance, but attorneys and activists were forced into action in 1984 when a federal court ruled that Berman's California bill violated the Civil Rights Act of 1964 by singling women out for preferential treatment. Berman resolved to introduce a similar bill—a bill mandating that women be given four months of job-protected, unpaid leave to prepare and care for their newborns—into the United States Congress and see how higher courts would react. The Women's Legal Defense Fund Team sent Pat Schroeder and representatives of NOW, the American Civil Liberties Union, the National Women's Political Caucus, and the National Women's Law Center into Berman's office to pressure him into taking a different tack. They insisted that a leave bill could not be written only for women. No matter the intent, it needed a more high-minded rationale, and a more inclusive-sounding umbrella, to pass both legal and political muster.

Parental and Disability Leave, they called their alternative scheme, a bill that would guarantee parents job-protected time off to take care of young or sick children. (They threw in the disability dimension—a mandate for similar time off in the case of "temporary disabilities"—to draw in wider support from organized labor.) That tactic, allegedly developed with an explicitly feminist raison d'être, created some of the strangest bedfellows Washington has seen in modern times. The United States Catholic Conference threw its considerable weight behind the "feminist" bill. The Junior League climbed on board. And when the House of Representatives voted on the measure, Henry Hyde, a feminist anti-Christ for his opposition to abortion, rose before his colleagues and declared, "There are very few bills that involve apple pie and motherhood. This one does not involve apple pie, but it does involve motherhood and it seems to me a social policy of encouraging motherhood is good. Therefore, for that reason, I will support this bill."

The crusade for what eventually became the Family and Medical Leave Act turned into an eight-year battle between American business, represented by the Chamber of Commerce, the National Association of Manufacturers, and the National Federation for Independent Businesses, and feminist leaders, who carried the standard of motherhood against business lobbyists decrying the amount of regulation already heaped on American business and the burdens family leave would put on mom-and-pop stores. Caught in the welter of pressures from the AARP, NOW, and the Women's Bureau of the AFL-CIO, Congress never got around to debating whether socializing childrearing functions was a desirable course, or whether Americans really wanted to put up the extra cash, and put in the extra time, to allow women the choice to pursue parenting and careers simultaneously.

Nor, against the backdrop of dramatic testimony of women forced to pursue motherhood either as a career or as a six-week disability leave, did anyone mention how many women the legislation would force into, not out of, double duty. The bills' female supporters delighted in the prospect of making businesses and corporations pay for a modicum of freedom for women. They ignored the bitter truth: When a colleague is on leave, the boss doesn't pay; another worker does, and, given the fact that women remain concentrated in heavily female offices and professions, that worker is usually a woman. They pitted woman against woman in workplaces all across the land, and they did so in the name of women's liberation.

Felice Schwartz was the Superwoman's woman—until January 1989. That month, the founder of Catalyst, the first American organization established to help fill the upper ranks of Corporate America with women, committed feminist treason. After almost three decades as an icon of female empowerment, on the pages of the *Harvard Business Review,* Schwartz offered a modest suggestion for the resolution of the work/family crisis: a separate career track for working mothers, what came to be called the "mommy track." In "Management Women and the New Facts of Life," Schwartz was speaking to corporate leaders and policymakers caught between the demand for more women in positions of power and the impact such promotions were having on the bottom line. "The cost of employing women in management is greater than the cost of employing men," Schwartz declared boldly in the first line of the piece, sending a wave of fury throughout feminist circles. "This is a jarring statement partly because it is true, but mostly because it is something people are reluctant to talk about." The problem, as Schwartz saw it, was that the first generation of women who pushed into high-level positions in the workforce had recast themselves as men. Intent on erasing long-held stereotypes, they had worked longer and harder and denied that they differed in any way from male employees. But the younger women coming up behind them didn't like the price those pioneers had paid. They wanted families as well as high-powered careers. And that meant babies, a reality around which, Schwartz said, women's rights leaders maintained "a conspiracy of silence."

Childbirth can't be reduced to a disability, "like a broken ankle," Schwartz argued. It is exhausting and confusing for women trying to cope with conflicting sets of demands. No matter how supportive their employers, women trying to do everything at once live with more stress and confusion than men trying to parent and work simultaneously. Whether by socialization or biology, women simply are more bound up with their children than are men, and no manner of feminist hectoring will change that reality. Rather than let those women languish professionally from sheer exhaustion, or watch midcareer professionals walk out the door in distress, Schwartz urged companies to give new mothers an out, a temporary "career and family" track that would keep them in the game with flexible schedules, but take them off the fasttrack while they tended their kids.

Schwartz's suggestion was hardly original. Dana Friedman, then at Conference Board, had written, "Somehow women need to accept the inevitability of making tradeoffs. Does this mean that women can't have it all? For several years of their careers, they may decide they don't *want* it all." And newspapers all across the land had discovered a startling new phenomenon, high-powered lawyers and businesswomen downsizing their lives and putting their career advancement on hold in order to spend more time with their children.

Brandishing polls showing that women wanted careers as well as families, feminist leaders insisted that it just wasn't so. How could it be when

The New York Times, the arbiter of truth, reported that 55 percent of women between the ages of eighteen and forty-four preferred to combine work and family? Anyway, they declared, if women were abandoning their jobs, they were being forced out by evil, male-centered structures and attitudes. Something had to be done.

They were ignoring—willfully or not—the more complicated ambivalence that Schwartz was addressing. The Department of Labor graphed an undiminished rise in the number of mothers of young children working outside the home, but the Department of Labor had a pretty basic definition of "working" that revealed little of the subtle ways mothers were cycling into and out of the business world to make room for their kids. Newspaper reporters were becoming freelancers. Editors were cutting back to four-day workweeks. Supermarket clerks were planning their shifts so they could tag-team childcare with their husbands. And consultants were opening their own, part-time businesses.

It wasn't supposed to be that way, at least in feminist mythology. Children weren't supposed to remain "women's responsibility," and women were supposed to follow the linear "male" model, so the activists who'd invented those dicta were infuriated that those they purported to speak for refused to follow the party line. Over and over again, ad nauseum, feminist leaders bemoaned those emerging patterns in women's lives, at least when they weren't denying their existence. They carped that men were able to pursue careers and families simultaneously. "So why can't women?" they whined.

Much to their chagrin, Alice Rossi answered that question directly: because of physiological differences that can't be willed away or swept under an ideological carpet. "The mother-infant relationship will continue to have greater emotional depth than the father-infant relationship because of the mother's physiological experience of pregnancy, birth, and nursing," she wrote in *Daedelus.* "A society that chooses to overcome the female's greater investment in children must institutionalize a program of compensatory education for boys and men that trains them in infant and child care. (Even then, women may still have the stronger bond with their offspring.) ... Any slackening of such compensatory training—for generations to come—will quickly lead to a regression to the sex-role tradition of our long past, as so many social experiments of this century have shown. We cannot just toss out the physiological equipment that centuries of adaptation have created. We can live with that biological heritage or try to supersede it, but we cannot wish it away."

Feminist leaders refused to heed Rossi, or the thousands of women refusing to behave like men. They could not accept the fact that women might want it all, but many are obviously unwilling to pay the price their fathers paid—in the missed dinners, neglected bake sales and games, and forgotten meetings with the principal. Men, after all, have never had it all, except in the most perfunctory way. They have been workers and parents, but parenting has been a sort of second job. Few mothers, no matter how career-obsessed, seem willing to turn their children into such part-time ventures.

Madeleine Albright described the result of those choices. "Women's careers don't go in straight lines," she once told a reporter for *Time* magazine, equating women, it seems, with mothers. "They zigzag all over the place." All Felice Schwartz did was to suggest that CEOs face this reality, the reality that many women want to play jacks with their kids, attend all of their school plays, or be the face they see when they wake up from their naps. Be flexible, she counseled employers. Let mothers return part-time. Allow them to re-enter the competition at their own pace. You'll gain more than you lose. You might gain a Madeleine Albright.

That prescription might have reflected reality. It might have been a formula for bridging the hostile divide between the "mommys" and childless women fed up with being forced to take responsibility for their decisions. But it was heresy. Activists from Maine to Michigan pilloried Schwartz for providing the enemy with ammunition. Dividing women into separate tracks, "career primary" and "career and family," was dangerous, said Betty Friedan, who accused Schwartz of "retrofeminism." The headline on a *Washington Post* column written about Schwartz's piece branded the notion "demeaning," an echo of the old racist "separate and unequal" doctrine. Pat Schroeder, whose own career followed precisely the kind of path Schwartz suggested, called her analysis tragic.

Schwartz was right, and millions of American women knew it. But no one ever accused the Sisterhood of fighting like girls.

*   *   *

In March 1999, I was asked to debate the "family-friendly backlash," as it has come to be called, on Minnesota Public Radio. My opponent was Teresa Rothausen, who teaches management in the graduate business program at the University of St. Thomas in Minneapolis. Rothausen had made news in Minneapolis several months earlier when she asked students in her Organizational Theory and Behavior class to debate whether businesses should be responsible for employees' ability to balance work and life. Her own position is clear: She believes that all of society, including business, has to "value dependent care."

During our hour-long debate, we agreed on virtually nothing, but the tone was friendly and courteous. At least until I asked Dr. Rothausen directly whether she was bothered by the fact that the programs she advocated violated the principle of equal pay for equal work. I fully expected her to fudge the issue, to change the topic or deny that working mothers are receiving greater rewards for their work than childless women since that was usually what happened when I was engaged in such a debate. So her reply threw me for a loop. "Well, other societies do things differently," she said. "Equal pay for equal work isn't the only principle for compensation."

The conversation was interrupted by one of public radio's noncommercials or a phone call from a listener, and we never managed to return to the issue. But during the weeks that followed our debate, Rothausen's comment haunted me. Okay, I thought, what are those alternative principles? There's equal pay for unequal work, and unequal pay for equal work, both of which we have tried at some point in the nation's history. Could she really be suggesting that we return to the bad old days of blatant, institutionalized discrimination? I doubted it, so I searched for a fourth possibility, combing through books and consulting with friends. None appeared. For a while, I began to think that I had misunderstood Rothausen, and thought about calling her on the phone. Upon further reflection, however, I realized that I had not, that she was simply stating with honesty what so many feminists want without admitting it: affirmative action for mothers.

In fact, that is what Betty Friedan & Co. have been advocating for years, although never so overtly. In 1997, Friedan suggested that American women had become distracted by the wrong right to choose. Forget abortion, she said. Women need the right to "the choice to have children, demanding policies in the workplace, schools and other institutions that take into account the realities of combining work and family."

I admit that I've spent hours puzzling over what the "right" to that choice—the right to choose combining mothering and work—means. I understand the "right to work," which would guarantee me a job, although not the presidency of IBM. I understand the "right to food," which would guarantee me nutrition, although not dinner at the Four Seasons. And I understand the "right to choice" about abortion, which guarantees that no one will force me to get rid of a fetus, or to keep one I don't want, in my womb.

Perhaps I am dense, but, to me, the "right" to choose both career and family means that no one can say: Look, if you want to work, you *may not* bear children. Or, if you want kids, you *may not* work. And, finally, thank goodness, women have gained that right. But having the right to opt for that choice doesn't guarantee that it will be easy, or stressless, or that you will be able to do both at once without keeling over in collapse. No American right comes with that kind of warranty. The right to vote isn't a promise that your candidate will win, just as the right to life doesn't mean that someone won't shoot you as you're making your way to your car in a dark alley. Rights are guarantees of opportunities, not outcomes.

Furthermore, how would we guarantee such a right? It would probably be with twenty-four hour, publicly funded daycare centers, childcare tax credits, special tax breaks for stay-at-home moms, and broad workplace reforms that would provide mothers with day-to-day and month-to-month flexibility. In other words, we would do precisely what we are already doing, transferring the benefits we used to give to men—in the old days when we thought of them as heads of households—to parents. In short, we would set up an affirmative action program for mothers that would shelter them from the difficulties created by their own choices.

Now, forgive me if I fall into some sarcasm here, but, as a lifelong feminist, I am confounded by the feminist principles behind this. Who would we transfer those benefits *from* in this feminist fantasyland? From women who use their reproductive freedom *not* to have children? Let's parse this out carefully: In the name of feminism, we are going to take time and money away from women and give it to men (since half the nation's parents are male, at least in name). And then we are going to say that we have protected the freedom of women to choose not to have children, which we assume is as sacred as the freedom of women to choose to bear them or abort them?

We now have laws that make it illegal to discriminate against pregnant women. And recent rulings under the Americans with Disabilities Act suggest that we are on the verge of discovering that it is illegal to discriminate against women who want to get pregnant and can't. What about those of us who don't want to be pregnant? Is reproductive freedom a one-way street? Sure, no one is forcing women like me to reproduce. But what does freedom of choice mean if those who exercise that freedom in one way are supported with tax breaks and financial assistance, work release, and massive lobbying efforts while those who exercise it differently are forced to pay?

I, like most women I know who are childless by choice or chance, feel more than a little betrayed by feminist support of maternal affirmative action. "The definition of womanhood can't be tied to biological processes," says Andrea McCormick, who works for a health insurance company in Harrisburg, Pennsylvania. "If women are going to be considered equals, then they have to act like equals and we have to demand that they be treated as equals, not whine that they need to be taken care of since they can bear children. How come the women's movement allows, even encourages this?"

Unfortunately, the answer to Andrea's question is all too obvious. Feminism has become the ladies' auxiliary of the parents' rights movement, and the words woman and mother have become synonymous, once again. In the names of both political correctness and political expediency, movement leaders have clung to the mythology desperately that the policies they support aren't reinforcing the vision of woman as mother, that they are "for parents." But if the goal is to liberate men, why have feminists poured so much energy into these proposals? And if the goal is to liberate mothers, what happened to the feminist ideal of liberating women from forced motherhood, to the notion that feminism must speak for us all?

Everyone knows that women without much money need better access to quality childcare, and that the workplace can be mighty unfriendly to those juggling two major responsibilities. But feminists, in particular, should know that you can't build the privilege of one group on the backs of another. You can't bolster the rights of a single segment of the population by diminishing the rights of another. You can't build a women's movement by telling women like me, "Sorry, if you refuse to have children, you'll have to ante up more than your requisite share." After all, as Sojourner Truth asked in 1851, "Ain't I a Woman?"

PART THREE

Balancing Act

6

No Kidding

Nora got herself pregnant with Sam's child, the result of a quickie in a cabana between courses at a family dinner. She wasn't peddling her body like some suburban slut. She opted for desperate measures because her beloved husband, Bo, who was sterile and suffering from acute pneumonia, needed a reason to live—and what other incentive would be so powerful? Across town, Cassie suffered a breakdown when her infant died at birth. But her mind was healed by the most powerful force in the universe, a miracle child she discovered in a manger on Christmas Eve.

And that's just on daytime television.

After dark, superstars Helen Hunt and Paul Reiser became Mad About Mabel. Offbeat Dharma and her blueblood husband Greg tried to adopt the infant of a supermarket checkout girl, inspiring Dharma's flaky parents to assemble the requisite village—a spiritual advisor, a folk singer, a historical guru, and a lactation expert—to help raise him. Phoebe of *Friends* gets pregnant with triplets as the surrogate mother for her half-brother and his wife. And Bill Cosby, the latter-day Art Linkletter, produces kids who, miraculously, say the darnedest things.

Meanwhile, in real life, Geraldo interrupted his impeachment discussions to broadcast photographs of the newborns of his staff members. Celebrity moms and dads gushed to Rosie not about their careers, their politics, or their sex lives, but about their kids. In the most heralded act of reproduction since, well, the Madonna, the modern-day wannabe presented Lourdes Maria to the world with the same audaciousness she exhibited when she bared her tits and ass in downtown Miami. Jodie Foster titillated her fans with a press release proclaiming her impending motherhood, although declining to state how she had achieved that state. And *The New York Times* waxed poetic about how much fatherhood had softened Yasir Arafat.

In the procreation-obsessed nineties, with motherhood, fatherhood, parenting, and children driving the zeitgeist of premillennial America, the conception craze isn't confined just to celebritydom. Anxious to make up for lost time, baby-boomer women all across the nation are racing their biological clocks to reproduction. Younger women, chilled by the difficulties their older sisters have had conceiving later in life, are opting to procreate during their prime. Single women are boosting the bottom lines of sperm banks, lesbians are turning in their turkey basters and making deals with their gay brothers, postmenopausal women are finding doctors to impregnate them artificially—and the nation is feting women whose abuse of fertility drugs is producing quintuplets, septuplets, and octuplets.

Kid-mania has seized America's imagination so thoroughly that you'd never know that another, more revolutionary, demographic trend was sweeping the nation. Having children, after all, is hardly a pathbreaking act. The *news* is the number of women who are not following that road to the maternity ward. Baby-boomer women—the first women in world history to grow up with the ability to have sex without reproductive consequences—have opted out of motherhood in record numbers. Choosing careers over family, committed to population control, or simply not interested in kids, one-fifth of them are childless by choice. In 1976, 84 percent of all women had reproduced by the time they turned thirty-four; by 1990, although the rate of infertility had remained stable and medical procedures for circumventing it improved drastically, that number had fallen to 75 percent. Demographers predict that the trend will continue and that as many as one-quarter of the women born between 1956 and 1972 will never give birth.

Population experts base most of their research about childlessness on women, but the same pattern seems to be repeating itself among the male population. According to the U.S. Census Bureau, as many as 19 percent of married couples choose not to have children; a decade ago, that figure was below 10 percent. The Kid-Free Zone, in fact, is the fast-growing segment of the nation's population.

Children may be today's fashion in popular culture, but the countercultural crowd that has embraced nonmotherhood is rewriting the history of American women. For two centuries, by whatever admixture of choice and necessity, only a minuscule percentage of women chose to remain childless. When money was tight or the national mood sour, the numbers would rise, as they did during the Depression of the 1930s. But when spirits and bank accounts recovered, as they did after World War II, for example, the numbers bounced back, and motherhood became the almost universal norm once again.

In the late 1960s and 1970s, however, the birth rate plummeted. Young adults lingered endlessly in adolescence, too self-absorbed to consider changing diapers. Protofeminists abstained from reproduction, a reflection of ideological suspicion of the patriarchal family. Careerists were too busy building stock portfolios out of junk bonds on Wall Street, Neal Cassady followers too drugged out on fantasies of living on the road, and the politically correct too preoccupied with the dangers of overpopulation to deal with morning sickness, protruding bellies, and Lamaze classes.

Then, just as boomer women began hitting their biological walls, everyone got a little bored with all this "revolutionary" change, or least its consequences. Classes in the Talmud or the Kabbalah replaced downtown clubs as New York's hot spots, the hip version of a quest for meaning that pushed Americans in the heartland back to church, or at least into voting for Ronald Reagan. Political idealism waned, or at least was transmogrified into Republicanism or the "new" Democratic vision, a donkey that looked strikingly like an elephant. Tubal ligations were reversed. Korean babies came into vogue, then Peruvian and Chinese ones. Clomid and Pergonal became the new drugs du jour. Suddenly, in 1998, a record number of children were born in the country.

But armed for the first time in history with effective birth control, millions of women refused to follow the script. Some opt out of motherhood because they are committed to population reduction on a planet they believe is already overtaxed. Some can't imagine where they would find the time to take care of children in lives already scheduled to the minute. Others just keep postponing and postponing, waiting for the time to feel right until time simply runs out, and they aren't upset enough at the consequences to run to the endocrinologist. Most simply don't want children—because they don't care much for kids, are too wrapped up their careers, can't afford the added financial burden, or have other plans for their lives.

Nothing provokes their ire more than being asked to explain that inaction. "People are never asked to justify their decision to have kids, so why should I be expected to justify my decision not to have them?" asks Ilene Bilenky, a nurse in Massachusetts.

By every measure, the childless are among the elite of American women: wealthier, more independent, and better educated than the average mother. The percentage of women who are voluntarily childless rises directly and dramatically with each advanced degree. Among those without high-school diplomas, only 10 percent have forsworn reproduction, rising to 19 percent among the two-year-degree set, reaching an astonishing 28 percent among four-year graduates. Childless women are twice as likely as working mothers to hold professional or managerial jobs, and according to the National Center for Health Statistics, they are more likely than mothers to be in egalitarian marriages, less traditional and less religious.

Despite the social stereotype of the childless as bitter and sour, most nonparents are content with their decisions, and surveys suggest that few grow to regret them. Whether at the end of their lives or just building their futures, they echo the comments of Abby and Tom Bohley of Colorado Springs, Colorado, who have been married and committed to childlessness for more than three decades. "I consider myself blessed," says Abby. "I've been able to do so many things that have enhanced my life, things that wouldn't have been possible if we'd had kids. As a couple, we are incredibly close. We invest a lot in our relationship and we enjoy it. A lot of our contemporaries who are grandparents are always talking about how old they are. But frankly, I feel pretty damn young."

Unlike the childless of other eras, today's nonmothers and nonfathers are unlikely to allow themselves to be demeaned, or to let their interests be drowned out by the cries of a million babies. Cut from the same cloth as the Soccer Moms who have whipped salivating politicians, marketers, and businessmen into a family frenzy, they are nonparents with an attitude, emboldened by feminism and the powerful ideology of "choice." They are losing their patience with the extra workloads heaped on them at the office, with their skimpy benefits packages and the rude assumption that their time is less valuable than a parent's. They have learned—from the strange glances thrown their way when they announce that they don't want children, from the platforms of the current crop of politicians, and from the tax cuts they do not receive—that all the family-friendliness sweeping America is not a victimless crime.

Traditionally, women who did not reproduce were virtually invisible, ashamed of their "barrenness" or too timid to call attention to their unwomanliness. In fact, for most of the nation's history, childless women were openly suspect—strangely pathological creatures violating the biblical command to be fruitful and multiply. In colonial America, married women without children were assumed to be suffering God's punishment for some unknown sin. If not meticulously virtuous, they ran the risk of being accused of witchcraft. In the early Republic, they were shunned for refusing to live up to the responsibilities of "republican motherhood," the ultimate female service to the new nation, which needed to populate its sparsely settled land with upstanding citizens—of European descent, of course.

Those same sentiments were echoed by the founding feminists. Lydia Kingsvill Commander called upon intelligent American women to have six children to keep the nation from being overpopulated with "loosely united, crude savages, content to hunt and fish, war with neighboring tribes." And, writing of the day the United States bombed Hiroshima, *American Home* magazine warned ominously that "on that day, parenthood took on added responsibilities of deep and profound significance." Women avoiding the most important career imaginable were "flabby, apathetic, indifferent, irresponsible members of society."

In the twentieth century, when psychologists became the arbiters of American behavior, those traditional voices were joined by a chorus of "experts" pounding home the message that women must, at all costs, and if at all possible, breed. Sigmund Freud laid the groundwork by teaching that women needed children to overcome childhood penis envy, and that lesson redounded for decades. "Any woman who does not desire offspring is abnormal," opined Dr. Max G. Schlapp, a world-renowned neurologist, at a lecture in New York well covered by the city's press in 1915. Half a century later, Erik Erikson, perhaps the most influential modern guru of human behavior, offered his own version of Freud. "The woman who does not fulfill her innate need to fill her 'inner space,' or uterus, with embryonic tissue," he wrote, "is likely to be frustrated or neurotic."

Female psychologists proved equally unable to resist maintaining the pressure on women to follow the biblical commandment to be fruitful and multiply. In her classic book on women's psychology, Judith Bardwick, for example, proclaimed that women uninterested in motherhood exhibited "pathological levels of anxiety, a distorted sex identity and a neurotic solution."

For hundreds of years, from biblical Palestine to modern America, the message has remained unchanged. In the African Igbo tribe, where celibacy was traditionally considered unnatural and immoral, the bellies of childless women were slit open before they were buried and their names erased from tribal memory. The Talmud, the central book of Jewish law, teaches, "He who brings no children into the world is like a murderer. A childless person is like the dead." In the New Testament, Timothy warned that women, who are still lugging around Eve's original sin, could be saved from it only by childbearing. And in Germany, Hitler lionized the most fertile Aryan women with the Mutterkreuz, the Mother's Cross.

That cycle remains unbroken, even in the postmodern, postfeminist land of the Empathic President and the "right to choose." Girls grow up learning that women cannot be happy or fulfilled without children. Women teach one another that without children, they can't keep their men. Adulation is heaped on women whose only accomplishment is overdoing fertility drugs and bearing septuplets. Every force in popular culture—from women's magazines and Lifetime "television for women" to Katie Couric, Madonna, and the First Lady—broadcasts the same message: Women are mothers.

In a land where motherhood is as intrinsic to Americanism as apple pie, baseball, and the Stars and Stripes, Ilene Bilenky is a traitor. Ilene, a registered nurse, clings to a small patch of Littleton, Massachusetts, with a vengeance—as if the dense shrubbery that shades her tiny cottage from the road could protect her from the reality of a world that considers her an eccentric. A dozen times a week, scores of times a month, she is reminded that she is "other" when she faces what seems to most women an innocuous question: "Do you have children?" It's a remarkably personal question—touching on intimate sexual and medical matters—that total strangers feel free to pose in a country where few dare to inquire so boldly about their neighbors finances.

If she's feeling feisty, Ilene is likely to snap back with her stock, "No, I was never interested." If she's tired and just wants to get home, or to move onto a topic of conversation that interests her, she's likely to utter a simple, "No." But the conversation rarely ends there. A forty-five-year-old woman isn't supposed to give a negative answer to that question unless she's prepared to follow it with a long discourse on her efforts at in vitro fertilization or the lack of motility in her husband's sperm. Childlessness is still socially suspect unless you have a pregnancy penned on your calendar for the following year, or are desperately seeking little Susan with the help of a fertility specialist. No matter the attitude she adopts, Ilene knows she will receive one of five stock responses, all of which she can recite by heart:

"Oh, it's different when they're your own."

"Oh, I'm so sorry. What's the problem?

"Aren't you lonely?"

"I know a wonderful doctor."

"Don't you worry you'll grow old and have no one to take care of you?

Annette Annechild, a Washington, D.C., psychotherapist without children, has heard a wider litany. "I've had women say to me, 'Don't you feel like your life isn't going to be complete without a child?' And couples who don't have children are constantly being asked, How come no babies, how come no babies?' As if they've failed if they don't produce a child."

When Amy Goldwasser, a twentysomething magazine editor in New York, expresses ambivalence about having kids, no one hesitates to set her straight. Progeny, after all, is destiny. "They try to sell me on children, like you'd try to sell someone on getting a dog," she says. "Or they dismiss me entirely by telling me I'll come around. It's so sexist. We still live in a world where the burden of caring for children falls on the woman, yet there's this assumption that women will become mothers. I'm sick of being the bad guy for not being 100 percent sure I'll have kids."

In December 1996, Ann Landers stepped right into the middle of this anger when she answered a writer who'd signed a letter "Childless and Happy in Pa." by suggesting that the woman might well change her mind. "I am 41-years-old, have been married for 17 years and am childless by choice," a reader from New England responded. "I knew when I was 16 that I did not want to have children. I have changed my mind about many things but not about that. Ann, you would not believe the insulting remarks people have made to me. I have been accused of being 'selfish,' 'lazy,' and a lesbian. . . . People who don't want children shouldn't have them, and nobody has the right to make them feel guilty. Not even you."

Compulsory motherhood, that's what Ilene calls the relentless social pressure to reproduce. Sure, most parents aren't aware of what they're doing. They just assume that having kids is "natural." But that's the crux of the dissension. If having children is natural, what does that make those of us who don't have kids, or don't want them? Unnatural? The myth that the reproductive instinct is woven into every strand of the DNA of every women on the planet provokes the same reaction in those who lack it as any another assumption of majoritarian normalcy.

And a myth it is. Genetic need? Dr. Richard Rabkin, a New York psychiatrist, put it succinctly: "Women don't need to be mothers any more than they need spaghetti. But if you're in a world where everyone is eating spaghetti, thinking they need it and want it, you will think so too. Romance has really contaminated science." Asked about maternal instinct, sociologist Jessie Bernard was equally pithy. "Biological destiny? Forget biology! If it were biology, people would die from not doing it."

The voluntarily childless aren't keeling over from violation of the sanctity of their biological imprint. Rather, they are revving up for a fight. Before "for the children" drove them to rage, all the childless-by-choice wanted was to be left alone—and that was relatively easy in the good old days when parents were content to keep their procreation and childrearing to themselves. Baby boomers, however, never do anything privately, or discreetly. Their private functions—be they sexual, soporific, or reproductive—have always become public. As they wrap their pleas for privilege in the mantle of parenting, they are provoking a new wave of identity politics.

What do the childless want? Well, to start, they want respect, the same respect that African-Americans and women, the physically challenged, the mentally handicapped, fat folks, native Americans, and gays have been demanding in the face of nasty stereotyping and overt discrimination of varying degrees. And they are waging their fight for respect on the same turf that has been the battleground for every other minority group in American history. Like sixties feminists who rejected titles like Miss and Mrs., they want a new label. "I'm not childless, I'm childfree," says Ilene. "Child*less* implies something is missing that should be present. I am currently companion*less*—I'd like a man/husband in my life and feel that absence. I was dog*less* until I bought a property where I could have dogs. I am cat*free* as they are not missing. And I am also childfree."

Following the lead of every other minority group, they want popular culture to reflect both their existence and their diversity. No more snide comments about DINKS—dual-income, no kids—with its implication that nonparents fritter away their cash on baubles or fancy trips while parents selflessly scrape together every nickel to buy Christmas presents for their five-year-olds. No more Alex Forrest, the childless, bunny-killing psychopath in *Fatal Attraction*. No more television programs where the only childless person over the age of thirty is some pathetic modern version of the fifties television sit-com *Our Miss Brooks*. "We need to get rid of the image that it's only okay to be childless if you're miserable about it, but that you're a monster if you are childless and happy about it," says Ilene.

But the list of grievances against parents and the blindness of a society caught in the glare of children has moved well beyond such passing respect. Family-friendly America has erected a stone wall of parental protection and inconsideration that leaves the childless isolated and embattled on the other side. And they want it to stop. All the tax cuts that force them to subsidize parenting. All the workplace benefits that make a mockery of the principle of equal pay for equal work. All the laws and regulations that sound like such "caring" support for mothers and fathers that convert them into second-class citizens.

The list mushrooms weekly, but try this small sampling: In recent years, California, Florida, Utah, and Oregon have passed laws increasing the penalties for spousal abuse if witnessed by a child. "I see," said one

Oregonian shortly after her state passed that law in June 1998. "If my husband beats the crap out of me, it's not that big a deal, just a misdemeanor. But if I have a kid who might be traumatized, then it becomes a serious crime, a felony, that will put him away for five years. Certainly tells me how much *my* well-being counts."

In towns and cities across the nation, mothers and fathers, worked up by the blare of media coverage about pedophiles using the Internet as a tool of seduction, are pressuring libraries and town boards to pull the plug on all connection to the World Wide Web. "Wait a minute, wait a minute, I lose *my* access to the Internet because parents can't control their own kids?" one childless woman screamed. "All this protecting the children nonsense is going too far."

In March 1998, Liz Langley, who pens a column called *Juice* for the *Orlando Weekly* in Florida, vented her spleen against a broad range of new "isn't pregnancy precious" benefits that she found intolerable, from special parking spaces for the almost-due to open discrimination against the nonpregnant in jury duty. " 'Nah,' was not on the list of optional excuses," she wrote of her experience trying to avoid that civic responsibility. But 'expectant mother' was. Why? How is it that sitting in a room for eight hours is something these berfrau's shouldn't suffer?"

For Lori Copeland, a thirty-four-year-old paralegal, of Hampton, Virginia, the most grating and degrading moment came when she and her husband Lane began shopping for a tiny corner of private space within America's parent-centric village, a simple house they could fix up to be their home. They would have preferred to live in an adult-only community since they value quiet. But, under federal law, only adults over the age of fifty-five have the right to live in such developments. Lori and Lane thought that at least they might move to a neighborhood far enough from a school that it would not be a magnet for kids. But when they asked the realtor to recommend such a community, the realtor balked. "I can't help you there," she said firmly. "That would be steering, and steering is illegal." Lori didn't believe her. Then she checked the law and discovered that realtors are legally barred from helping buyers "discriminate" in housing. Under the federal housing code, creating a neighborhood barring nonparents is entirely legal. Creating a "childfree" one, however, is as illegal as establishing an all-white enclave.

Like many of the thirtysomething women who chose not to reproduce, Lori points to such policies as examples of the treatment of "the last minority," the minority that can still be legally discriminated against in everything from work assignments to housing and federal tax policy. "I'm fed up with the cult of parenthood," she says. "And I'm fighting every step of the way." Lori has fought TWA over the widespread airline policy of selling seats at reduced rates to children accompanying their parents. "They take up the same seat an adult does, so why does the child's ticket cost less," she asks. "Isn't charging me more for that same seat age discrimination?" And, like scores of childless women and men, she has fought with restaurants and cruise lines, resorts and public parks for "adults-only" space.

Few issues send the childless into longer or more ear-splitting tirades than the lack of such "adult-only" spaces in which they might shop, dine, or swim without being drowned out by wailing infants or rammed into by rambunctious toddlers. But the trend is flowing in the opposite direction, toward opening up every corner of the nation—the most upscale restaurants, the most serious playhouses—to parents with kids in tow. In Ilene Bilenky's hometown in Massachusetts, for example, a restaurant just off the village green set aside one room as "No Kids." Although other rooms in the restaurant welcomed children, parents complained, and the owners bowed to their sentiments.

Oddly, in a country that cherishes the privacy clause of the U.S. Constitution and keeps abortion legal, the hardest-fought struggle of childless women has been the most intimate one, the struggle with gynecologists over the right to control their own bodies. Until 1969, the American College of Obstetricians and Gynecologists actually published a formula, based on how many children a woman had and her age, to determine who was "eligible" for voluntary sterilization. A twenty-five-year-old, for example, was ineligible unless she had already given birth to at least five kids, but a forty-year-old could get away with having only three. Even today, with such guidelines consigned to the dustbin by feminism, gynecologists still routinely refuse requests for sterilizations, insisting that they are "protecting" women from future regret.

Ilene Bilenky was lucky. Her gynecologist didn't balk at tying her tubes—but not out of respect. "He assumed I was a lesbian," she said, still laughing at the encounter. "Later, I thought, if I were a lesbian, why would I need my tubes tied?" Ilene's former fiancé, however, a Marine Corps officer, was required to undergo counseling before doctors at a military hospital would perform a vasectomy. "That's so rich," Ilene says. "They require counseling for people who don't want to have kids and let just anyone become a parent."

For Joe Hoenigman, a financial and tax advisor in Carlsbad, California, nothing rankles more than what he calls the "discriminatory child-rearing subsidy." He and his wife, who works for a nonprofit organization, dealt with the social isolation of childlessness by joining the San Diego chapter of the Child Free Network, which is largely a social group. But Joe hasn't found any such easy solution to the problem of federal tax policy toward those without children—although he has tried, with letters to congressmen, discussions with friends, and op-ed pieces in the newspaper. Politicians "think that people with kids are more deserving than those without children," he wrote in the *San Diego Union-Tribune* just after the five-hundred-dollars-per-child tax credits were enacted. "They also think it is the easiest way to sell the voters on the idea that they, as a group, are more caring than their political opposition. What the proponents of this type of child-oriented subsidy forget is that most households do not include children.

"Cutting taxes for people who have children at home and placing the tax burden squarely on the backs of taxpayers who do not have children is financial discrimination. . . . [T]he child-rearing subsidy will cost one group of taxpayers billions of dollars every year for the enrichment of people with no claim to the money other than the propensity to procreate. In effect it is the moral equivalent of a law which would fine people every year because they did not have children and use fewer government services. Yet, it originates from the same people who want to curtail Aid to Families with Dependent Children (AFDC) payments for children born to women already on welfare."

If the tax issues infuriate Joe, who is straight and married, they send childless gay men and lesbians into a rage. "First, they tell us that we shouldn't have kids," says Tom Butenhoff, who owns a gift and frame shop in Margaretville, New York. "Then they prevent us from adopting. Finally, they turn around and sock us with a tax penalty because we don't have children. I don't believe in spending my life pining about things I can't do anything about. But, tell me, how can anyone defend this as nondiscriminatory?"

For the most part, the battles waged by nonparents have been private affairs, individual forays against a society that considers their complaints vaguely loopy, if not shockingly self-centered. If the childless by choice have one thing in common, it is an almost pathological independence. Few would ever dream of banding together to declare themselves a dreaded "interest group." So they have not launched a formal organization, like NON—the National Organization of Nonparents—which attracted hundreds of members, mostly young, well-educated women, in the mid-1970s. Instead, they have been like a band of anarchist guerrillas, unorganized and unfocused, sowing controversy and chaos wherever they live and work.

Fed up with the cushy treatment awarded to mothers and denied to her, when Sarah, a childless travel agent in Seattle (routinely voted the Best City to Raise Children), changed jobs, she gave herself a daughter. With the photograph of her child prominently displayed on her desk—it was actually a picture of her young cousin—she takes a long lunch to take her kid to the doctor or skips out early to deal with childcare emergencies. Few are so bold. But where once they volunteered to work Saturdays to help out colleagues with children, childless men and women are refusing because parents no longer consider their help a favor, but a right. Faced with losing their Internet access, or higher property taxes without open accountability from the parents who control local school and library boards, they are showing up at public meetings to vent their anger.

Those raids on family-friendly America provide a certain satisfaction, but the result is almost universally demoralizing. Mark Dawson, a childless design anthropologist in Boston, suggested that the manager of his local supermarket post "adults-only" hours, say from six to nine o'clock certain nights of the week, to allow grownups to push their carts through the aisles without having to maneuver around a bunch of six-year-olds playing hide-and-seek behind the cereal. "Next thing I knew, they give me a horrified look," he says, "make the sign of the cross in the air, and I have to shop someplace else."

Gradually, however, random acts of disruption are merging into a cohesive force. When the National Transportation Safety Board issued a new Federal Motor Vehicle Safety Standard that required automobile manufacturers to install a new type of kiddie car seat restraint system on all new cars, a group of childless men and women organized a petition campaign to protest the price increase they would be forced to bear because parents are too lazy or irresponsible to snap their kids in properly where they belong. Congressional action limiting the Earned Income Tax Credit of childless adults earning as little as $9,000 a year to $332—while those with a single child could claim up to $2,210—and reducing the food stamp eligibility of those same poverty-stricken grownups just because they have no children provoked letter-writing and calling campaigns to member of Congress. Lawsuits are being researched, grievances filed, and alliances formed—with the elderly, with gay rights activists, and with older parents disgusted at the greediness of the younger generation.

With the adoption of every new parental entitlement—bought, like the entitlements extended to men or to whites in earlier eras, at the expense of someone else—those cries increase in volume and stridency. The childless are overcoming their fear of being branded as "child-haters," and are honing the rhetoric of both feminism and the antientitlement movement into pointed questions about whether the benefits and tax breaks granted to parents really are, in the end, "for the children."

A sleeping giant has begun to stir.

Ilene Bilenky should have anticipated the stares from her fellow employees, the cold shoulders and the backroom whispers that greeted her that rainy May evening when she opened the heavy metal doors that confined her patients to the locked psych ward of the hospital in suburban Boston where she works as a night nurse. A letter she'd fired off to *The Boston Globe* as part of her erratic crusade to give voice to the frustrations of the childless had appeared in the newspaper that morning. It was not the heartwrenching plaint of a woman haunted by infertility, but a *cri de coeur* against a world indifferent to the interests, the very existence, of the other childless women, the millions of women who are childless by choice.

"I am so utterly tired of the *Globe*'s constant pandering to its assumed audience of married people with kids," she wrote, responding to an article urging companies to give employees with children more flexibility in their work hours, vacation schedules, and job assignments. "Who do the authors think will pick up the undesirable travel/hours assignments left by those favored in 'family friendly' policies? The authors try rather weakly to claim that happy family employees will be more productive. Maybe. Maybe not. Those of us burdened by the 'flexing' to people who choose to be in families may not see it that way."

Driving to work that night, Ilene was too distracted by the truckers who turn I-95 around Boston into their personal drag strip to give much thought to how her coworkers on the psych ward might react to this attack on parental perks. She was bracing herself for the wrenching tedium of the night shift, for the groans of the demented and the ravings of the confused—not a lesson in political correctness. Ilene had barely begun to check her charge sheets, however, when she sensed an unmistakable chill in the air. As the night wore on, it turned into permafrost. No one spoke to her. She was excluded from the idle chatter by the coffeepot. Her coworkers kept her at a distance normally reserved for the incontinent. Finally, a colleague took pity on Ilene and gently explained the ostracism: Someone had posted her letter on a bulletin board by the cubbyholes used for interoffice mail.

Ilene peered out at her coworkers, knowing precisely what they were thinking. At the age of forty-five, she'd heard it often enough. "She doesn't respect the fact that people have kids," one coworker complained when Ilene refused to change her schedule so that a mother could spend a month of Saturdays with her children. "Insensitive," another branded her when she groused about the extra hours she worked because of a hospital policy requiring supervisors to consider "family obligation" when assigning forced overtime. "Self-absorbed and shortsighted," a third spat when she criticized tax credits for children.

Selfish, that's what Ilene Bilenky was in the eyes of her coworkers. A woman so wrapped up in her own petty concerns that she could find no room in her life for a child. Even worse, a woman who dared insist that those concerns might be as important as those of parents. "Selfish," says Ilene, a huff embedded in her voice. "They decide to have children because they want someone to take care of them in their old age, or because they want to prove to themselves that they can do a better job than their parents, or they want to pass on the family name, or whatever—all of which are entirely selfish reasons. Then they turn around and accuse me of being selfish because I don't want to take responsibility for the selfish choice they made—and, these days, at least, having a kid is a choice. Well, I consider having children to be a very expensive private hobby. I'm not asking anyone to pay for my hobbies and I certainly don't think I should be expected to pay for anyone else's."

Ilene's characterization of parents may seem over the edge, but so is the response to her complaints. Confronted with the accusation that they are paying less and receiving more, parents may balk, insisting that it just isn't so. But, as we've seen, the figures tell a different story. Remember that Clinton's proposed tax credit for stay-at-home moms, for example, will cost taxpayers $1.3 billion over the next five years, shifting the tax burden from parents of young children onto the rest of us. The child tax credits of 1997, which covered all kids under the age of sixteen, is depriving the treasury of $100 billion over five years that parents won't pay the government. Someone else will make up for that loss. Remember, every time a federal or state program reduces the taxes of one group, or offers it free or subsidized services, someone else winds up paying more.

For beleaguered, stressed-out parents, these benefits are a lifeline to sanity, so confronted with numbers they cannot dispute, they move from denial to a plea for understanding. "How else can we take care of our children and cope with our competing demands?" they ask plaintively, forgetting that for years, American families managed that feat with neither public nor corporate assistance. In 1930, after a decade of smaller families and the looser social mores of the Flapper Era, more than one-quarter of working women—more than three million women—were married, almost all of them with children. In 1940, one-third of working women were managing the double day—and that was before vacuum cleaners, disposable diapers, and take-out food. By 1960, the vaunted age of the two-parent family, when Harriet baked cookies and Ozzie brought home the bacon, more than half of the nation's working women were juggling home, kids, and paid employment. And if you look at the life history of African-American women, the notion that you can't do it all without help becomes a cruel conceit.

Forced to concede statistics and the weight of history, some supporters of parental privilege fall into name-calling—selfish, short-sighted, mean, and ridiculous are a few hurled about with abandon. "We're the majority, and why should the majority bend to the minority?" one mother asked me, never considering how much she sounded like a heterosexual bigot talking to a lesbian, or a Christian countering a Jew who wanted the Nativity scene pulled from City Hall. "No one forced you to remain childless."

In response to piece I wrote about the childless for *Mirabella,* a British magazine editor spat out a classic rejoinder. "I think that the childless women who say that they are unhappy about working mothers are the ones that really want children themselves—they're bitter," wrote Marcelle D'Argy Smith, editor of *Woman's Journal.*

Most parents maintain some semblance of civility in the face of challenges to their perks. But, in the end, they fall back on the script they learned in Moral Oneupsmanship 101. They defend their advantaged turf on four grounds: Conservatives wave the flag of the traditional family as the backbone of a stable society, while liberals stand firm as defenders of women's right to have it all. And parents of all political persuasions trumpet, alternately, the intrinsic morality of safeguarding children, who can't lobby for themselves, and the importance of nurturing the next generation of scientists and philosophers, political leaders and artists. That's when the fur starts flying. Listen to some of the back-and-forth:

What do tax credits for affluent parents have to do with shoring up the "traditional family," whatever that means? "Somehow the family managed to thrive and mankind to reproduce itself for centuries without federal tax credits," says Ann Coulter, the author of the bestseller about the impeachment of Clinton, *High Crimes and Misdemeanors.* At thirty-five, Ann is childless, but insists she plans to remedy that situation. "Oh, but what parents do benefits all of society," mothers and fathers argue, trying to bolster their case for special help. "Really?" asks Ilene. "What if a couple chooses to have fifteen kids? Does that benefit society? What about couples insisting that insurance companies pay thousands of dollars for in vitro fertilization treatments? Is that about the public good?"

"But what about the children?" parents ask. "Which children?" Ilene responds. "All the children." parents press on. "Do all children really need help, or are you using 'for the children' as a cover for what you, as a parent would like?" she counters.

Ilene, for one—although she is typical in this regard—is openly contemptuous of any such argument that isn't limited to children, and parents, with real economic need. "The notion that if we don't help middle-class parents their children will turn into ax-murderers is extortion," she says. "If one of their kids takes an ax and slaughters his classmates, I'm not accepting any responsibility. That's on their parents."

Finally, the polemical debate reaches the parental trump card: But children are our future. "I know mothers work very hard indeed and yes, it is unfair, but you have to cover for them sometimes," wrote D'Argy Smith, the British magazine editor. "They're continuing the human race, for God's sake, so you have to do it."

As Ilene has said: "Sure, all those folks became parents because they were sitting around one night, worrying about the future of the nation and decided, 'we better go upstairs and do something about it.'"

The issue, finally, becomes a problem in logic. Or at least in village dynamics, since the assumption that everyone should bear at least some of the costs of raising the next generation—whether through tax credits, spending, special employee benefits, or reduced work schedules—springs from the belief that it takes a village. Now it's odd that Republicans are supporting these kinds of proposals since they cheered Bob Dole longest and loudest at the 1996 Republican convention when he mocked Hillary by insisting that "it takes a family, not a village." But, on this one, as on so many others, the Republicans are not consistent with their own verbiage.

The notion seems to be that when individual villagers undertake projects that benefit the entire community, all the members of the village should support their efforts. Raising children, of course, is seen as the most preeminent of all possible projects. By that logic, it is my communal responsibility, as a childless woman, to relieve parents of some of the burden of raising kids, no matter how wealthy they are. I should feel proud to be paying to educate their children, from birth through university, no matter how able they are to pay for it themselves, no matter how scholarly inept their children may be. I should know that I'm doing the right thing by subsidizing their lunches, providing them with parks and other safe places to play, funding research into how to educate them effectively, and underwriting antismoking campaigns to scare them away from tobacco.

At work, I should understand that the pot of money available to fund employee benefits cannot be divided up equally, or according to merit or seniority, because they need a larger share to pay for childcare, summer camp, and health insurance—no matter how fat their own paychecks. And I should never complain if I have to work weekend shifts, since no one could possibly have anything more important to do on a weekend than to spend time with the children. And I'm not supposed to feel ripped off when my boss asks me to take over as, say, the city editor of the newspaper for six months while the regular editor is on maternity leave and then I'm shoved back into reporting when she comes back to claim her job, because I need to be supportive of women.

And I am supposed to do and feel all of these things because the lifestyle choice of parents—which is what having kids is—happens to make a valuable contribution to society.

We generally do not presume to reward and punish private decisions based on their impact on the communal good, or at least history teaches us about the dangers of doing so. But let's say that we decide to make an exception in the case of parents because their work seems so uniquely important. What do we do if their lifestyle choice of having kids does *not* make a valuable contribution to society? Having ten children, for example, can be a detriment to society. By the logic of the village, overactive parents should not only have their rewards withdrawn, but should be penalized, right? Or, by that same logic, lousy parents who turn out delinquents instead of good citizens should be barred from continued reproduction, or at least fined heavily for their negative impact on the community.

Since parents' critical reproductive and parenting functions are what the village is rewarding, perhaps we should consider guaranteeing that they carry both out in a socially responsible way, say, by requiring pregnant women to eat well and walk regularly, or new mothers to spend all their time making their infants feel loved. Furthermore, since part of the social contract implicit in It Takes a Village is that society needs to support individual projects that are socially valuable, we might also consider rewarding the childless for their *failure* to reproduce, since, if everyone has a passel of kids, the village will become overcrowded, which will jeopardize our collective quality of life. The schools would become over-crowded, the playgrounds chaotic, and the food supply short. So, given the good the nonreproducers are creating, should the community not support them in some concrete way, just as it supports parents?

Moreover, since we've decided that what parents do is so valuable that we need to increase our social support of them, which means reprioritiz-ing, to whom should we give less social support? Should we cut back on medical care for the elderly, who have already made their valuable contri-bution to society? Should we stop spending money on ramps for wheel-chair-bound adults? If we haven't reached full employment, should we provide parents with preferential hiring, even if it means firing them once their kids are out of the house?

And what would these priorities say about us as a society? If, as Bill Clinton suggests, we need to protect parents from discrimination at work but feel no responsibility to confer that same protection on nonparents, are we giving employers license to exploit those without kids? If we offer housing subsidies, for example, only to people with children, then we are saying that it's not so bad if our citizens sleep in the streets as long as they don't have anyone under age thirteen with them.

What kind of village would that be?

Today's childless know precisely what kind of village that is, because they live in it. Asked what place nonparents have in the American village and what the village owes them in return for supporting those who have children, Michelle Gaboury, who is raising two children in Acton, Massa-chusetts, is utterly candid, speaking for millions of parents. "You get in re-turn that you don't have children."

Little wonder, then, that the childless feel demeaned and discarded. "What drives me and other childless people crazy is that everyone acts as if this is as it should be because what parents are doing is better, more im-portant," says Ilene Bilenky. "They act as if parenting were holy, a sacred calling that elevates them in terms of entitlements above the rest of us mere mortals.

"That doesn't work. As a society, we have to recognize and respect the needs of everyone."

7

When the Bough Breaks

After living through the race wars, the gender wars, the sexual orientation wars, and the smoking wars, I dread the prospect of enduring the parenting wars. I can already imagine nonparents declaring nationwide strikes against flex-time, family leave, on-site daycare centers and corporate summer camps, walking picket lines with signs emblazoned in oversized letters, "Equal Pay for Equal Work." Or the Internal Revenue Service, which never thinks to ask parents for proof that they really have all those kids who provide the ticket to tax relief, thrown into chaos by militant nonparents declaring six dependent children, as a scam or political protest—whichever works its magic.

The battle will be joined over the demand for "adults-only" seating on airplanes and at restaurants because research indicates that children spread more disease, or more noise, or whatever other argument those just looking for a little peace and quiet decide to proffer. And nonparents will stand their linguistic ground, waving their hands in the air to proclaim, "Don't call me childless, what makes you think that I'm less," and demanding to be called "childfree" instead.

Separatists will stream out of the closet arguing that the provisions of the Fair Housing Act that force them to live among children until they turn fifty-five constitute age discrimination. And to every retort about the contribution parents make to the future of society, they will offer up a proud list of their predecessors—Frederick Douglass, Mozart, Michelangelo, Nobel Peace Prize winners such as Jane Addams, Albert Schweitzer, or Mother Teresa—whose work has enriched all humanity.

Nonmothers and nonfathers will begin sporting buttons and pins, STOP BREEDING PRIVILEGE and NO KIDDING. If we're lucky, they won't declare Mother's Day to be Childfree Pride Day and tread down Pennsylvania Avenue by the thousands chanting "two, four, six, eight, we don't have to procreate," following the path of the Bonus Boys, antiwar protesters, gay activists, and every other group of Americans that has felt a need to make that symbolic journey to demand redress from the government.

The newly empowered childfrees will sow havoc at school board meetings, over both bloated budgets and curricula that don't teach nonreproduction as an "alternative lifestyle." They'll tie "family-friendly" corporations into legal knots with lawsuits alleging that the equal protection clause of the Constitution must be applied to nonreproducers. America will be Balkanized, yet further, into new warring factions enervated by mutual recriminations and competing moral superiorities.

Don't think that I'm kidding, or mocking those who've wound down that long road in their quest for redress of grievances and respect. Who, in 1975, would have imagined bands of gay men and lesbians racing through suburban malls screaming, "We're here, we're queer, and we're not shopping," or one million gay men and lesbians marching under a rainbow banner in Washington, D.C.? Who, two decades earlier, would have anticipated women burning their bras on the boardwalk in Atlantic City during the Miss America Pageant?

Portents of a strikingly similar rebellion are sparking up all across the land. Remember the workplace flareups, the scuffles over breastfeeding, the emergence of a "nonparenting gap" in voting, delineated elsewhere? They're the tip of that venerable iceberg everyone likes to invoke. Although most hesitate to discuss it, labor union activists admit that their childless members routinely block attempts by national officials to incorporate childcare and other "parent-friendly" clauses in their contracts, demanding that union clout be used to win "something for everyone" rather than benefits that favor the minority. For example, Ridgeview, Inc., a sock manufacturer headquartered in North Carolina, maintains a first-rate daycare center at its nonunionized plant in Newton, North Carolina, by management design. But no such facility exists at their unionized factory in upstate New York, because workers didn't bargain it into their contract.

Skirmishes between parents and nonparents over school property taxes and school bond issues are turning ugly—although retirees usually take the fall in their defeat. But when voters in Milton, Massachusetts, rejected a $1.2 million tax increase to pay for new teachers, teacher aides, and school buses in 1998, even *The Boston Globe* couldn't ignore what had happened, an almost silent coalition of opposition between "elderly residents on fixed incomes" and "childless households."

Attorneys specializing in housing discrimination are researching lawsuits on behalf of young childless couples who want the same rights as senior citizens to live in "child-free" communities. And gay lawyers who once thought their clients' inferior work assignments and miserly benefits' packages were the result of discrimination on the basis of sexual orientation are discovering that their status as nonparents is frequently the underlying problem. At the moment, they have little legal recourse because it is perfectly legal to discriminate against the childless in housing, or in workplace benefits, because civil rights laws offer nonparents no explicit protections. But as parents turn to the courts to demand even more rights, turnabout is inevitable.

Log on any night to one of the Internet chat groups where the childless share their fury, and you will hear the first stirrings of rebellion—laced with the same bitterly biting humor minorities always direct toward the privileged. Last February, one thread fantasized a new television network, Childfree TV, "Television for Grownups," with a broadcast lineup including *The Childfree Say the Darndest Things* and a game show called *Whack a Sprog*. And another thread took off after Pope John Paul II, a "senile, celibate old man in a dress," delivered a homily on the Day of Life in February 1999 urging couples not to deny themselves the "gift and joy of parenting" out of "selfishness and hedonism."

We can stop the war before it deteriorates even further into open name-calling, into a squabble over who is more selfish—parents who use up planetary resources by having children because they want to pass along their DNA, or the childless, who are too self-involved to contribute to the future of the nation. But first we have to keep our eyes focused on what we *can* do.

1. Let's identify who really needs social assistance and give it to them and stop pretending that we're designing programs to bolster "the family" or help poor starving children unless that's what we're doing. Now, I'm no fool. I recognize that asking politicians and lobbyists to 'fess up to their real agendas is like asking the president to tell us the unexpurgated truth about his sex life. But the rest of us don't have to play along. So let's sort the wheat from the chaff and admit which of these programs offers the remote possibility of cushioning the lives of the needy and which are backhanded attempts to counter the birth dearth in the white population, placate greedy yuppies, reinvigorate marriage, cut taxes, or make sure that professional women intent on having it all don't throw up their hands in despair and decide that the kitchen looks pretty good. After all, if our goal is to increase the birth rate—though I'm not sure why that *would* be a goal—the Family and Medical Leave Act is unlikely to fill up our maternity wards. And if we're trying to make sure that no child goes to bed hungry, or grows up without a book of his own or a bedroom without rats for roommates, we're not going to make much of a dent by giving six-digit-income suburbanites five-hundred-dollar tax credits for their kids.

2. Acknowledge that people without kids might feel put upon by the current parenting craze, and that the privileges and benefits we are extending to parents might be insidious violations of the principle of equal pay for equal work.

3. Abandon high-minded attempts to create a "family policy." I know, I know, but, "What about the family?" Let's be real: No two Americans can agree on what the family is for more than ten minutes. Religious conservatives have managed to concoct a definition that excludes half of what the rest of us think of as families. Such liberals as Pat Schroeder, paraphrasing Robert Frost's well-known line about "home" in *The Death of the Hired Man,* define "family" as "where you go at night and they have to let you in"—and then propose "family" policies that don't follow that "inclusive" definition.

The "profamily" movement—both the Schroeder wing and traditionalists convinced all of America's problems will disappear if we return to mom-dad-and-two-kid living units—have probably generated more entirely stupid proposals than any other modern political lobby. In its 1977 report, for example, the Carnegie Council on Children, which represented the former wing of the movement, declared that America needed a "family policy" that would be as comprehensive as our national defense policy in order to change the context in which children live. The linchpin of the program they designed was "full employment" for parents "so that no American child will suffer because a parent cannot find work or earn enough to provide a decent living" and so that kids will "enjoy the self-respect and stability that this brings to the family."

Sounds wonderful, right? It conjures up a warm and fuzzy vision of every single child in the nation watching his parents go off to work each morning and enjoying the fruits of that labor in food, education, shelter, and clothing. But let's play it out: Parents raising kids would be guaranteed jobs. But what happens when their kids grow up? Do those "retired" parents have to give up their jobs to make way for the up-and-coming parents in a society that has not achieved full employment? And since jobs for the childless would be limited not by their skill or experience, but by the number of parents needing work at any given moment, I imagine the august minds at the Carnegie Council believed we would wind up with a supremely peaceful and cooperative society. Yep, that certainly seems like the kind of fine idea we'd expect from such a prestigious group.

And then there's the crowd that's crazy about the family, per se. To take just one example, Paul Weyrich, the head of the Free Congress Foundation, a conservative think tank, has churned out dozens of proposals that would "save" the family by forcing all families to conform to his image. He would limit cash welfare benefits to intact families and offer "matching grants" to heads of intact families with full-time jobs whose incomes are insufficient to support their dependents. So, if a woman's husband runs off to Siberia with a hot mama, she and her kid get squat, because the family is not "intact." That's brilliant, punish the kids because the father is a jerk.

The best Weyrich brainstorm is restoration of the "family wage," which would permit employers to do just what the U.S. military has traditionally done, adjust pay according to the number of dependents a worker has at home. That certainly would do wonders for productivity! Imagine how morale would soar if the lazy moron in the corner took home a paycheck twice as hefty as that of her coworkers because she'd had the perspicacity to pop out eight children.

The search for family policy is about as productive as searching for butterflies in the Arctic. It's time to give up. Call a truce. Can the rhetoric. Let's ban the use of the word "family" for five years and force everyone to be precise about what they mean when they say they want to help children. Then maybe we can actually accomplish something. Or at least we can if we decide precisely what we are trying to achieve with these transfers of time and money from the childless to parents.

4. We need to open up a national conversation about what claim middle-class and upper-middle-class parents have on the childless. Should we single parents out for preferential treatment just because they have chosen to bring children into the world? Should we extract extra work and tax dollars from nonparents without so much as a "by your leave" in order to hold parents harmless from their decision to procreate? Is the contribution parents make to society so uniquely important that we should violate every conceivable principle of fairness and justice in order to reward them? Or is this very concept a kind of majoritarian tyranny by which we denigrate the decisions and lives of the minority?

I am well aware that posing these questions gets translated into some antichild or antifamily statement, which makes the search for an answer virtually impossible. These days not giving preferences to families with kids—even asking whether or not we should—is seen as hostility to the family, or lack of concern with the future of the next generation.

But, listen: I accept the proposition that discrimination can be justified in the face of a compelling social interest. We drafted men into our military, violating every tenet of freedom, because we believe in the concept of a citizen's army. We demand a portion of workers' paychecks, breaching the bulwark of private property, because we subscribe to the notion that we, as a collective, owe it to one another to share the costs of the roads we travel, the borders we defend, and the safety net we are committed to providing.

So, I'm prepared to entertain arguments about why there is a compelling need for us to transfer the wealth and energies of nonparents to those raising kids. But I still haven't heard them framed in any terms that justify giving the children of upper-middle-class parents tax credits and childcare deductions, leave from work to watch Susi dance *Swan Lake,* or flex-time to check on the nanny. And no childless person I know finds anything socially compelling about subsidizing the owners of three-hundred-thousand-dollar houses in the suburbs.

Nebulous appeals to fairness or other lofty principles won't be any more effective than middle-class desire in convincing us that our interests ought to take a back seat. On what principle do parents base their demands for privilege? Equity? Fairness? Need? Clearly they reject equality, since the point of equality is to abolish privilege. And equity is usually based on merit, which also wouldn't give parents much of a leg up. Fairness is a suckers' game since it is entirely in the eye of the beholder. So that leaves parents staking claim to extra perks on the basis of need—which turns everything into Queen for a Day, where everyone lines up to tell his or her sob story, and whoever generates the most ergs on the applause meter gets the ermine-lined cape or extra vacation. If that's how we play the game, the poor will walk off with the goodies—but affluent parents won't be able to keep intoning mushy phrases about "for the children" to grab onto their coattails.

Ultimately, none of these principles allows parents to skirt the one indisputable fact that pulls the rug out from under almost any moral argument they offer: Having children is a choice. Amitai Etzioni, the nation's foremost communitarian, put it succinctly: "Potential parents must consider what is important to them: more income or better relationships with their children. Most people cannot 'have it all'!" And the childless are decreasingly willing to subsidize their attempts to try.

So what do we do to stave off the parenting wars? Compromise. We have to face the fact that a growing number of Americans are eschewing parenting, and that they too might make valuable contributions to society, that they too have a right to a good life, the right to use their time and hard-earned money to pursue their own interests and pleasures, which is precisely what adults do when they choose to have children. Everyone has a claim on our collective resources, and we can't dole them out fairly if we write any group off or start playing the "who makes a more valuable contribution to society" game.

So we need to follow the lead of the most progressive companies in Corporate America, which have seen the handwriting on the wall and moved beyond *Working Mother* magazine's definition of family-friendliness to equitable treatment of all workers, parents and nonparents. "Companies we held up as models a few years ago because they were accommodating to working parents or offered child-care benefits, we're now saying they are not going far enough," says Marcia Brumit Kropf, a vice-president at Catalyst, a New York research group. "Their policies are pitting one set of employees against the other."

The least enlightened companies heed that call with linguistic quick fixes. They change the name of the work/family office to the work/life office, but do nothing to adjust the thrust of their programs. Others understand that they have to offer something to workers without kids, so they add a few insubstantial fringe benefits and pitch them as perks for nonparents. But the childless aren't so easily mollified, especially by benefits worth a fraction of what childcare or summer camps cost. Geri Recht, a consultant for Towers Perrin, a multinational management consulting company, suggests to clients that they might placate childless workers with concierge services to help them arrange vacations, or subsidies for home computers. Heinz USA, for example, subsidizes half of the cost of two massages per month. Whoopee!!! say the childless, who can't help but wonder how such concessions forge equality, since parents enjoy the massages and home computers as well as childcare and flex-time.

Keener human resources minds recognize that the childless aren't dogs who are easily satisfied with linguistic or cosmetic bones and that any fix that does not bridge the inequality is no fix at all. When Terri Ireton, manager of work and life programs at Blue Cross and Blue Shield of Massachusetts, began to hear rumblings of discontent from childless employees, she realized that her company rules gave mothers more control over their time, but treated the childless like slaves. "A lot of our benefits are around family issues," she concedes. "One of the things we heard strongly was that everyone wanted some flexibility in their lives." So Blue Cross revamped corporate flex-time arrangements to make sure mothers weren't the only ones being given control over their time. Telecommuting, compressed workweeks, job sharing, and part-time work are now open to all employees, regardless of parental status.

Monica Brunaccini, director of human resources for the Consolidated Group, a HealthPlan Services company in Framingham, Massachusetts, realized that she needed to reconceptualize the human resources approach forged by the work/family movement. "What really constitutes a family?" she asks. "In one area it may be a grandmother and grandfather raising their grandchild. In another it could be a single parent and her two kids. In another it could be two people who've lived together for several years—same sex or different sex. Staying in those typical definitions of single or married, childless or with children doesn't work anymore. We need to shift our paradigm and look at things more realistically."

At the nation's most sophisticated companies, that paradigm shift has been translated into flexible benefits plans that give workers a flat dollar amount of benefits, which they can allocate in accordance with their needs. Employees with kids might increase their life insurance coverage or add dependents to their health insurance plans. Nonparents might opt for dental and vision, or forgo life insurance in favor of a greater contribution to a 401(k) retirement savings account. The bottom line is that inequities disappear because everyone receives a total benefits package of the same value. No two companies structure their flexible benefits plans, often called cafeteria plans, along the same lines. At Consolidated Natural Gas in Pittsburgh, for example, the company's twenty-eight hundred workers can select from three levels of basic benefits. Those who select the lowest level of coverage are compensated with extra vacation days or cash in hand.

At Eastman Kodak, the model employer from the point of view of the childless, even-handedness is carried well beyond anything envisioned elsewhere in the country. "Our [values] say there's no room for exclusion of anybody, so you can't just [focus] on the mainstream population of those married with two children," says Mike Morley, senior vice-president of human resources. "You have to believe that diversity is a business imperative. Once you get those fundamentals in place, some of the activities important for your organization will become pretty obvious."

Those "activities" include not only a first-rate flexible benefits plan, but a leave-of-absence program that recognizes that nonparents also have commitments and concerns outside of the workplace. Kodak no longer offers maternity or paternity leave. Instead, employees may apply for "personal unique opportunity leave," which allows parents to spend time with their newborns, or take care of sick children, and childless employees to pursue their interests, whether they be volunteering, studying full-time, or traveling.

Corporate America's new work/life thrust is a blow for equality and the concept of equal pay for equal work. It probably won't satisfy the family-friendly crowd whose priorities still dominate politics and the media. But they are caught in an ideological time warp, demanding the very preferences, such as flex-time and childcare, that Corporate America has begun to discard as discriminatory, morale-busting, and not all that popular with working parents themselves.

The ultimate irony of all that family-friendliness in the workplace is that most parents show little enthusiasm for it. In 1998, Aon Consulting surveyed workers, asking them how important different kinds of benefits were to their commitment to their employers. Childcare, flex-time, and part-time work didn't even make it into the running. The AFL-CIO's poll of working women reflected similar apathy toward family-friendly initiatives. And Alice Campbell, the work-life director at Baxter International, a worldwide health-care products company, and consultant Marci Koblenz, discovered the same indifference in an eighteen-month survey of Baxter employees. Traditional programs designed to assuage work-life tensions didn't turn out to be very relevant. Fewer than 15 percent of Baxter's employees, for example, told them that more help with childcare would be of any use.

Cutting-edge companies have discovered that they were led down the garden path to nowhere by a small coterie of advocates of on-site childcare and family programs, by a drumbeat of magazine and newspaper articles that held such programs up as the cure for employee stress. Workers don't want paternalism that holds them hostage to a given corporation for daycare or medical care. They don't want companies to tell them what benefits they need, how to do their work, and when they have to do it. Whether they are parents or nonparents, they want flexibility that gives them the room to use the benefits money set aside for them as they choose, and to complete their work in their own way. They want "worker-friendly" programs, not "family-friendly" ones. Turning a deaf era to family advocates, Corporate America has begun to provide them.

*   *   *

Political America, attuned to electoral advantage rather than the bottom line, heeds different winds—usually those that howl loudest. So politicians craft "children's" policy in response not to public demand, but to the trumpeting alarmism of lobbying groups who claim to speak in the name of the children. Do the interests of the owners of for-profit daycare centers necessarily coincide with those of the nation's young? Do teachers demand salary increases because higher pay for teachers correlates with higher test scores? No one stops to consider these questions. Lobbyists, after all, are the key to money and votes.

Likewise, "family policy" isn't rooted in grassroots demand, but in ideological stirrings. After all, when American adults are queried by pollsters about their major concerns, crime, Social Security, and the state of the economy tend to top their priority list, not tax credits for stay-at-home moms or the expansion of the Family and Medical Leave Act. The political contest that has fueled family-friendliness doesn't leave much room for dissenting voices. After all, minority groups never have much success in the political arena—at least until they take to the streets. Yet the public policy solutions to turn "parent-friendly" programs into "citizen-friendly" ones are remarkably straightforward.

First, government *must* be concerned about children. Many childless people disagree, mounting libertarian arguments that would leave children captive to their parents' whims or fates. But while kids are the primary responsibility of their parents, someone has to make sure that those parents don't beat them, rape them, or leave them without supper. The only someone available is the government. Doing more, however—intervening to try to guarantee that all kids really receive equal opportunity, or the best possible life—is a fantasy unless we decide to collectivize child-rearing entirely to ensure equal conversation around the dinner table, equal concern for education, and equal willingness to sacrifice. Over and over again, we have tried to use child policy to abolish the inequities that exist among adults, and that is a fool's mission.

There's no way to help children without stepping on the toes of their parents, which just creates a new set of problems. For example, if the nation wants to give its poorest and most vulnerable children a decent shot at growing up healthy, safe, and educated, research suggests that there's one thing it should guarantee them: two good parents. Admitting that in liberal circles is a bit like crying, "The Jews killed Jesus," on the Lower East Side of Manhattan. But the Christian Right can't always be wrong. The single factor that correlates with every bad outcome a kid can achieve is being raised by a single mother.

In fact, it is the staggering increase in the proportion of kids living in single-parent, mostly single-mother, families—from 11 percent in 1970 to 25 percent in 1990—that is responsible for most of today's child poverty. Look at black America: The poverty rate for black kids raised in single-parent households has remained constant, at above 65 percent. The poverty rate for black kids in two-parent families declined from 26 percent in 1970 to 19 percent in 1988.

Where the Christian Right often gets it wrong is that grim reality isn't the result of the moral superiority of two-parent families. It's simple economics. Having two parents increases the likelihood of having two parents who are working. And even if they are working at cruddy jobs, they will have twice as much money for food and rent, clothing, health care, and transportation.

But there's no way government can wave its magic wand to give kids the kind of families they need. Conservatives think that we would reverse the tide of single-parent households by defining marriage as a contract broken only at legal peril, by making divorce more difficult to obtain, by requiring a waiting period for a marriage license or premarital counseling. But that's silly. The government can't legislate away divorce, out-of-wedlock children, or single parenthood any more than it can legislate away child abuse.

Nor will kids wind up in nurturing homes if we follow the liberal fantasy formula of a Swedish-type state with stipends for parents, universal childcare for mothers working outside the home, and paid parenting leaves. Does anyone really believe that such a system would miraculously save America's youth from poverty and drugs, indifference to homework, and the lure of sex? And how many Americans would be willing to send more than half of their paychecks to the government, as the Swedes do, to replace the salaries of high-priced lawyers, stockbrokers, or consultants who might decide to take off a couple of years to stay home with their kids?

Using the tax system to socially engineer kids into meaningful equality won't work. Using the tax system to socially engineer anything has never worked, and we are unlikely to thwart decades of American history by trying to reinvent that wheel. The problem with social engineering in a pluralistic society is that there will always be conflict over what kind of boat we want to build. Long ago we reached social consensus about engineering feats that bolster the needy, that ensure that no one goes hungry, sleeps outside in the snow, or begins work at the age of eight without learning to read. But, beyond that, every time we try bending the tax system to social ends, we wind up causing more conflict than we resolve.

Take childcare as an example. The federal government allows working parents to deduct a portion of what they spend on baby-sitters and daycare centers from their income tax bill. What happens? Conservatives rant and rave that we are rewarding women for working, which they interpret as penalizing women who stay home with the children. Rather than admit that he is zooming down a slippery road, Bill Clinton responds by offering stay-at-home moms special tax breaks. That, of course, does nothing for parents who deal with childcare by working split shifts, or leaving their children with grandparents or other relatives. What should we do about them? Offer them tax breaks to avoid the inevitable charge of discrimination?

Where does it end? If we're going to give parents tax deductions to compensate them for their childcare expenses, should we not give similar deductions to taxpayers who spend money on other sorts of essential domestic work? Once we subsidize the first group of parents for their use of childcare, rather than for economic need, we start sliding into absurdity.

So, forget childcare deductions. Get rid of them entirely, or at least cap them by need. They are patently unfair to those of us without children, as well as to those who raise their children themselves. If we left them intact for families earning under thirty thousand dollars—which is about the median family income—and then reduced the value of the credit by 1 percent for every fifteen hundred dollars earned above that level, phasing it out entirely at fifty thousand dollars, we would generate an added $8 billion in tax revenue over the next five years. We could then channel those funds into direct subsidies for childcare for parents who really can't afford not to work. That way we subsidize *need* rather than random parenting.

What about those child tax credits recently enacted? They are insulting, suggesting that supporting a dependent adult is less important than supporting a dependent child. Raising the deduction for all dependents would at least have maintained the pretense that we care as much about grownups as about kids. Furthermore, child tax credits can't possibly solve the problem they are allegedly designed to address, which boils down to time, not money. The political oratory behind those tax credits offered them up as a way to reverse the trend of disinvestment in America's children. The oratory wasn't entirely empty: Less is being invested in today's children than in their parents. But the investors who have withdrawn their capital don't come from the government, which has increased spending on children in every possible category, from health to education. It is parents. Mothers and fathers both work outside the home, dads disappear from the family entirely, and couples break up with increasing frequency. Adults, then, are putting their interests before the interests of their kids. Tax credits for children won't change those realities.

The parental rights crowd argues that parents will use that extra five hundred dollars per child to save for their children's college tuition or buy them health insurance—although most of those who benefit from this largesse already have health insurance and enough money to pay the bill at a state university. Anyway, if the goal is to give parents money to spend on their kids, why don't we require them to use that money that way? After all, it's not *their* money. It's mine. It's only theirs if we all receive the same tax break. And if I'm going to fund it, should I not have some say over how it is used?

Or they expect us to believe that parents are going to use the five-hundred-dollar-per-child credit to "buy" more time with their kids, which is hard to swallow, since parents don't seem to be taking advantage of flextime, job sharing, or part-time work for that purpose. When Arlie Hochschild, professor of sociology at the University of California, interviewed employees at an unnamed Fortune 500 company for *The Time Bind: When Work Becomes Home and Home Becomes Work,* she discovered that despite employee complaints about the stress and strain of competing demands, few on any level—professional, managerial, or labor—took advantage of "family-friendly" policies designed to give them more time with their kids. Among eligible workers with children under the age of thirteen, only 3 percent worked part-time and less than 1 percent shared a job. Although one-third of parents had flexible hours, 56 percent of them regularly worked weekends and 72 percent regularly worked overtime.

Asked to explain why he and his wife didn't use flex-time to read books with the kids, and why, instead, they both opted for ten to twenty hours a week in overtime, Mario Escalla, a factory worker, said candidly, "Fifty percent for need, 25 percent for greed, and 25 percent is getting away from the house." Company professionals were even worse, routinely working until 7:00 or 8:00 P.M. rather than leaving at 5:00 P.M. to be with the kids, who were home with the nanny. And they weren't sticking to the office for fear that the boss would brand them as slackers. Rather, they said, they felt more valued at work than at home, and their friends were at the office, not in their neighborhoods.

As a society, we cannot compensate for reduced parental investment in kids, just as we cannot shield children from the other decisions and realities of their mothers and fathers. Parental-rights advocates limn a portrait of moms and dads desperate for more time with their children, but foiled in that desire by greedy employers and a government that seizes so much of their wages that they have to take second jobs. That portrait might well be accurate for some segment of the population. But given research like Arlie Hochschild's, it is disingenuous, at best, to suggest that it is an accurate reflection of the state of American parenting.

No matter how alluring the notion of casting a safety net around all children or all parents, the current child-friendly federal and state efforts are mere pretenses in that direction, because it is clear that we can't accomplish that feat without throwing ourselves into chaos. Are we to offer the nation's children every possible protection and then, when they turn eighteen, throw them off the public dole like bums and let them discover what adult America really is like? Shore up parents with health insurance, housing, jobs, and stipends until their youngest child reaches the age of majority and then force them to fend for themselves? Offer tax breaks to well-to-do couples whose children already have a parental safety net? And tell childless adults that, no matter their circumstances, they deserve no assistance because they don't have kids? That's nonsense. We have a country with either a safety net for everyone or a safety net for no one.

So, what does this mean in practical terms? Children have to remain the primary responsibility of their parents. They alone decide to create kids. They alone, then, bear the burden of what Amitai Etzioni calls that "moral act" unless they fall into poverty or extreme need. Parents'-rights advocates might call that "parent-blaming," but today's children suffer from the empty-nest syndrome not because society has failed them, but because "parents have flown the coop," as Etzioni remarks. Do both parents really *need* to work full-time, he asks, or are they working for VCRs, matching shoes, and designer frames? Do they both have to climb the corporate ladder to success? "Careerism is not a law of nature," Etzioni says, and parents are choosing to put their public lives before their responsibilities to their kids.

The best we, as a society, can do is to make sure that no one—no child or adult—falls so low as to be homeless or hungry, ill without medical care, or without hope of a job. And the easiest way to accomplish that is to throw "parental" entitlements into the dustbin of bad ideas and, if we really care about children and families, use the money we save by ending subsidies to parents earning sixty thousand dollars a year or more to make sure that every kid in the nation has enough food, a decent education, and a safe place to live. Think about what we might accomplish for the poor with the $8 billion saved from childcare deductions and another $85 billion from child tax credits channeled into education in inner-city neighborhoods, job training, housing, or medical care.

Asking the childless to ante up their share of the money to help families and individuals on the bottom fifth of the earnings ladder, where almost 25 million families have a median annual income of a chilling $8,872 a year, or even the second fifth, where the median reaches only $22,098, is asking them to do their fair share to erase hunger and desperation from the face of the wealthiest nation on earth. Expecting the childless to relieve middle-class parents of the burdens they took on when they decided to conceive is financing someone else's politics of want, vaguely sugarcoated with the sweet suggestion of cooing infants.

If we play that game, the counter-demands will fly, and they are unlikely to be coated with anything but venom.

In January 1999, as I was writing this book, I paused one evening to listen to Bill Clinton deliver his sixth State of the Union address. As I forced myself to stay alert during an oratorical marathon worthy of Fidel Castro, a presidential plea for something I actually cared about deeply pierced my flagging consciousness: "And let's make sure women and men get equal pay for equal work by strengthening enforcement of equal-pay laws." My heart wanted to soar. It had been too long since I had heard that eloquently simple principle lofted from such a prestigious pulpit. But three sentences later, the president continued his litany by admonishing the nation about the importance of protecting parents from discrimination in the workplace. The contradiction was deafening, and I have wondered since, repeatedly, how it could have fallen on so many deaf ears, especially in a society that has become notably more adept at listening.

Over the past generation, most Americans have come to appreciate that you cannot give lip service to freedom of religion while treating Christian beliefs and traditions as the social norm, entrenched in everything from Nativity scenes on courthouse lawns to New Testament readings in public schools. We have, all too gradually, learned that a society that writes its history from the point of view of the white majority—teaching its young to glory in the victories of white cowboys over indigenous people or to envy the opulent lifestyles of white plantation owners who created their Taras on the backs of black slaves—demeans not only minorities, but the very concept of justice it purports to instill. And we have grown to understand the trauma that straight society wreaks on young men and women who awaken to their sexuality with an attraction to the same gender only to have their emergence from the closet greeted with lectures on sin, derisive insults, or dead silence.

Yet we seem to remain tone deaf to the larger lesson, the underlying principle: that singling out any one group for special privilege—on the basis of gender, religion, ethnicity, or lifestyle—implicitly, even explicitly, turns members of all nonprivileged groups into second-class citizens. And a society that pretends to tolerance and diversity is ultimately torn apart by such inequity.

Throughout American history, we have repeatedly been seduced into neglecting this principle by arguments that sounded weighty and important at the time—and, in retrospect, entirely absurd. For decades we refused to concede African-Americans the justice and dignity of equal rights because we convinced ourselves that they were savages whose sloth and perfidy would thwart the advance of a great nation. We spurned efforts to grant women the vote because we were sure that they were too hysterical, too emotional to exercise political responsibility intelligently. And we rejected pleas for laws barring discrimination on the basis of sexual orientation because we allowed ourselves to become hysterical over the possibility that gay men would recruit our children.

Today, we justify violating the doctrine of equal pay for equal work, of equity in taxation or fairness in the workplace, alternately by invoking the plight of our children and by bemoaning the stress on our parents. It may be that a generation from now, we will look back on cries of parental oppression and ask, "How could they have conceived of a voluntary activity as oppressive?" or, "What kind of parents could have defined childrearing as such a chore?" Or it may be that those concerns will stand the test of time. But in either event, history cannot look kindly on a nation that can protect its parents and children only by demeaning its childless citizens, by creating one set of rules for those who breed and a different set for those who do not. Freedom and equal rights for one group can never be purchased or guaranteed at the expense of another.

The cruelest comedy of the current family craze is that it comes at a moment in history when conservatives oppose affirmative action and civil rights legislation for gay men and lesbians by mounting that very argument. It has arisen at a time when purported liberals speak passionately about diversity, tolerance, and equality for all. And it has flowered just as we seem to be embarking on a national dialogue about respect.

In the end, of course, respect is the core issue. Cheryl Brant, Ilene Bilenky, and the other childless men and women quoted in this book aren't just talking about taxes and benefits packages. That's the least of their complaint. Respect, after all, isn't measured only in dollars and cents, or workplace flexibility. As any woman who has ever walked past a construction site and been assaulted by wolf whistles and macho verbal bravado knows, it's a quality of interaction, an attitude that pervades even the most casual encounter. Lack of respect for the childless is intrinsic to the conceit that no civilized individual could possibly argue with the privileges being doled out to parents, and to the convenient amnesia about how abrupt a break with tradition those parental entitlements really are.

During one of our interviews, Cheryl Brant asked me, both rhetorically and seriously, "What does it mean to say that we respect people's choices when we penalize people who don't follow the pack?" It means, I think, that we still haven't learned the full lessons of the race, gender, and sexual orientation wars. The battle for human dignity is a constant struggle between the convenient and the necessary. The childless are just today's inconvenience.

Notes

All Animals Are Equal

3 "Cheryl's grandmother, Anna Diehl": The information on Anna Morgan Diehl and her daughter and granddaughter is based on interviews with Susan Diehl Scott and Cheryl Brant.

3 "That promise, however, went only so far": For more information on women's education and higher education, see Barbara Miller Solomon, *In the Company of Educated Women* (New Haven: Yale University Press, 1986); Nancy F. Cott, ed., *Education, History of Women in the United States*, Vol. 12 (Bethesda, Md.: University Publications of America); and John L. Rury, *Education and Women's Work: Female Schooling and the Division of Labor in Urban America, 1870-1930* (Albany: SUNY Series, Women and Work, 1991).

4 "But wherever they worked, women rarely earned even half the wages": The best surveys of women's wage work in this period consulted for this section are Alice Kessler-Harris, *Out to Work* (New York: Oxford University Press, 1982), and Leslie Woodcock Tentler, *Wage-Earning Women* (New York: Oxford University Press, 1979). See also Linda K. Kerber and Jane DeHart-Mathews, *Women's America* (New York: Oxford University Press, 1982), and the section on industrialization and women's work in Nancy F. Cott, ed., *Root of Bitterness* (New York: E.P. Dutton, 1972). Tentler has a particularly thorough discussion of the question of marriage and women's work and an extremely comprehensive set of charts and figures on women's wages and the discrepancy in wages between men and women.

8 "In 1997, with enormous public hoopla": The $5 billion figure was used regularly in congressional hearings dealing with the kiddie tax credit. The dependent care tax credit is at a maximum of $960 for high-income families, and the $1,500 tuition tax credit is part of the president's HOPE Scholarship plan. An analysis of the elimination of EITC for the childless was written by Robert

Greenstein and Isaac Shapiro, "The Consequences of Eliminating the EITC for Childless Workers," for the Center on Budget and Policy Priorities, July 9, 1998. At present, low-income childless workers (earning up to $10,030) can claim a maximum EITC of $341. Those with one child are eligible for a maximum credit of $2,210 if they earn up to $26,473. See IRS publications on the EITC. The food stamp regulation for the childless came from program information published by the Department of Health and Human Services.

8 "In June 1999, childless Americans saw their status further eroded": Clinton announced his plan to allow states to use surplus unemployment funds to pay for parental leave in late May 1999. See the Associated Press story filed after the president's graduation speech at Grambling State University on May 23, 1999.

9 "and employers might soon be given tax breaks by the federal government": Granting tax breaks to employers providing daycare to their employees is under consideration by the U.S. Congress. The law mandating employee postpartum leave is the Family and Medical Leave Act, which Clinton signed into law just after his inauguration.

9 "In May 1999, the White House announced that it was drafting": The press first caught wind of Clinton's proposed civil rights legislation for parents when *The Washington Post* ran a front-page story on the plan on April 17, 1999. Dozens of stories and editorials followed quickly, from which I drew considerable information. In particular, see Roger Clegg's "Legislation to Protect Workers with Children Is Bad Policy," *Legal Times,* May 10, 1999; Timothy Noah, "Breeder Blues, *Slate,* April 19 and April 21, 1999; Stuart Taylor, Jr., "At Last, the Stupidest Law of All," *National Journal,* May 3, 1999; Mary Leonard, "Plan for Parents' Rights Opens a Domestic Divide," *Boston Globe,* April 25, 1999; and Joanne Jacobs, "Working Parents Don't Need the Protection," *San Jose Mercury News,* April 26, 1999.

9 "On May 16, in his commencement address at Graceland College": Gore's call for universal daycare at Graceland was cited in the *New York Times* story on the event, May 17, 1999. His remarks about the family lobby were made at his Family Re-Union in Nashville on June 21, 1999.

10 "as Representative Carolyn McCarthy said": The McCarthy quotation is from a *New York Times* story on gun control, June 14, 1999. The Mikulski quotation is from a *Times* story, "Democrats Try Pitching to Maternal Instincts," July 4, 1999. The *Times*'s observation, written by Frank Bruni, was part of the June 14 piece.

10 "The hoppers of the House of Representatives": The legislation mentioned was under consideration as of July 1999, according to a search of the Thomas database that permits searches of the bills in the hoppers of both houses. It is located at www.thomas.loc.gov.

10 "No matter that in Cheryl's demographic group alone": The figures on the

number and percentage of childless are from the U.S. Census Bureau, Technical Working Paper 14, and "Fertility of American Women."

12 "men like Allan Carlson, president of the Rockford Institute": Allan Carlson's comment about the childless being "free riders" was made during his presentation of "Taxation and the Family: Philosophical and Historical Considerations" at a Family Research Council briefing on Capitol Hill in April 1992.

14 "After almost two decades languishing in the congressional hopper, the Equal Pay Act was finally poised": The best brief history of the Equal Pay Act, which includes the information about the National Office Management Association study and the Westinghouse case, is contained in Alice Kessler-Harris, *A Woman's Wage* (Lexington, Ky.: University Press of Kentucky, 1990), the chapter called "The Double Meaning of Equal Pay."

16 "Corporate America was following, in a helter-skelter fashion": For information on the Australian wage, see John Niland, *Wage Fixation in Australia* (Sydney: Allen & Unwin, 1986).

16 "In New York City at the turn of the last century": For references on wage disparities, see Kessler-Harris, *A Woman's Wage* and the fourth note to the Introduction, "In 1997, with enormous public hoopla."

17 "The apparently general approval of 'equal pay for equal work'": Copal Mintz's letter to the editor appeared in *The New York Times* on June 12, 1963. The quotation from Schwellenbach is cited in Kessler-Harris, *A Woman's Wage*, pp. 105–106. The response to Mintz appeared in *The New York Times* on June 26, 1963.

18 "By the time that President John F. Kennedy": The information on the crowd at the signing of the EPA comes from the bulletin "Equal Pay: A Thirty-five Year Perspective," published by the Women's Bureau of the Department of Labor, June 10, 1998.

20 "The first skirmishes have run the gamut": The problem of the Colorado couple seeking university housing is contained in a series of e-mail messages posted on the National Fair Housing Advocate Discussion Forum on the Internet in July 1997.

20 "Two seasons ago, the new-found fury": The episode of *The Drew Carey Show* mentioned aired on September 24, 1997.

20 "And Bill Maher managed to ruffle": The episode of *The Bill Maher Show* referred to aired on May 12, 1998.

20 "A voting gap—a parent gap": According to Voters News Service. The figures on the presidential election are from the postelection polling of Voter/Consumer Research, explicated in *Family Policy*, December 1996.

1

Unequal Work for Unequal Pay

25 "By midmorning, even the brightly-colored plastic blocks": The section on Neuville is based on interviews there with Steve Neuville, the owner of the company, and Chris Gates, who runs their daycare center.

26 "Over in Cary, on the edge of the famed Research Triangle": The section on SAS is based on an interview with John Dornan of SAS and a tour of the company's facilities.

27 "But it isn't just SAS": The material on NationsBank is taken from, "Company Banks on Work/Family Programs' Payoffs," *Miami Herald*, February 10, 1997, and "Will We Ever Close the Gap?" *Charlotte Observer*, September 1, 1997.

27 "In Winston-Salem, the men and women still left working": The material on R.J. Reynolds comes from an interview with Steve Carr in Winston-Salem, N.C.

28 "They had no idea that they were breaking": Background on "family-friendly" benefits beginning with Robert Owen at New Lanark, through Kellogg, the wartime defense industry, KLH, and Polaroid, was based on information in Hal Morgan and Kerry Tucker, *Companies that Care* (New York: Fireside/Simon & Schuster, 1991).

30 "So, after a morning visiting Neuville": The interviews around Neuville were conducted at the grocery store and various restaurants near the Neuville plant.

32 "Ask Donna Klein of Marriott Corporation": Donna Klein's quotations are based on my interview with her.

32 "Klein convinced executives from Omni": The information on the Atlanta Children's Inn is based on my interview with Klein, as well as reporting from the *Atlanta Journal and Constitution*, March 27, 1997, July 3, 1997, and October 9, 1997.

34 "An extensive survey commissioned by the AFL-CIO": The AFL-CIO survey mentioned was sponsored by the Working Women's Department.

34 "Karen Nussbaum, head of the Working Women's Department": Nussbaum's quotations are from my interview with her.

34 "Look at what the 'best' companies": *Working Mother* magazine began its annual Best Companies survey in 1985. *Business Week* conducted its first survey in conjunction with the Center on Work & Family at Boston University. It ran on September 16, 1996. The Women's Bureau of the Department of Labor began printing its Honor Roll of family-friendly companies as part of its Working Women Count survey in 1995.

34 "Fel-Pro Incorporated is precisely": Morgan and Tucker provided information on Fel-Pro, BE&K, IBM, Stride-Rite, and Hallmark. For IBM, see also, "Paying Attention to Families Pays," *Charlotte Observer*, April 12, 1992. For Hallmark,

see the March 1996 issue of *Personnel Journal*. For Stride-Rite, see the July 1993 issue of *Personnel Journal*.

35 "According to Hewitt Associates' annual survey": The figures about the Hewitt Associates survey are based on its 1997 report, as detailed in a press release from the company on April 19, 1997.

36 "Survey after survey confirms that same picture": The Families and Work Institute survey results were published in the company's "1998 Business Work-Life Study."

36 "They cite the case of the pharmaceutical giant": For Johnson & Johnson, "Reframing the Business Case for Work-Life Initiatives," p. 9, Ellen Galinsky and Arlene A. Johnson, Families and Work Institute, 1998. For Fel-Pro's claim about reduction of turnover in response to its camp, see Barbara Adolf and Carol Rose, *Children at Work* (1982). Merck's claim of three dollars in savings appeared in the *Christian Science Monitor*, June 30, 1988, and *The New York Times*, July 20, 1988. John Fernandez's estimates of how much family-friendly programs reduce absenteeism is from his *Childcare and Corporate Productivity* (Lexington, Mass.: D.C. Heath, 1980).

36 "By the time *Business Week* published": The *Business Week* survey mentioned appeared in the magazine on September 16, 1996.

37 "How can turnover and absenteeism drop": The BLS statistics were cited by Gillian Flynn in her "Backlash: No Spouse, No Kids, No Respect," *Personnel Journal*, September 1996.

37 "How can a company like Chase": The statistics on Chase Manhattan Bank's Brooklyn Center appeared in an article on childcare in *Forbes*, January 11, 1999.

39 " 'There's a brand new uprising nationally' ": Jane Yallum's quotation is from "Single and Childless Workers Say They're Not Getting Fair Share of Benefits," *Pittsburgh Post-Gazette*, June 19, 1998.

39 "Listen to Sandy Graf": The Sandy Graf material is from an interview with her via e-mail.

39 "Erin Galvin seethes almost daily": The Erin Galvin material is from my interview with her via e-mail.

40 "A childless woman who works in a hospital laboratory": The information from the woman who works in the hospital lab was part of an on-line discussion at childfree.net on October 30, 1998.

40 "Like most childless workers": The Kiriacon quotations are from my interview with him.

40 "Nonparents, of course, have no equivalent": The Tracy quotations are from my interview with him.

41 "'Who wants to be labeled a childhater?'": The Bilenky quotations are from my interview with her, much of which appeared in *Mirabella*, November/December 1998.

41 "But gradually, as employers and consultants use confidential surveys": The *Personnel Journal* survey appeared in April 1996.

41 "By every measure, they are working more and reaping less": These survey results are available from the Conference Board in New York.

42 "In a survey conducted for *Fortune* magazine": The *Fortune* survey cited was a childcare survey conducted for the magazine by Ellen Galinsky and Diane Hughes and published in 1987. This study and various other are discussed in Fairlee Winfield, *The Work and Family Sourcebook* (New York: Panel Publishers, 1988).

42 " 'It has created something of a hornet's nest' ": The quotations from Mary Young are based on my interview with her. Further information from her came from her 1997 research report, "What's Behind Work/Family Backlash," prepared for William Olsten Center for Workforce Strategies.

43 "American Express Financial Advisors": The Paul Demke quotation appeared in Amy Gage's column of December 3, 1998, in the *St. Paul Pioneer Press.*

43 "most corporate executives wave their hands dismissively": The Fernandez quotation is from his *Childcare and Corporate Productivity* (Lexington, Mass.: D.C. Heath, 1980).

44 "'It never comes back to you'": The construction supervisor quotations are from Roy Clark, who was interviewed by telephone.

44 "Jeff Guiler, a professor of management": Jeff Guiler's quotation is from "Single and Childless Workers Say They're Not Getting Fair Share of Benefits," *Pittsburgh Post-Gazette,* June 19, 1998.

45 "But listen to what happened in April 1997": *The Wall Street Journal* interactive discussion, "Child-Free Employees See Another Side of Equation," was conducted on April 2, 1997.

46 "A similar exchange occurred in August 1994": The Louv columns appeared in the *San Diego Union-Tribune* in August 1994.

48 "In July 1998, for example, Alicia Martinez": The information on the Alicia Martinez case is based on interviews with her attorney, a statement from MSNBC, and the court papers filed in the case.

49 "The most notorious case involves Lieutenant Emma Cuevas": The most thorough account of the Emma Cuevas case was printed in *Time* magazine, February 24, 1997, which was the source of the quotations from Cuevas and Finch.

50 "No one has yet asked Cuevas' attorney": Maloney's bill was introduced as H.R. 3531, the New Mothers' Breastfeeding Promotion and Protection Act, on March 24, 1998.

50 "The controversy and legal maneuvering isn't confined": Information on the Upton case was culled from *The Standard-Times,* August 19, 1997, and *The Boston Globe,* April 22, 1997.

51 "In 1998, an attorney affiliated with the Rutherford": The Friedlander suit was filed in U.S. District Court for South Carolina in December 1997.

53 "Running against this tide": The Purnick story was patched together from interviews with many *Times* employees and a copy of Purnick's speech, which
was circulated widely in the newsroom and provided to me by a *Times* reporter. Background on the *Times*'s earlier problems with female employees
was taken from Nan Robertson's *The Girls in the Balcony* (New York: Fawcett
Ballantine, 1992). The Susan Chira quotations are taken from her book, *A
Mother's Place* (New York: HarperCollins, 1998). The information on generational tensions in the workplace, including the quotations from Jennings and
Bernstein, is from "Generational Warfare," *Forbes,* March 22, 1999. The reaction from Steve and Cokie Roberts appeared in their column of May 28, 1998,
in the New York *Daily News.* The *Philadelphia Inquirer* response, contained in
piece by Melissa Dribben, ran on July 2, 1998. The Shellenbarger piece, written for *The Wall Street Journal,* ran in the *Charlotte Observer* on June 29, 1998.
The *Slate* column cited ran on May 20, 1998. The e-mail from Keller was sent
on May 20, 1998, and was provided to me by one of the dozens of *Times* employees who got their hands on it.

2

Pregnant Payoffs

PAGE

62 "On a gray, gloomy morning in 1991": A transcript of the hearing discussed,
Reclaiming the Tax Code for American Families, was published by the Government Printing Office as part of the records of the 102d Congress, first session.

66 "Lisa and Richard Doe": The taxes of these two families were prepared by Ann
Morris, an accountant in Oneonta, New York.

70 "So, let's talk about the much-heralded": An excellent short history of the per-
sonal income tax is provided by Joel Slemrod and Jon Bakija, *Taxing Ourselves*
(Cambridge, Mass.: MIT Press, 1996), pp. 22–25. The 1948 Revenue Act, FHA
and VA changes are outlined in Sylvia Ann Hewlett and Cornel West, *The War
Against Parents* (New York: Houghton Mifflin, 1998) pp. 98–108. A thorough
look at these tax changes is provided in Rudolph G. Penner, ed., *Taxing the
Family* (Washington, D.C.: American Enterprise Institute, 1983). Also see Jon
Bakija and Eugene Steuerle, "Individual Income Taxation since 1948," *Na-
tional Tax Journal,* Vol. XLIV, No. 4, part 2, and Edward J. McCaffery, *Taxing
Women* (Chicago: University of Chicago Press, 1997).

72 "Those tax cuts will cost the U.S. Treasury roughly $100 billion": The rough
figure of $100 billion over five years as the cost of the child tax credits was
widely used during the discussion of the enabling legislation. I took the figure
from Eugene Steuerle, "Taxation of the Family," the statement of the former
economic coordinator of the Treasury Department before the Ways and
Means Committee of the U.S. House of Representatives on April 15, 1997.

72 "Tax analysts and gurus justify this sort of tax shift": The clearest discussion of horizontal equity I have read appears in Slemrod and Bakija, op. cit., pp. 73–81.

74 "'Having children is largely a voluntary choice'": The quotation on taxation and children appears on pp. 77–78 of Slemrod and Bakija, op. cit.

75 "Public education was never intended": For background on Horace Mann, see Lawrence A. Cremin, ed., *Republic and the School: Horace Mann on the Education of Free Man* (New York: Teachers College Press, Columbia University, 1957), Mary T. Mann, *The Life of Horace Mann* (New York: Ayer Company Publishers, 1977), reprint of the Washington, D.C.: National Education Association edition of 1937.

76 "Every year between 1975 and 1997": The figures on spending on and cost of education are from Victor R. Fuchs, "Are Americans Underinvesting in Children," in David Blankenhorn et al., eds., *Rebuilding the Nest: A New Commitment to the American Family* (Milwaukee: Family Service America, 1990.)

77 "Take New York as an example": The information on the higher education budget of the State of New York for 1997 was pulled from the budget as published on-line by the state.

78 "The federal government kicks in billions more": These figures are based on the budget for the Department of Education for 1997.

78 "When Bill Clinton first suggested the Hope Scholarships": The quotation from Merkowitz appeared in a *Philadelphia Inquirer* story on December 26, 1996, and the Gladieux comment in a piece that ran in the *Baltimore Sun* on December 1, 1996.

79 "Richard and Lisa's daughter, for example, attends the University of Maryland": The figure for the state contribution to the University of Maryland system appeared in the *Baltimore Sun* on August 29, 1998.

80 "The first time an American woman tried to write off childcare expenses": For a discussion of the Smith tax case, see McCaffery, op. cit. The case is cited as *Smith* v. *Commissioner,* 40 BTA 1038(1939).

80 "Until 1954, the prevailing winds stormed": Excellent surveys of the history of childcare deductions and spending are contained in John Fernandez, *Childcare and Corporate Productivity* (Lexington, Mass.: D.C. Health, 1980), Martin Feldstein and James M. Poterba, *The Empirical Foundations of Household Taxation* (Chicago: University of Chicago Press, 1996), Mary Frances Berry, *The Politics of Parenthood* (New York: Viking, 1993); and Karen Brown and Mary Louise Fellows, eds., *Taxing America* (New York: New York University Press, 1997).

81 "But the childcare crisis—a crisis in availability, affordability and quality": For an excellent overview of the various research on childcare usage and preferences see, "Emptying the Nest," *Mother Jones,* May/June 1991. Included in that article are the results of polls from Withlin Worldwide, the Pew Research Cen-

ter, Louis Harris, and the Independent Women's Forum. The IWF hired the Polling Company to update their poll in early 1998. The results are published in *Ex Feminia,* April 1998.

81 "Furthermore, surveys conducted by the U.S. Department of Labor": The information on vacancy rates et cetera in daycare centers comes from a 1990 HHS survey.

81 "And in those same surveys, 95 percent": The information on satisfaction with current childcare arrangements comes from a 1990 survey conducted by the Department of Health and Human Services that found that 96 percent of Americans were satisfied or highly satisfied with their current childcare arrangements, including 95 percent of those with incomes below fifteen thousand dollars per year. This survey was discussed in the *CRC Foundation Watch,* June 1998. In considering these figures, the readers should remember that the income bracket with the largest number of at-home mothers is $20,000 to $24,999. Currently, the median income of dual-income families is $57,637. This compares to a median income of $38,835 for families with mothers at home. This information is from the *Mother Jones* article already cited.

81 "Once again, the poor are being used": The question of what percentage of the federal childcare largesse is targeted to the poor has provoked considerable controversy in recent years. For discussion of the figures and the regressivity of this funding, see Feldstein and Poterba, op. cit., and McCaffery, op. cit., as well as Andrew J. Cherlin, ed., *The Changing American Family and Public Policy* (Washington, D.C.: The Urban Institute Press, 1988), p. 19.

82 "Bill Clinton, at least, seems to have been persuaded": Clinton's proposal for a tax credit for stay-at-home parents was released during his 1999 State of the Union address.

82 "Senators and representatives rushed": The transcript of the April 6, 1995, hearing of the Joint Economic Committee was published by the Government Printing Office.

3
For the Sake of Which Children?

PAGE

91 "On October 10, 1983, millions of American parents": The background on the Reve Walsh case and John Walsh's crusade was culled from a variety of news sources, most especially the *Miami Herald.* See the *Herald*'s reporting of July 27, 1982; October 9, 1983; July 27, 1986; July 28, 1991; as well as *The Boston Globe,* September 28, 1986. Information on dairies' posting of photographs of missing children on milk cartons, and the results, were reported by Peter Brewer of the AP in a story that ran in *The Boston Globe,* February 15, 1987,

and included discussion of the American Academy of Pediatricians' warning that the missing children campaign was exaggerated. Reporting designed to calm the hysteria and warn readers about charities misusing the facts appeared in the *Miami Herald,* July 27, 1985; in Diana Griego and Louis Kilzer's story in the *Denver Post,* May 26, 1985; and in Ellen Goodman's column of July 9, 1985. The tale of the boys in Des Moines came from the *Chicago Tribune,* August 20, 1984. The report about the boy at Zayre's in Palm Beach County from the *Miami Herald,* August 30, 1984. For the story of Laura Bradbury, I relied most heavily on the *Los Angeles Times,* October 21, 1985.

94 "When a Boston infant died": The case of Louise Woodward electrified the nation during much of 1997, from February, when she pled not guilty to charges of shaking eight-month-old Matthew Eappen to death, through her trial in October and the judge's reduction of her conviction to manslaughter on November 10, 1997.

94 "In 1998, thanks to the reportorial endeavors": The phthalates story ran on ABC's *20/20* as "Are Babies at Risk for a Chemical Found in Toys?" in November 1998.

94 "By the fall of that year, peanut butter panic": The information on school reactions to peanut butter allergy scares, and the figures from the CDC, are from "Nothing's Safe," *The New York Times,* September 23, 1998. For information on the Food Allergy Network, log on to their website at www.foodallergy.org.

95 "In 1998, the crusaders for cleaner air and water": Boxer first introduced her Children's Environmental Protection Act on April 16, 1997. It would require the EPA to set safety standards at levels that protect children, rather than adults, to publish a list of products safe for children, and to conduct research on the health effects of pollutants on children.

95 "In February 1999, in his *National Liberty Journal*": Falwell's warning about Tinky Winky appeared in his *National Liberty Journal,* February 1999.

96 "No mention was made of the study released by a Berkeley biologist": The relationship between folic acid and chromosomal damage was explicated by B. C. Blount et al. in the *Proceedings of the National Academy of Sciences,* 94:3290-5, 1997. The Berkeley biologist mentioned in conjunction with this study, Bruce Ames, was a coauthor.

97 "At the end of the Year of the Child in 1979, a survey": The 1979 survey mentioned ran in *The Boston Globe,* December 16, 1979.

98 "The first comprehensive parental defense scheme": The report of the National Commission on Children was issued in 1991 as *Beyond Rhetoric: A New American Agenda for Children and Families.*

99 "By every measure, the children of "traditional" families are thriving": For information on the relationship between poverty and single parenthood, see Wade Horn, "Children and Family in America: Challenges for the 1990s," Heritage Lecture No. 345, June 23, 1991.

100 "The new conservative thinking about children": Dana Mack, *The Assault on Parenthood: How Our Culture Undermines the Family* (New York: Simon & Schuster, 1997).

101 "The most startling approach" Sylvia Ann Hewlett and Cornel West, *The War Against Parents* (New York: Houghton-Mifflin, 1998).

102 "The attachment to the project of Hewlett": Sylvia Ann Hewlett, *When the Bough Breaks* (New York: Basic Books, 1991).

104 "Ted Kennedy branded": The quotations of praise for Hewlett and West appeared on the jacket of their hardback book and in the accompanying press kit.

104 "By almost every measure, the average American kid": Information on infant mortality, mothers' mortality, the decreasing birth rate, and the increasing educational level of parents are available from dozens of disparate sources. But a good overview of the statistics is available in Andrew Cherlin, ed., *The Changing American Family and Public Policy* (Washington, D.C.: The Urban Institute Press, 1988). Those statistics are available both in the introductory pages, especially pp. 8 to 10, and throughout.

104 "They are decidedly more affluent": The information on parental income comes from Charlin, op. cit. Parental spending on children is from "The Millennium Generation," *The Washington Post,* June 29, 1998.

105 "The health of today's kids": The health statistics are available in Cherlin, op. cit. Parental opinion of children's health is cited on pp. 55.

105 "Most nights—five out of seven": The percentage of children who regularly have dinner with their parents is from a Nickelodeon-Yankelovich Youth Monitor poll discussed at the February 19, 1992, hearing of the House Select Committee on Children, Youth, and Families. Perhaps the most thorough analysis of the figures about how much time parents spend with their children, appeared in "The Myth of AWOL Parents," *U.S. News and World Report,* July 1, 1996.

105 "The public schools in his neighborhood": The figures on spending on education and teachers' salaries are from Victor R. Fuchs, "Are Americans Underinvesting in Children," David Blankenhorn et al., eds., *Rebuilding the Nest: A New Commitment to the American Family* (Milwaukee: Family Service America, 1990.)

106 "And it hurts the national pride": The information on SAT and other test scores is available in Charlin, op. cit.

106 "The rate of juvenile violent crime": The statistics on juvenile crime were drawn from the Child Welfare League of America, "Children '98: America's Promise Fact Sheet."

106 "Kids around him are drinking": The decrease in youth drug and alcohol consumption has been demonstrated by dozens of surveys and studies. See, for example, "Teen Drug Use Falls," *Miami Herald,* August 18, 1999.

108 "Nonetheless, if our cries about the plight of our children": The best source of information on children in poverty—the risks poverty creates in education, health and violence—is *Poverty Matters,* a 1997 report from the Children's Defense Fund.

108 "Their planned universal health coverage for pregnant women and for children": The Balanced Budget Act of 1997 provided $24 billion in federal funds over five years for children's health, with $20 billion of the funds set aside for the Children's Health Insurance Program (CHIP). In most states, that program includes coverage for pregnant women.

110 "Listen to William Rasberry": The Rasberry quotation is from his column in *The Washington Post* on May 4, 1998.

112 "Michelle Gaboury is convinced that she deserves": The material on the Gabourys came from my interviews with them.

112 "'It's the kind of place that inspired'": The Francis X. Clines piece quoted ran as "A Mayor Yields to a Special Interest," *The New York Times,* January 9, 1994.

115 "Read this, from the first page": Shirley P. Burggraf, *The Feminine Economy and Economic Man* (Reading, Mass.: Addison-Wesley, 1997).

116 "In Western and Eastern Europe": The lack of impact of "family-friendly" policies on the birth rates in Western and Eastern Europe is documented in Charlin, op. cit., pp. 24 and 236.

4
Family Frenzy

118 "In a different age with an altered sensibility": Schroeder discusses the tour in detail in her *Champion of the Great American Family* (New York: Random House, 1989). Further information came from media reports about the event, including "Giving Families the Vote," *Miami Herald,* January 23, 1988; "Dr. Brazelton's Family Crusade," *Washington Post,* December 22, 1987; "Family Power," *Charlotte Observer,* March 7, 1988; "American Family in Great Need of Attention," *The State,* February 24, 1988; "Focusing on Family Issues," *Boston Globe,* January 19, 1988: The quotations used are from those articles.

119 "Goldberg lent the group star power": The mini-bios of Goldberg and Brazelton are taken from the coverage of the tour, as cited above.

120 "Under Ronald Reagan, Republicans had turned": The clearest example of Reagan's political use of children and the family can be gleaned from reaction to a report produced by a presidential commission in November 1986. See *Washington Post,* "Family Screed," November 17, 1986; *Boston Globe,* "Federal Study Urges Efforts to Encourage Child Rearing," November 14, 1986; *Philadelphia Inquirer,* "Social Setback," November 14, 1986. The quotations from the report are taken from those articles. A good sense of the climate cre-

ated is analyzed by Joan Beck in her "Beware Leaders with 'Family Policy,' "
Chicago Tribune, November 26, 1988.

121 "Jimmy Carter charged Vice-President Walter Mondale": The problems over the
Carter/Mondale conference are discussed in "Family Screed," above, as well as
Ellen Goodman's column, "Family Feud," which appeared in *The Washington
Post* on February 27, 1980; William Rasberry's column, "All on the Family,"
Washington Post, April 21, 1980; "Family Matter," *Washington Post,* May 31,
1980; "Conference on Families," *Washington Post,* June 4, 1980; "Band of Con-
servatives Walks Out," *Washington Post,* June 7, 1980; "Uproar at Family Con-
ference," *Washington Post,* June 11, 1980. See also Gilbert Steiner, *The Futility of
Family Policy* (Washington, D.C.: The Brookings Institution Press, 1981).

122 "In 1956, parents were the majority of the electorate, at 55 percent": See *Next
Generation Reports,* September 1998.

122 "In virtually every poll, every survey, parents with children at home": Many
polls indicate this trend. See, for example, the post-1996 election Voter/Con-
sumer Research survey conducted by Consumer Research of Bethesda, Maryland, that found that even when controlling for age, marrieds with children in
the home are more apt than other Americans to describe themselves as "very
conservative."

122 "Seizing the family initiative became an irresistible temptation": The 1986 Democratic Policy Committee statement is detailed in "Party's Policy Paper
Takes a Neutral Stance," *Philadelphia Inquirer,* September 23, 1986, and in
"Democrats Are Asked to Build on Local Record," *Boston Globe,* September
22, 1986. See also George Will, "Democrats Discover the Family," *Washington
Post,* October 2, 1986. Wright's response was offered right after the broadcast
of the State of the Union speech, on January 27, 1987. Every major newspaper
covered the speech. See, for example, the coverage of *The Boston Globe* and the
Miami Herald on the 28th. This conference is also discussed in Andrew J.
Cherlin, ed., *The Changing American Family and Public Policy* (Washington,
D.C.: The Urban Institute Press, 1988).

123 "Then came the annual Democratic party issues conference": For background
on the Democratic retreat, see "Family Dominates Democratic Retreat,"
Washington Post, January 25, 1988.

123 "More than a decade before, Edelman had acknowledged": The Edelman quotation appeared in Mickey Kaus, "The Godmother: What's Wrong with Marian Wright Edelman," *New Republic,* February 15, 1993.

124 "Smelling possibility after eight grueling and humiliating years": The Women's
Agenda Conference in Des Moines was well covered by the media. See, in particular, the *Washington Post* reports from January 24 and January 20, 1988,
and Ellen Goodman's column written from the event, which ran on January
30, 1988. But probably the best news report of the event was "Family Affairs,"
Chicago Tribune, February 3, 1988.

124 "Dick Gephardt tapped as his official advisor": The problems Democrats faced in dealing with family issues were detailed in Robert Kuttner's Op-Ed piece, "The Democrats' Family Problem," which ran in *The Washington Post* on March 6, 1988. It provides a clear sense of Klein's position.

124 "Bruce Babbitt announced his candidacy": Babbitt announced his candidacy twice—once in a renovated mill in New Hampshire and then at a daycare center in Iowa. See *The Boston Globe,* March 11, 1987.

124 "In July 1988, the Democratic National Convention in Atlanta": The 1988 Democratic National Convention was held in Atlanta and ran from July 20 to July 23. The details presented were drawn from the almost endless coverage of the event by major newspapers.

124 "'Mark this down in your memory book'": The Ellen Goodman column, which is nationally syndicated, ran on August 6, 1988.

125 "After all, their pollsters and campaign managers argued, 57 percent of mothers": The percentage of kids under the age of five with mothers employed outside the home almost doubled from the mid-1970s through 1988. But it has leveled off since then. As of 1994 the figure was still at the 1988 level of 52 percent. That figure, however, is misleading since it lumps together part-time and full-time work. Eighteen percent of preschool children have mothers who work part-time. These figures are from the U.S. Bureau of the Census, "Who's Minding Our Preschoolers," 1994.

126 "As the number of children born in the nation soars": The baby boomlet demographics are available from the Census Bureau online at www.census.gov. It is beautifully detailed and analyzed in "The Millennium Generation Is Making Its Mark," *Washington Post,* June 29, 1998.

128 "Bookstores are replete": The baby books mentioned are Linda Rosenkrantz and Pamela Redmond Satran, *Beyond Jennifer and Jason, Madison and Montana: What to Name Your Baby Now* (New York: Griffin, 1999); Linda Acredolor and Susan Goodwyn, *Baby Signs: How to Talk with Your Baby Before Your Baby Can Talk* (New York: NTC Contemporary Publishing, 1999); and Gwen Gotsch and Judy Torgus, *The Womanly Art of Breastfeeding* (New York: Plume, 1997).

128 "Corporate America has discovered that kids": The information on marketing to children and the quotations from Kitei are from "The Millennium Generation Is Making Its Mark," *Washington Post,* June 29, 1998.

129 "Take Bright Horizons Family Solutions": The information on the marketing by Bright Horizons, including the *Charlotte Observer* quotation, is from "Bright Horizons Leads Companies into World of Naps, Diapers," *Charlotte Observer,* June 22, 1992.

130 "Child advocacy groups are no different": The information on the Florida Children's Campaign comes from its website, www.floridakids.com.

130 "Nancy and Jim Chuda, who lost their daughter": The Children's Health Environmental Coalition Network is based in Malibu, California. Information on

its activities and the support it has attracted was taken from the group's website, www.checnet.org. The story of Nancy and Jim Chuda also appears on the Children's Television Workshop website as "Environmental Crusaders for Kids."

130 "Consider the surveys and polls": The information on the Children's Partnership, including the work done for the group by Schrayer, was printed in its *Next Generation Reports,* September 1998, *Looking to the New Millennium: Elections and Kids.*

130 "Celinda Lake, Alysia Snell, and Dave Sackett": The "Great Expectations" poll can be read or downloaded at www.usakids.org or ordered from the Coalition for America's Children in Washington, D.C.

131 "Deborah Wadsworth, executive director of Public Agenda": Wadsworth's poll about American attitudes toward children is part of the Public Agenda survey, "Can Government Help Children and Families?" That information and her quotations were part of her presentation "Communicating with the Public About Children's Issues," delivered at a forum sponsored by the Coalition for America's Children, part of its Campaign '98, June 23, 1998.

131 "And Glen Bolger of Public Opinion Strategies": Glen Bolger's remarks were delivered at the same forum as Wadsworth's, above.

133 "In the 1998 elections, one candidate in Florida": The Tamargo tale was covered by the *Tampa Tribune.* The story was taken from their reporting, "Mud Flies in District 58 House Race," November 2, 1998; "Candidate's Advertising Strategy Backfires," November 3, 1998; and the newspaper's explanation for its changes in endorsement of Tamargo, which ran on November 3, 1998.

134 "Just after Memorial Day 1998, Senator Barbara Boxer": The information on the Boxer fund-raiser was provided to me by a reporter covering the event.

134 "Just before 9:00 P.M. on Tuesday, January 26, 1999": Clinton's 1999 State of the Union address was broadcast nationally. The copy I used for reference purposes ran in *The New York Times* on January 20, 1999.

134 "43.5 million Americans tuned": Information on the number of viewers who watched the State of the Union address and the length of the speech was carried on the Associated Press wire the night of the speech and ran in newspapers nationwide the following day. The number of proposals contained therein are my count from his printed text.

135 "The next day, a wide swath of experts": Samples of the criticism lobbed at his Social Security and education proposals were reported by the *Miami Herald* in "Federal Mandates Don't Lead," January 26, 1999, and "Fed Chief: Wall Street No Place for Social Security Fund," January 21, 1999. The poll numbers were reported by the *Miami Herald* on January 21, 1999.

135 "That thundering wave of approval": A *Los Angeles Times* poll conducted right after Clinton's State of the Union address showed that less than half the citizenry expected to vote for the president for a second term in office.

136 "'I think he is doing a good job'": The quotation from Stacey Schwartz appeared in a story printed about the president's trip through Pennsylvania printed in the *Philadelphia Inquirer* on January 26, 1995

136 "'The era of big government is over,'": Clinton delivered his 1996 acceptance s142ch on August 28. It was reprinted widely in major newspapers.

142 "As Michael Kelly, Democratic apostate": The Kelly quotation ran in *The Washington Post,* March 3, 1999, p. A23.

142 "In 1987, Ben Wattenberg, a demographer": Ben J. Wattenberg, *The Birth Dearth* (New York: Pharos Books, 1987).

143 "Ellen Goodman, one of the nation's leading newspaper columnists": The Goodman column mentioned ran nationwide on August 4, 1987.

143 "Two years later, in *The Atlantic Monthly*": Jonathan Rauch's piece, "Kids as Capital," appeared in *The Atlantic Monthly,* August 1989.

144 "Then Bill Clinton weighed in": Clinton's statement about couples deferring childbearing, which formed part of a discussion of support for childcare, was found on the Zero Population Grown website, July 22, 1995.

5

The Maternal Mystique

PAGE

147 "Betty Friedan hung up": The Friedan interview was conducted as indicated, by phone.

148 "By the late 1990s, the National Organization for Women": For a sampling of NOW's current activities, and an ad for their cookbook, log on to the group's website at www.now.org.

149 "It wasn't just NOW": For background information on the Institute for Women's Policy research, see "A Feminist Approach to Policy Making for Women and Families" by Heidi Hartmann and Roberta Spalter-Roth, prepared for the Seminar on Future Directions for American Politics and Public Policy at Harvard University, March 10, 1994. The results of the meeting at Arlington Hill, Vermont, on December 4–6, 1992, were published by the IWPR as the "Arlington Hill Working Paper" on December 10, 1992.

150 "And, on its website, the White House Office": The White House website, www.whitehouse.gov, can lead you to information on the office on women's initiatives or you can go directly to www.whitehouse.gov/WH/EOP/Women/OWIO.

150 "Early suffragists decried social": Finally, we have available multiple histories of early feminism. See, for example, Christine A. Lunardini, *From Equal Suffrage to Equal Rights: Alice Paul and the National Woman's Party, 1910-1928* (New York: New York University Press, 1986); Marjorie Spruill Wheeler, *Votes For Women* (Knoxville: University of Tennessee Press, 1995); and William O'Neill, *Everyone Was Brave* (New York: Quadrangle, 1969).

151 "Such feminists as Inez Milholland": Inez Milholland, often referred to as Inez Boissevain, was a New York lawyer and suffragist who collapsed during a pro-suffrage speech in Los Angeles in 1916 and died several weeks later.

151 "Motherhood wasn't just a tactic": Ellen Key was a prominent Swedish social reformer who argued that mothers should be paid by the state to raise children. Her classic work, in which she argues forcefully about the role of women as mothers, is *The Century of the Child,* first published in Swedish in 1900. The most recent American edition is from Ayer Company Publishers, 1972. The Goldman quotation is from her "Marriage and Love," published in 1910 by Mother Earth Publishing Association. It is included in her *Anarchism and Other Essays* (New York: Dover Publications, 1969). The Gilman quotation is from her *Women and Economics,* first published in 1898. One of many reprintings is Harper & Row, 1966.

151 "Elizabeth Cady Stanton brushed off": The Stanton quotation was reprinted in Marian Faux, *Childless by Choice* (New York: Anchor, 1984). Duffey's opinion was expressed in her *The Relations of the Sexes* (New York: Ayer, 1976). For Gilman, see her *Women and Economics,* op. cit.

152 "The Board of Trustees of Barnard College": The Barnard decision is detailed in Carl N. Degler, "Revolution Without Ideology: The Changing Place of Women in America," *Daedalus,* 93, Spring 1964.

152 "That philosophy dovetailed seamlessly": Watson was a professor at Johns Hopkins University. His classic work on childrearing, published in 1928, was *The Psychological Care of the Infant and Child.*

153 "The new guru of childrearing": For a sampling of Gesell's thinking, see Gesell et al., *Infant and Child in the Culture of Today* (Northvale, N.J.: Jason Arsonson, 1996).

153 "Helene Deutsch and other psychologists": For background on Deutsch's positions, see Janet Sayers, *Mothers of Psychoanalysis* (New York: W. W. Norton, 1993), and Paul Roazen, *Helene Deutsch: A Psychoanalyst's Life* (Transaction Publications, 1991).

153 "At an American Academy of Arts and Sciences": Rossi's immodest proposal was included in her "The Woman in America," which appeared in *Daedalus,* Spring 1964.

154 "Rossi pointed the finger of blame squarely": Rossi's reaction to Dr. Spock was to the early printings of his book, *Common Sense Book of Baby and Child Care,* which was first published in 1946. His positions on women's role changed considerably over time.

155 "And then came Friedan": *The Feminine Mystique* was most recently reissued by W. W. Norton in November 1997.

155 "The National Organization for Women, founded by a disparate": A good history of NOW placed in the wider context is online as the *Feminist Chronicles,* at the Feminist Majority Foundation website, www.feminist.org. It also includes many key original documents.

156 "In her classic book, *The Dialectic of Sex*": Firestone, *The Dialectic of Sex* (New York: Bantam Books, 1970).

157 "Kate Millet, one of the movement's leading writers": Millet's classic work was *Sexual Politics* (Garden City, N.Y.: Doubleday, 1970).

157 "In her weightier philosophical and historical tract": Juliet Mitchell, *Woman's Estate* (New York: Vintage, 1971).

157 "'Motherhood . . . is forced on women by men'": See Rich's *Of Woman Born* (New York: W. W. Norton, 1995).

157 "'Daycare centers buy women off'": The Firestone quotation comes from *The Dialectic of Sex,* op. cit.

157 "After a decade or more of battling": Friedan's *Second Stage* was published in 1981, and most recently issued in paperback by Harvard University Press in 1998. The quotations from her are from a profile of Friedan that ran in *The Boston Globe* on November 16, 1981. Her continuing evolution in this direction became even clearer in her *Beyond Gender* (Washington, D.C.: Woodrow Wilson Center Press, 1997).

159 "Every 'special protection' ever conferred": In *Conflict and Compromise* (New York: Touchstone, 1996), Ronald Elving shows how the framers of the FMLA struggled to avoid the concept of special protection and why. For an excellent analysis of this issue historically, see the chapter on protective labor legislation in Alice Kessler-Harris, *A Woman's Wage* (Lexington, Ky.: University Press of Kentucky, 1990).

159 "It was an old struggle": An excellent, and succinct, discussion of the conflict between Alice Paul and the old-line suffragists is contained in Carl Degler, *At Odds* (New York: Oxford University Press, 1980), pp. 400–405.

160 "In one of its first issues": The Shulman contract ran in *Ms.* as part of an article on marriage contracts, Spring 1972.

160 "In 1975, Letty Pogrebin": The Letty Cottin Pogrebin book mentioned here is *Getting Yours* (New York: David McKay., 1975).

160 "Men grudgingly began picking up": The information on the hours men and women spend in housework comes from a study by John P. Robinson, "Who's Doing the Housework," *American Demographic,* December 1988.

161 "Nancy Folbre, an economist": Nancy Folbre, "The Pauperization of Mothers: Patriarchy and Public Policy in the US," *Review of Radical Political Economics* 16:4, pp. 72–88. Reprinted in *Families and Work: Toward Reconceptualization,* Naomi Gerstel and Harriet Gross, eds. (New York: Temple University Press, 1987).

162 "Adjust public policy to meet": The IWPR generates publications prolifically. For a list of them, go to their website at www.iwpr.org. The group's tendency to equate woman with mother is particularly clear in "Looking Toward the Workplace of the 21st Century," the Yulee Lecture delivered by Heidi Hartmann at George Washington University on March 28, 1996, and testimony by

Hartmann and Robert Spalter-Roth before the Subcommittee on Employment and Productivity of the U.S. Senate Committee on Labor and Human
Resources, July 18, 1991.

163 "These women were given voice": The books referred to by Roiphe, Peters, and
Chira are Anne Roiphe, *Fruitful* (New York: Houghton-Mifflin, 1996); Joan
Peters, *When Mothers Work* (New York: Perseus, 1998); and Susan Chira, *A
Mother's Place* (New York: HarperCollins, 1998).

164 "A group of philosophers have gone": A short survey of the position and role
of the new maternalist philosophers can be found in Carolyn M. Morell, *Un-
womanly Conduct: The Challenges of Intentional Childlessness* (New York:
Routledge, 1994). For the original works of these women, see Sara Ruddick,
Maternal Thinking (New York: Beacon, 1995); Nancy Chodorow, *The Repro-
duction of Mothering* (Berkeley: University of California Press, 1999); Carol
Gilligan, *In a Different Voice* (Boston: Harvard University Press, 1993); and
Virginia Held, ed., *Justice and Care: Essential Readings in Feminist Ethics*
(Boulder, Colo.: Westview, 1995).

165 "No challenge required more formidable intellectual gymnastics": For a good
discussion of the history of pregnancy leaves, see Pogrebin's *Getting Yours*. See
also Schroeder, op. cit.

166 "Concerned only with the first two goals": Ronald D. Elving has written a superb chronicle of the long fight over the FMLA, *Conflict and Compromise*
(New York: Touchstone, 1996).

168 "Felice Schwartz was the Superwoman's woman": Schwartz's original article, "Management Women and the New Facts of Life," ran in *Harvard Business Review,* January–February 1989. Schwartz's account of the controversy
is contained in her *Breaking with Tradition* (New York: Warner Books,
1992).

169 "Schwartz's suggestion was hardly original": Information about the position
taken by Dana Friedman comes from Schwartz's book, op. cit.

170 "Much to their chagrin": Rossi, op. cit.

171 "Madeleine Albright described the result": The Albright quotation appeared in
Nancy Gibbs's profile of her that ran in *Time* on February 17, 1997.

171 "The headline on a *Washington Post*": The *Washington Post* headline was on
Judy Mann's column about the controversy that ran on March 15, 1989. The
quotations from Friedan and Schroeder were published in Schwartz's book,
op cit, on pp. 111 and 120, respectively.

174 "And recent rulings under the Americans with Disabilities Act": The ADA ruling mentioned is the Bragdon decision issued by the Supreme Court on June
25, 1998. In that decision, the Court held that Sidney Abbott was protected as
a person with a disability under the Americans with Disabilities Act, because
her HIV infection is an impairment that substantially limits her major life activity of reproduction. That conclusion, that the inability to reproduce is a

disability, opens up the ADA for millions of infertile women to seek redress under the law.

174 "The definition of womanhood can't be tied": Andrea McCormick was interviewed by telephone and e-mail for this book.

6

No Kidding

PAGE

180 "And *The New York Times* waxed poetic": The *Times*'s swoon over Arafat as a father was contained in a piece on Suha Arafat that ran on February 4, 1999.

180 "Choosing careers over family, committed to population": For statistics on the voluntarily childless, see Joyce C. Abma and Linda S. Peterson, "Voluntary Childlessness Among U.S. Women: Recent Trends and Determinants," presented at the Annual Meetings of the Population Association of America, April 6–8, 1995; "Is Your Family Wrecking Your Career?" *Fortune,* March 17, 1997; Diane Crispell, "Planning No Family, Now or Ever," *American Demographics,* October 1993; and Bill Stoneman, "Boomers Skipping Babies," *American Demographics,* January 1998.

181 "Children may be today's fashion in popular culture": The best history of childlessness is Elaine Tyler May, *Barren in the Promised Land* (Boston: Harvard University Press, 1997). See also Jean E. Veevers, *Childless by Choice* (1980), Marian Faux, *Childless by Choice* (New York: Anchor, 1984), Carolyn Morell, *Unwomanly Conduct* (New York: Routledge, 1994).

182 "Nothing provokes their ire more": Quotations and anecdotes from Ilene Bilenky are from my interviews with her.

182 "By every measure, the childless are among the elite": Many studies have now been conducted to detail the demographic characteristics of the voluntarily childless. See Susan O. Custavus and James R. Henley, "Correlates of Voluntary Childlessness in a Select Population," in Ellen Peck and Judith Senderowitz, *Pronatalism: The Myth of Mom & Apple pie* (New York: Thomas Y. Crowell, 1974); Bill Stoneman, "Boomers Skipping Babies," *American Demographics,* January 1998; Joyce C. Abma and Linda S. Peterson, "Voluntary Childlessness Among U.S. Women: Recent Trends and Determinants," presented at the Annual Meetings of the Population Association of America, April 6–8, 1995

182 "Despite the social stereotype of the childless as bitter and sour": The quotation from the Colorado Springs couple appeared in Scott Smith, "No Babies, No Maybes," *The Gazette* (Colorado Springs), April 23, 1998.

183 "Traditionally, women who did not reproduce": For traditional attitudes toward the childless, see Elaine Tyler May, op. cit.

183 "Those same sentiments were echoed": For Lydia Kingsmill Commander, see

her *The American Idea: Does the National Tendency Toward a Small Family Point to Race Suicide or Race Development?* (New York: Barnes, 1907). The piece from *American Home* was Louisa Randall Church, "Parents: Architects of Peace," and ran in November 1946.

183 "In the twentieth century, when psychologists became the arbiters": An excellent analysis of Freudian prescriptions about motherhood is contained in Judith Blake, "Coercive Pronatalism and American Population Policy," a paper presented for the Commission on Population Growth and the American Future, 1972, and reprinted in Ellen Peck and Judith Senderowitz, eds., *Pronatalism: The Myth of Mom & Apple Pie* (New York: Thomas Y. Crowell, 1974). The Erickson quotation is from "Inner Space and Outer Space: Reflections on Womanhood," *Daedalus,* 1964, p. 590. For Bardwick, see her *Psychology of Women* (London: Harper and Row, 1971). The Schlapp quotation is taken from Leta Hollingworth, "Social Devices for Impelling Women to Bear and Rear Children," *American Journal of Sociology,* 1916.

185 "Annette Annechild, a Washington, D.C., psychotherapist": The Annette Annechild quotations were taken from *The Washingtonian,* February 1997.

185 "When Amy Goldwasser, a twentysomething magazine editor": Goldwasser was interviewed by telephone.

186 "In December 1996, Ann Landers stepped right into": The responses to Landers ran on December 27, 1996.

186 "And a myth it is": The quotations from Rabkin and Bernard both appeared in Betty Rollin's "Motherhood: Need or Myth," *Look,* September 22, 1970, reprinted in Peck and Senderowitz, op. cit.

187 "The list mushrooms weekly": Oregon, for example, in June 1998 boosted the penalty for abuse if a child is present. The Associated Press carried the story on June 3, and it ran statewide the next day.

188 "In towns and cities across the nation": A classic example of the Internet moves came on November 24, 1998, in Loudoun County, Virginia, where officials pulled the plug on library Internet connections after a federal judge ordered that they remove Net-filtering software.

188 "In March 1998, Liz Langley": Liz Langley's column ran in the *Orlando Weekly* on March 26, 1998.

188 "For Lori Copeland, a thirty-four-year-old paralegal": Lori Copeland was interviewed by phone for this article.

188 "But, under federal law, only adults over the age of fifty-five": The federal Fair Housing Act of 1968 is contained in the US Code Chapter 45. It prohibits discrimination on the basis of "familial status," which is defined as "one or more individuals (who have not attained the age of 18 years) being domiciled with" a parent, legal guardian, designee of parent, or custodian. The protections also extend to pregnant women. See the US Code or check, on line, www.fairhousing.com for the full text of the law and relevant cases.

189 "Oddly, in a country that cherishes the privacy clause": The old policy on sterilization was maintained by the American College of Obstetricians and Gynecologists and was modified in its "The Question of Sterilization," published in 1971.

190 "For Joe Hoenigman, a financial and tax advisor": The background on Hoenigman came from Dan Fost's " Child-Free with an Attitude," *American Demographics,* April 1996.

190 "If the tax issues infuriate Joe, who is straight": Tom Butenhoff was interviewed at his frame shop in Margaretville, New York.

191 "So they have not launched a formal organization": For information on NON, see Elaine Tyler May and Veevers, op. cit.

191 "Fed up with the cushy treatment": This travel agent has posted at childfree.com. Her name is not printed for obvious reasons.

191 "Those raids on family-friendly America": Mark Dawson's story was posted on the chat group at childfree.com on May 22, 1998.

191 "Gradually, however, random acts": The NTSB established a new federal motor vehicle safety standard requiring new cars to have uniform child restraint anchorages built in. The rule became effective on September 1, 1999.

192 "Ilene Bilenky should have anticipated": Ilene's letter to the *Globe* was published on May 26, 1997.

194 "In 1930, after a decade of smaller families": The statistic for 1930 is from Kessler-Harris, op cit, p. 229. The figures for 1940 and 1960 come from Carl N. Delger, "Revolution without Ideology," *Daedalus,* 93, Spring 1964.

195 "'We're the majority'": The mother in question was a friend in the Catskills.

195 "In response to a piece I wrote": The Smith quotation appeared in an article about me in the *Independent,* February 7, 1999.

195 "What do tax credits for affluent parents have to do": Ann Coulter was interviewed by phone for this book.

196 "Finally, the polemical debate reaches the parental trump": Smith, op. cit.

198 "Today's childless know precisely what kind of village": The quotation from Michelle Gaboury is from my interview with her in Acton, Massachusetts.

7
When the Bough Breaks

PAGE

200 "For example, Ridgeview, Inc., a sock manufacturer": The information on Ridgeview comes from my interview with Erskine White at the company's headquarters in North Carolina.

201 "Skirmishes between parents and nonparents": The information on voters' rejection of a school tax increase in Milton, Massachusetts, is from *The Boston Globe,* June 7 and June 21, 1998.

201 "Log on any night to one of the Internet chat groups": For a sampling of the

tenor of these child-free discussions, try the chat group alt.support.childfree, or browse the message board of the Childfree Association at www.childfree.com.

202 "In its 1977 report, for example, the Carnegie Council on Children": The Carnegie Council's report was published as Kenneth Keniston, *All Our Children* (New York: Harcourt Brace, 1977).

203 "To take just one example, Paul Weyrich": For an example of Weyrich's position, see his contribution to the discussion, "Can Government Save the Family," *Policy Review: The Journal of American Citizenship*, September–October 1996.

205 "Amitai Etzioni, the nation's foremost communitarian": The Etzioni quotation is from his *The Spirit of Community* (New York: Crown, 1993).

206 "Companies we held up as models": The Kropf quotation is from her remarks in "Child-Free Employees See Another Side of Equation," *Wall Street Journal Interactive*, April 2, 1997.

206 "Geri Recht, a consultant for Towers Perrin": The Towers Perrin and Heinz information are from Joyce Gannon, "Single and Childless Workers Say They're Not Getting Fair Share of Benefits," *Pittsburgh Post-Gazette*, June 19, 1998.

206 "Keener human resources minds recognize": The material about Ireton and BC/BS are from *Personnel Journal*, September 1996.

207 "Monica Brunaccini, director of human resources": The Brunaccini quotations and information are from Gillian Flynn's column in *Personnel Journal*, September 1996.

207 "At Consolidated Natural Gas in Pittsburgh": The information on Consolidated Natural Gas is from the *Pittsburgh Post-Gazette* article cited above.

207 "At Eastman Kodak, the model employer": The information on and quotations about Kodak are from *Personnel Journal*, September 1996.

208 "The ultimate irony of all that family-friendliness": The Aon Consulting survey is described in "They Want More Support—Inside and Outside Of Work," *Workforce*, November 1998.

208 "And Alice Campbell, the work-life director at Baxter": The Baxter study was outlined in "Work and Family," *Business Week*, September 1997.

210 "In fact, it is the staggering increase": For the clearest view of the conservative position on the plight of children raised in single-parent families, filled with the attendant statistics and footnotes, see Wade Horn, *Children And Family In America: Challenges For The 1990s*, Heritage Lecture No. 345, June 23, 1991.

212 "Or they expect us to believe that parents are going to use": Arlie Hochschild, *The Time Bind: When Work Becomes Home and Home Becomes Work* (New York: Henry Holt, 1997).

214 "They alone, then, bear the burden": The Etzioni material is from his *The Spirit of Community* (New York: Crown, 1993).

214 "Asking the childless to ante up their share": Median income figures used are the U.S. Census Bureau's 1997 figures.

Bibliography

Scores of books, articles, government reports, and research papers were consulted as part of the preparation for this book. The primary sources, however, were:

Abbot, Pamela, and Claire Wallace, *The Family and the New Right* (London: Pluto, 1992).

Berry, Mary Frances, *The Politics of Parenthood* (New York: Viking, 1993).

Blankenhorn, David, et al., eds., *Rebuilding the Nest: A New Commitment to the American Family* (Milwaukee: Family Service America, 1990).

Blau, David, ed., *The Economics of Child Care* (New York: Russell Sage Foundation, 1991).

Blau, Francine D., and Ronald G. Ehrenberg, eds., *Gender and Family Issues in the Workplace* (New York: Russell Sage Foundation, 1997).

Brown, Karen, and Mary Louise Fellows, eds., *Taxing America* (New York: New York University Press, 1997).

Burggraf, Shirley P., *The Feminine Economy and Economic Man* (Reading, Mass.: Addison-Wesley, 1997).

Cherlin, Andrew J., ed., *The Changing American Family and Public Policy* (Washington, D.C.: The Urban Institute Press, 1988).

Children's Defense Fund, *Poverty Matters* (Washington, D.C., CDF, 1997).

Coontz, Stephanie, *The Social Origins of Private Life* (London: Verson, 1988).

Degler, Carl, *At Odds* (New York: Oxford University Press, 1980).

Edelman, Marian Wright, *Families in Peril* (Cambridge, Mass.: Harvard University Press, 1987).

Elving, Ronald D., *Conflict and Compromise* (New York: Touchstone, 1996).

Etzioni, Amitai, *The Spirit of Community* (New York: Crown, 1993).

Faux, Marian, *Childless by Choice* (New York: Anchor, 1984).

Feldstein, Martin, and James M. Poterba, *Empirical Foundations of Household Taxation* (Chicago: University of Chicago Press, 1996).

Fernandez, John, *Childcare and Corporate Productivity* (Lexington, Mass.: D.C. Heath, 1980).

Firestone, Shulamith, *The Dialectic of Sex* (New York: Bantam Books, 1970).

Friedan, Betty, *Beyond Gender* (Washington, D.C.: Woodrow Wilson Center Press, 1997).

Friedan, Betty, *The Second Stage* (Cambridge, Mass.: Harvard University Press, 1998).

Gerstel, Naomi, and Harriet Gross, eds., *Families and Work* (Philadelphia: Temple University Press, 1987).

Gilman, Charlotte Perkins, *Women and Economics* (New York: Harper & Row, 1966).

Hewlett, Sylvia Ann, and Cornel West, *The War Against Parents* (New York: Houghton Mifflin, 1998).

Hochschild, Arlie Russell, *The Second Shift* (New York: Avon, 1989).

Hochschild, Arlie Russell, *The Time Bind: When Work Becomes Home and Home Becomes Work* (New York: Henry Holt, 1997).

Howe, Louise Kapp, ed., *The Future of the Family* (New York: Simon & Schuster, 1972).

Keniston, Kenneth, *All Our Children* (New York: Harcourt Brace, 1977).

Kessler-Harris, Alice, *Out to Work* (New York: Oxford University Press, 1982).

Kessler-Harris, Alice, *A Woman's Wage* (Lexington, Ky.: University Press of Kentucky, 1990).

Leira, Arnlaug, *Welfare States and Working Mothers* (Cambridge, England: Cambridge University Press, 1992).

Mack, Dana, *The Assault on Parenthood: How Our Culture Undermines the Family* (New York: Simon & Schuster, 1997).

Mawyer, Martin, *Defending the American Family* (Green Forest, Ark.: New Leaf Press, 1995).

May, Elaine Tyler, *Barren in the Promised Land* (Cambridge, Mass.: Harvard University Press, 1997).

McCaffery, Edward J., *Taxing Women* (Chicago: University of Chicago Press, 1997).

Millet, Kate, *Sexual Politics* (Garden City, N.Y.: Doubleday, 1970).

Mintz, Steven, and Susan Kellogg, *Domestic Revolutions* (New York: Free Press, 1988).

Mitchell, Juliet, *Woman's Estate* (New York: Vintage, 1971).

Moen, Phyllis, *Women's Two Roles* (New York: Auburn House, 1992).

Morell, Carolyn M., *Unwomanly Conduct: The Challenges of Intentional Childlessness* (New York: Routledge, 1994).

Morgan, Hal, and Kerry Tucker, *Companies that Care* (New York: Fireside/Simon & Schuster, 1991).

Moss, Peter, and Nickie Fonda, eds., *Work and the Family* (London: Temple Smith, 1980).

National Commission on Children, *Beyond Rhetoric: A New American Agenda for Children and Families* (Washington, D.C.: 1991).

O'Neill, William, *Everyone Was Brave* (New York: Quadrangle, 1969).

Peck, Ellen, and Judith Senderowitz, eds., *Pronatalism: The Myth of Mom & Apple Pie* (New York: Thomas Y. Crowell, 1974).

Penner, Rudolph G., ed., *Taxing the Family* (Washington, D.C.: American Enterprise Institute, 1983).

Robertson, Nan, *The Girls in the Balcony* (New York: Fawcett Ballantine, 1992).

Schroeder, Patricia, *Champion of the Great American Family* (New York: Random House, 1989).

Schwartz, Felice, *Breaking with Tradition* (New York: Warner Books, 1992).

Sidel, Ruth, *Keeping Women and Children Last* (New York: Penguin, 1997).

Slemrod, Joel, and Jon Bakija, *Taxing Ourselves* (Cambridge, Mass.: MIT Press, 1996).

Sochen, June, *Movers and Shakers* (New York: Quadrangle/New York Times, 1973).

Steiner, Gilbert, *The Futility of Family Policy* (Washington, D.C.: The Brookings Institution Press, 1981).

U.S. Congress, *The Family First Act: Hearing before the Joint Economic Committee,* Congress of the United States, 104th, April 6, 1995.

U.S. Department of Labor, *The Working Women Count: Honor Roll Report,* 1997.

U.S. Department of Labor, *Working Women Count: A Report to the Nation,* 1994.

U.S. Senate, *THE FMLA of 1993, Hearing before the Subcommittee on Children, Family, Drugs and Alcoholism of the Committee on Labor and Human Resources,* U.S. Senate, 103d, Jan 22, 1993.

Veevers, J.E., *Childless by Choice* (Toronto: Butterworths, 1980).

Wattenberg, Ben J., *The Birth Dearth* (New York: Pharos Books, 1987).

Acknowledgments

Gratitude too frequently becomes a cliché, delivered in the form of a lengthy list of prominent and not-so-prominent individuals writers offer to appease, mollify, thank, and show off. Lest I fall into that trap, I opt for brevity.

This book could not have been written without the time, thinking, and generosity of dozens of childless men and women, corporate executives, human resources directors, political operatives, and public policy specialists who shared their time and expertise with me. In particular, I wish to thank Cheryl Brant and Ilene Bilenky, who opened their lives and their hearts to me so that I could delineate vivid portraits of the lives of childless women.

Thanks to the October birthday crowd, who gather for our annual family reunion. My gratitude also to Al Rose, who has never failed to keep me centered; to Robert Jones, who jump-started me on this professional path and has kept me on track for almost a decade; to Michael Solomon of *Mirabella*, the guru of titles; to Luis Feldstein-Soto, extraordinary journalist and crackerjack attorney; to Patrick Wright, who spent all too much of his week on the mountain digging through my prose; to Gail Winston, the first parent who told me I wasn't crazy; to Laurie Abraham of *Mirabella* magazine, who refused to be afraid of this topic when so many other magazine editors were; and to my friend and co-conspirator whom I know as La La, the Queen of Mean, without whom I cannot imagine ending each day.

I wish to acknowledge, and—I swear—not ironically, the contribution of all those people I know and have met who hated this topic, who refused to believe that the childless suffer from discrimination or to consider the possibility that such discrimination might be unwarranted. The importance of skeptics to the development of any project is often underestimated. Opposition, after all, makes the adrenaline flow, sharpens the wit, and goads a writer on. I feel no need to mention your names. You know who you are—thank you.

I would like to express particular appreciation for the ever-gracious assistance of Lisa Bankoff, my agent, who has put up with me through five previous books, and who suffered through this sixth even when it made her uncomfortable; for the constant, almost daily, help and patience of her assistant, Patrick Price; and for the encouragement of my editor, Liz Maguire, who understood where I was going well before I myself had a road map, and who struggled through it with me even while living out many of its key moments.

Finally, as always, I would like to thank Dennis, the center of my family, whose legacy does not have two legs and will not pay anyone's Social Security. But it includes a grace, wisdom, and fierce honesty that the world needs so desperately.

Index

Absenteeism, 36, 37
Act for Better Child Care, 125
Adoption and Safe Families Act, 150
AFDC, 85
AFL-CIO, 34, 208
    Women's Bureau of, 168
    Working Women's Department of,
        34
Albright, Madeleine, 171
Alcohol Beverage Control,
    Department of, 84
Allstate, 35
American Academy of Arts and
    Sciences conference, 153
American child, average, 104–7
American Civil Liberties Union, 167
American Council on Education,
    78–79
American Enterprise Institute, 142
American Express, 35
American Express Financial Advisors,
    43
American Home, 183
American Way of Life, 18
Americans with Disabilities Act, 48,
    52, 174
Angelou, Maya, 104
Annechild, Annette, 185

Aon Consulting, 208
*Assault on Parenthood, The: How Our
    Culture Undermines the Family,*
    100
Atlanta Inn for Children, 33
Atlantic Monthly, The, 143
Audrey Cohen College, 78

Babbitt, Bruce, 124
Baby boomers, 139–41
"Baby boomlet," 126, 129
Bakija, Jon, 73–74
Baltimore Sun, 69
Barnard College, 54, 102, 103, 152,
    153
Barrett, Bill, 62
Baxter International, 208
Bauer, Gary, 64, 65
BE&K, 35
Berman, Howard, 166, 167
Bilenky, Ilene, 41, 184–85, 187,
    189–90, 192–94, 195–96, 216
Bipartisan movement, 72
Birth Dearth, The, 143
Blaney, Jeff, 49
Board of Tax Appeals, 80
Boeing, 129
Bolger, Glen, 131

Boston Globe, The, 53, 201
Boxer, Barbara, 95, 134, 162
Boys Town, 85
Brant, Cheryl, 1–3, 5, 6, 7, 10–11, 216–17
Brant, Glenn, 5
Brazelton, T. Berry, 118–20, 152
Breastfeeding, 25, 48–50
Bright Horizons Family Solutions, 129
Brown, Roger, 129
Brunaccini, Monica, 207
Burggraf, Shirley P., 115
Bush, George, 125, 126
Business Week, 34, 36
Butenhoff, Tom, 190–91
Buy, Buy Baby, 127–28

California Children and Families First Initiative, 132
Campbell, Alice, 208
Campbell, Bill, 33
Carnegie Council on Children, 137, 203
Carson, Allan, 12
Carter, Bill, 93
Carter, Jimmy, 121
Catalyst, 168
Celebrity parenthood, 179–80
Census Bureau, U.S., 11, 181
Centers for Disease Control, 95
Charlotte Observer, 129
Chase Manhattan Bank, 37
Chemical scares, 94
Child Care Action Network, 162
Child-free Network, 45
Child Tax Credit, 20
Child Welfare League of America, 86, 123
Children, missing, 91–93
Children's Defense Fund, 85, 98, 123

Children's Environmental Protection Act, 95
Children's Health Environmental Coalition Network, 130
Chira, Susan, 57–58, 163, 164
Christian Coalition, 86
Christian Right, 210
Civil Rights Act of 1964, 48, 52, 155, 165, 167
Clegg, Roger, 53
Clines, Francis X., 112
Clinton, Bill, 8, 11, 12, 18, 29–30, 43, 51, 52, 68, 78, 82, 85, 98,108, 109, 123, 134–37, 138, 139, 140–41, 142, 144, 145, 149, 150, 195, 198, 214
Clinton, Hillary, 134, 196
CNN, 135
Coalition for America's Children, 131
Cohen, Bernard, 14
Cold War, 15, 121
College Board, 79
Columbia University, 78, 124
Columbine High School, 9, 95, 127
Commander, Lydia Kingsvill, 183
Commissions on the Status of Women, 155
Comprehensive Childhood Immunization Initiative, 150
Conference Board, 41
Congress, U.S., 93. *See also* House of Representatives; Senate
Consolidated Group, 207
Contract With America, 83
Copeland, Lori, 188–89
Corporate America, 16, 36, 43–44, 71, 206, 208
Coulter, Ann, 195
C-SPAN, 135
Cuevas, Emma, 49–50
Cutler, Lynn, 125

Daedalus, 170
Daughters of the American
    Revolution, 13
Dawson, Mark, 191
Demke, Paul, 43
Democratic National Convention,
    124–25
Democratic Policy Commission, 122
Democrats (party), 9–10, 64, 83, 120,
    121, 122, 124, 125, 126, 137
Demographics of American
    workforce, 37
Deutsch, Helene, 153
Dialectic of Sex, The, 157
Diehl, Anna, 3–4, 6
Diehl, George, 4
Diehl, Susan, 4–6
Divorce statistics, 5
Dobson, James, 137
Dodd, Chris, 9, 52
Dole, Bob, 11, 196
Dowd, Maureen, 60
Drew Carey Show, The, 20
Duffey, Elizabeth, 151
Dugger, Celia, 53, 54, 57
Dukakis, Michael, 125
Duke Power, 35
DuPont, 129

Eastman Kodak, 207–8
Eckel, Sara, 60
Edelman, Marian Wright, 97, 98, 123,
    132
Education, Department of, 78
Eisenhower, Dwight David, 15
Elections, 9, 11
Eli Lilly, 35
Employee turnover, 36, 37
Employer-sponsored daycare, 5
Equal Employment Opportunity
    Commission, 51, 165

Equal Pay Act, 14, 15, 16–17, 18, 43
    era of, 47
Equal Rights Amendment, 121, 124,
    148, 159
Equal work for equal pay, 8–9, 15
Exxon, 119
Exxon *Valdez,* 60

Fair Housing Act, 199
Fair Labor Standards Act, 52
Fallows, Deborah, 105
Faludi, Susan, 150
Falwell, Jerry, 96
Families and Work Institute, 36
"Family friendly," 7, 12, 18, 19, 27, 36,
    100, 212
Family and Medical Leave Act, 10, 47,
    52, 101, 131, 141, 142, 150, 168,
    202, 209
Family First Act, 83
Family First Tax Credit, 84–87
Family Research Council, 64
Family Ties, 119
Family status benefits, 8–9
FBI, 93
Federal Housing Authority, 71
Federal income tax, history of, 70–72
Fein, Esther, 53, 54, 57
Fel-Pro Incorporated, 34–35, 36, 37
*Feminine Economy and Economic
    Man, The,* 115
Feminine Mystique, The, 155
Fernandez, John, 36, 43–44
Ferrara, Peter, 86
Finch, Mary, 50
Firestone, Shulamith, 156–57
Florida Children's Campaign, 130
Folbre, Nancy, 161
Food Allergy Network, 94–95
Food stamps, 8, 12, 85, 87, 100, 109
Forbes, 58

Fortune, 42
Free Congress Foundation, 203
Friedan, Betty, 137, 147–48, 149, 155,
    156, 157–59, 171, 172
Friedlander, Andrew, 51–52
Friedlander, Glenda, 51–52
Friedman, Dana, 169

Gaboury, Michelle, 112, 113–14, 115,
    117, 198
Gaboury, Paul, 113
Gallup organization, 84, 135
Galvin, Erin, 39–40
GE, 96
General Electric v. Gilbert, 165–66
Georgetown University, 78, 166
Gephardt, Dick, 124
Gesell, Arnold, 153
Getting Yours, 160
Gildersleeve, Virginia, 152
Gilligan, Carol, 164
Gilman, Charlotte Perkins, 151, 152,
    155
Girls in the Balcony, The, 59
Gladieux, Lawrence, 79
Glueck, Grace, 59
Goldberg, Gary, 118–20
Goldman, Emma, 151
Goldwasser, Amy, 185–86
Goodman, Ellen, 125, 143
Gordon, H., 17
Gore, Al, 9, 52, 142, 150
Goucher College, 153
Graf, Sandy, 39
Grams, Rod, 83–84, 85
Great American Family, 119
Great American Family Tour, 118,
    120
Green, Edith, 18
Greenberg, Stanley, 123
Grey Lady. *See New York Times, The*

Gross Domestic Product, 70
Gross National Product, 76
Guggenheim, Elinor, 162
Guiler, Jeff, 44
Gun control, 10, 132
Gun lobby, 9

Hallmark, 35
Hartmann, Heidi, 149, 162
Hastert, Dennis, 62
Head Start, 20, 150
Health and Human Services,
    Department of, 63, 81, 98
Height, Dorothy, 18
Heinz USA, 206
Held, Virginia, 164
Henneberger, Melinda, 54
Henriquez, Bob, 133
Hepburn, Katharine, 5
Heritage Foundation, 86
Hewitt Associates, 35
Hewlett, Sylvia Ann, 71, 101, 102–3,
    104, 109, 132, 137
Hildebran, 27
Hilton, 33
Hiss, Alger, 16
HMOs, regulation of, 132
Hochschild, Arlie, 212
Hodge, Scott, 86
Hoenigman, Joe, 190
Hoffman, Jan, 54
Home Alone, 95
Honey, I Shrunk the Kids, 95
Hope Scholarships, 78, 79, 86, 141
Horizontal equity, 72–73
Horn, Wade, 98
House of Representatives, 10, 62, 83,
    86, 167
House Select Committee on Children,
    Youth, and Families, 62, 121
Howard University, 78

Hull, Jane Dee, 133
Hutchinson, Tim, 83
Hyatt Regency, 33
Hyde, Henry, 167

IBM, 35, 54
Institute for American Values, 100
Institute for Women's Policy Research, 149, 162
Internal Revenue Service, 7, 64, 72, 80
Inverse correlation, 116
IRS. *See* Internal Revenue Service
IWPR. *See* Institute for Women's Policy Research

Jackson, Jesse, 125
James, Kay Cole, 98
Jennings, Marianne, 58
Joe Camel, 27, 132
Johnson & Johnson, 36, 47, 129
Joint Economic Committee, 83
Jong, Erica, 150
JWP Businessland, 50

Kaus, Mickey, 60
Keller, Bill, 59, 60–61
Kellogg Company, 28
Kelly, Edna, 18
Kelly, Michael, 142
Kennedy, John F., 18, 71
Kennedy, Ted, 104, 123
Key, Ellen, 151
Kiddie car seats, 192
King, Martin Luther, Jr., 14
Kiriacon, John, 40, 41
Kitei, Michael, 128
Klein, Donna, 32–33
Klein, Ethel, 124
KLH, 28
Koblenz, Marci, 208
Kozol, Jonathan, 104

Labor, Department of, 15, 51, 81, 170
Lake, Celinda, 107, 130–31
Landers, Ann, 186
Langley, Liz, 188
Latchkey kids, 93–94
Lee, Linda, 54
Lelyveld, Joseph, 61
Levy, Frank, 144
Liederman, David, 86–87, 123–24
Louv, Richard, 46–47

Mack, Dana, 100, 108, 109
Macomb Journal, 60
Maher, Bill, 20
Maloney, Carolyn, 50
Mann, Horace, 75, 76, 77, 78
Marriott Corporation, 32, 33
Martinez, Alicia, 48–49, 52
McCarthy, Carolyn, 10
McCormick, Andrea, 174
Megan's Law, 150
Merck, 36, 129
Merkowitz, David, 78–79
Mesko, Mike, 45–46
Mfume, Kweisi, 66
Microsoft, 28
Mikulski, Barbara, 10, 66
Miles, Minnie, 18
Milholland, Inez, 151
Miller, George, 121, 123
Millet, Kate, 157
Minnesota Public Radio, 172
Mintz, Copal, 17
Mitchell, Juliet, 157
Mondale, Walter, 121
Montessori, 26
Moral Majority, 120, 158
Morris, Dick, 78
Morse, Wayne, 15
Mother's Place, A 164
Motorola, 129

Ms., 160, 161
MSNBC, 48–49, 135

Nation, The, 158
National Center for Missing and
    Exploited Children, 93
National Center for Policy Analysis,
    86
National Commission on Children,
    98–99, 107, 108, 109
National Congress of Mothers, 151
National Equal Pay Commission, 15
National Journal, 53, 142
National Liberty Journal, 96
National Office Management
    Association, 15
National Organization for
    Nonparents, 191
National Organization for Women
    (NOW), 148–49, 155–57, 162,
    167
National Partnership for Women and
    Families, 149–50
National Women's Law Center, 65,
    167
National Women's Party, 159
National Women's Political Caucus,
    167
NationsBank, 27, 38
NBC, 127
Neuville Industries, 25, 26, 27, 29, 31,
    33
Neuville, Steve, 25–26, 28–29, 30,
    31–32
New Mothers' Breastfeeding
    Promotion and Protection Act,
    50
New Republic, 123
New York, 55
New York *Daily News,* 61
New York Post, The, 55

New York Times, The, 10, 17, 37, 52,
    53, 55–56, 57, 58, 59–61, 170,
    180
New Yorker, The, 133, 158
Nixon, Richard, 71, 81
Noah, Timothy, 53
NON. *See* National Organization of
    Nonparents
NOW. *See* National Organization for
    Women
Nussbaum, Karen, 34

Office of Management and Budget,
    145
Ojito, Mirta, 54
Omni, 32
Oreskes, Mike, 53
Owen, Robert, 28

PANDER, 53
Parental and Disability Leave, 167
Parental quality, 131–32
Parents' Bill of Rights, 103, 104
Patagonia, 45
Pataki, George, 133
Paul, Alice, 159
Peanut allergies, 35
    related panic, 94–95
Pepper, Claude, 15
Personnel Journal, 41
Peters, Joan, 163–64
Peterson, Esther, 18
Philadelphia Inquirer, 14, 61, 136
Pogrebin, Letty Cottin, 160
Polaroid, 28
Politically Incorrect, 20
Poverty line, 108
Pregnancy Discrimination Act of
    1978, 161, 166
Price, Ann, 45–46
Princeton University, 78

Progressive Policy Institute, 65
Pronatalist policies, 145
Public Agenda, 131
Public Opinion Strategies, 131
Purnick, Joyce, 53, 54–57, 58–59, 60–61

Rabkin, Dr. Richard, 186
Ramsey, JonBenet, 127
Rasberry, William, 110
Rauch, Jonathan, 143–44, 145, 146
Reagan, Ronald, 98, 120, 121, 124, 167
Recht, Geri, 206
Red Scare, 97
Reddy, Helen, 160
Reiner, Rob, 132
Revenue Act of 1948, 70
R.J. Reynolds, 27
Republicans (party), 8, 64, 83, 120, 121, 122, 144
Richards, Ann, 124–25
Ridgeview, Inc., 200–201
"Right" folks, 145–46
Robert Morris College, 44
Roberts, Cokie, 61
Roberts, Steve, 61
Robertson, Nan, 59
Rockefeller, John D., IV, 98
Rockford Institute, 12
Roiphe, Anne, 163
Rossi, Alice, 153–55, 170–71
Rothausen, Teresa, 172
Ruddick, Sara, 164
Rutherford Institute, 51

Sackett, Dave, 130–31
San Diego Union-Tribune, 46
Sarpalius, Dave, 62
SAS, 26–27, 54
"School choice," 76–77

School property taxes, 75–76
Schrayer, Elizabeth, 130, 131
Schroeder, Patricia, 62, 63, 64, 69, 70, 83, 118–20, 162, 165, 171, 202
Schwartz, Felice, 168–69, 171
Schwartz, Harvey, 50–51, 52
Schwartz, Stacey, 136
Schwellenbach, Lewis Baxter, 17
Senate, 10, 83
Sesame Street Live, 51
Shanahan, Eileen, 59
Shapiro, Robert, 64–65
Shellenbarger, Sue, 61
Shulman, Alix Kates, 160
Slemrod, Joel, 73–74
Slate, 53, 60
Small Talk, 128
Smith, Henry, 80
Smith, Lillian, 80
Smith, Marcelle D'Argy, 195
Smith, Susan, 127
Snell, Alysia, 130–31
Social Security, 87, 99, 103, 105, 109, 142, 143, 144, 209
Sontag, Debbie, 53, 54, 57
Spartanburg Herald-Journal, 51
Spock, Benjamin, 119, 152, 153, 154
Stanton, Elizabeth Cady, 151
Stark, Pete, 85, 86
State income taxes, 77
State University of New York, 77
Steurele, Gene, 64
Stride-Rite, 35
Sulzberger, Arthur, Jr., 61
SuperWoman, 159–60, 161
Swetnick, Robert, 49

Tamargo, Deborah, 133
Tax Fairness for Families Act, 64
Tax Reform Act of 1986, 64
Taxing Ourselves, 74

Taxpayers' Relief Act of 1997, 68
Teletubbies, 96
Ten Commandments of workplace
    etiquette, 38–39
Terminal want, 111–12
Time, 50, 171
*Time Bind: When Work Becomes Home
    and Home Becomes Work, The,*
    212
Towers Perrin, 206
Tracy, David, 40
Treasury, Department of, 72
20/20, 94

United States Catholic Conference,
    167
Universal Studios, 129
University of California, 212
University of Chicago, 40
University of Maryland, 144
University of Michigan, 74
Upton, Joanna, 50–51, 52
Upward Bound, 20
Urban Institute, 64

Veterans Administration, 71
Vietnam War, 93
Village dynamics, 196–98

Wade, Betsy, 59
Wadsworth, Deborah, 131
Wall Street Journal, The, 45, 61, 79
Walsh, John, 91–92, 93
Walsh, Reve, 91–92
War Against Parents, The, 71, 101
War on Poverty, 8
Washington Post, 171
Watson, John B., 152

Wattenberg, Ben, 142–43, 145, 146
Wessel, David, 79
West, Cornel, 71, 101, 102–3, 108, 109,
    132, 137
Westinghouse, 15–16
Weyrich, Paul, 203
When the Bough Breaks, 102
When Mothers Work, 163
White House, 9, 14, 29, 30, 69, 78, 81,
    122, 124, 149
White House Conference on Child
    Care, 150
White House Conference on Early
    Child Development and
    Learning, 150
White House Conference on Families,
    121
William Olsten Center for Workforce
    Strategies, 42
Willis, Ellen, 158
Wittman, Marshall, 86
Wolf, Frank, 63, 64
Woodward, Louise, 94
Woman's Estate, 157
Women and Economics, 151
Women's Agenda Conference, 124
Women's Bureau of the Department
    of Labor, 15, 34
Women's Legal Defense Fund, 149,
    166
Working Mother, 18, 29, 30, 34, 42, 45
    Best companies list, 35–36
Working Woman, 26
World War II, 4, 15, 28

Yallum, Jane, 39
Year of the Child, 97
Young, Mary B., 42

Printed in the United States
By Bookmasters